The Architecture of McKIM, MEAD & WHITE
in Photographs, Plans and Elevations

McKIM, MEAD & WHITE

With a new introduction by

Richard Guy Wilson
Professor and Chairman of Architectural History
University of Virginia School of Architecture

DOVER PUBLICATIONS, INC.
New York

Published in Canada by General Publishing Company, Ltd., 30 Lesmill Road, Don Mills, Toronto, Ontario.

Published in the United Kingdom by Constable and Company, Ltd., 3 The Lanchesters, 162-164 Fulham Palace Road, London W6 9ER.

This Dover edition, first published in 1990, is an unabridged republication of *A Monograph of the Work of McKim Mead & White 1879–1915*, originally published in four volumes by The Architectural Book Publishing Co, Paul Wenzel & Maurice Krakow, New York, 1915–1920. The introduction by Richard Guy Wilson was written specially for this edition, and an index has been provided. Some obvious typographical errors in the original have been tacitly corrected.

Manufactured in the United States of America
Dover Publications, Inc., 31 East 2nd Street, Mineola, N.Y. 11501

Library of Congress Cataloging-in-Publication Data

McKim, Mead & White.
    [Monograph of the work of McKim, Mead & White, 1879–1915]
    The architecture of McKim, Mead & White in photographs, plans, and elevations / McKim, Mead & White ; with a new introduction by Richard Guy Wilson.
        p.   cm.
    Reprint. Originally published: A monograph of the work of McKim, Mead & White, 1879–1915. New York : Architectural Book Pub. Co., 1915–1920.
    Includes index.
    ISBN 0-486-26556-0 (pbk.)
    1. McKim, Mead & White. 2. Architecture, Modern—19th century—United States. 3. Architecture, Modern—20th century—United States. I. Wilson, Richard Guy, 1940–   . II. Title.
NA737.M4A4   1990
720′.92′2—dc20   90-43684
                                                            CIP

Contents

The original plate numbers, with all the omissions and interpolations, have been retained in this volume.

To preserve the spread on plates 31–31A, plate 32 has been moved forward.

CONTENTS OF VOLUME 1

CONTENTS OF VOLUME TWO

CONTENTS OF VOLUME THREE

CONTENTS OF VOLUME FOUR

Introduction

A Monograph of the Work of McKim Mead & White 1879–1915, as the publication reproduced here was originally titled, is one of the most important American architectural books ever produced. Published between 1915 and 1920 and composed of photographs and drawings with no text except for brief captions, it stands with Frank Lloyd Wright's nearly contemporaneous Wasmuth books (published in Germany, significantly) as testimony to a coming-of-age by American architects. Like the Wright volumes, though in substantially different ways, the McKim, Mead & White *Monograph* would influence architecture both in the United States and abroad.

Architects from across the United States avidly subscribed to the *Monograph,* and in turn they replayed its forms, details and styles in hometown libraries, banks, commercial structures, colleges and schools, monuments and statues, public buildings and houses. Certainly, some of the firm's influence can also be laid to first-hand knowledge of its buildings, and some to its great role as a training office. A number of former McKim, Mead & White employees went out and set up firms for local clienteles—W. H. Whidden in Portland, Oregon, Louis Kamper in Detroit, A. Page Brown in San Francisco—while other graduates and their firms became nationally significant— Cass Gilbert, Henry Bacon, Carrère & Hastings, York & Sawyer. All of these and many more helped spread the message about an American Renaissance that was being born in artists' studios and architects' offices. But finally, in the modern age it is a building's appearance on the printed page that confirms its stature. That is what the *Monograph* did for a great body of architecture, making available to architects from Atlanta to Honolulu examples of the new American classicism.

The *Monograph* also made a significant impact abroad, in ways that are still being uncovered and recognized. As early as 1891, the English architect and writer Robert Kerr had disowned James Fergusson's deprecating remarks of 1862 on American architecture and had claimed that its "old-fashioned character . . . prosaic and dull . . . has completely changed."[1] Kerr's new view came from an appreciation of Henry Hobson Richardson and also of the new classicism that was beginning to appear in works such as Madison Square Garden (plates 30–37), the Villard Houses (pls. 7–11) and the Boston Public Library (pls. 100–109), which was still under construction. By 1910, the English architect and educator Charles Reilly would report, after visiting New York and Washington and observing the new American classicism of the firm and its contemporaries, that "America has seized the lead" and "has established an architecture" that is the "conscious heir, as ours, let us hope is in yet the unconscious, of those forms and thoughts . . . born in Greece more than 2,000 years ago."[2] Reilly would later author a book devoted to the firm.[3] In England, from Liverpool to London, and in colonial cities abroad, from Victoria to New Delhi, Sydney and Johannesburg, can be found buildings and details that indicate that the *Monograph* lay close to the drafting tables. Even farther afield, in cities such as Moscow and Tokyo, are projects that attest that the *Monograph* was known. Like the seminal publications by Serlio, Palladio, Letarouilly, Le Corbusier and Wright with which it aspires to be ranked, the *Monograph* helped change the world of architecture.

The firm of McKim, Mead & White was founded in New York City in September 1879. Though always principally a New York firm, it set up branch offices in other cities and its practice grew to a nationwide scale. The firm's size (its employees at times numbered over one hundred), the scale and complexity of its projects, and its longevity (its name continued in existence until 1956) all indicate a new type of particularly American—and modern—architectural practice. The three founding partners had known each other since the early 1870s; McKim and Mead had been in partnership since mid-1877, and White joined in 1879. Charles Follen McKim (1847–1909) studied at the Ecole des Beaux-Arts between 1867 and 1870.[4] The only original partner to have an academic architectural background, McKim quite clearly was the firm's style setter. First among equals, it was he who established its goals, and he must be seen as the most influential figure in the history of the firm. The name of William Rutherford Mead (1846–1928) came appropriately second on the masthead: he was the office manager and the practical conscience who kept his sometimes too ambitious and mercurial partners down to earth. The libertine style of life and sensational demise of Stanford White (1853–1906) have made him the best known of the three.[5] One of the greatest decorative talents America has produced, White possessed tremendous energy and was responsible for more work than either of his partners.

Charles McKim's architecture tended toward solidity, monumentality and at times austerity, as in Pennsylvania Station (pls. 300–310) and the Vanderbilt house at Hyde Park (pls. 83, 84), whereas Stanford White's work generally possessed lightness and even frivolity, as in the New York Herald Building (pls. 62–64A), and ornamental richness, as in the interiors of the Henry W. Poore house (pls. 155, 156). Such characterizations can be misleading, however, for McKim also designed the lush University Club in New York (pls. 130–140C), and White produced the restrained Cullum Memorial at West Point (pls. 116–119). And William Mead was not just an office manager but also was responsible for significant work such as the plan of the Rhode Island Statehouse (pls. 183–190) and the design of the New York Life Insurance Company building in Kansas City (pl. 22). But despite these individual achievements, McKim, Mead & White existed as a partnership; the members criticized, interacted with and learned from one another. White once admonished an art magazine: "No member of our firm is ever individually responsible for any design which goes out from it."[6] Certainly, as the years passed and the projects grew in size and complexity, each of the partners became more individually responsible for his own work. But it was never an office of isolated teams, and ideas and work continued to be traded back and forth.

In addition to the three partners who gave the firm its name, there were many hundreds of employees who made contributions. One formidable designer was Joseph Morrill Wells (1853–1890), to whom the Russell and Erwin Building in New Britain, Connecticut (pl. 18), can be attributed. Wells's stand for classicism and his impact on the firm have assumed almost legendary stature.[7] In 1906, shortly before White's death and McKim's withdrawal because of ill health, three new partners were added: William Mitchell Kendall (1856–1941), Burt Leslie Fenner (1869–1926) and William Symmes Richardson (1873–1931). In 1909, Teunis J. van der Bent (1863–1936) became a partner. All of these men had been longtime employees and had worked closely with the founders; they all tended to continue the dominant direction of the firm's work in a commitment to classicism. And yet, as shown in the *Monograph*, shifts did occur; commissions for skyscrapers like the New York Municipal Building, 1907–1913 (pls. 320–327), which McKim—if he had been in better health—would have discouraged, now entered the office. Beyond the few high rises, the work of these later partners (shown extensively in the last hundred pages of this volume) is hard to differentiate from that of the founders. The Pyne house (pls. 349–351A) by Kendall could be by McKim, the Waterbury Station (pl. 311) by Richardson might have been White's work, and the Burke Foundation Hospital (pls. 380–383), in which Fenner played a role, evinces Mead's usual good sense.

Over the years the work of the firm had been extensively published, albeit piecemeal, in architectural periodicals. *Architectural Record* had devoted an entire issue to the firm in 1895; the commentary by Russell Sturgis, a former teacher of both McKim and Mead, criticized their classical direction.[8] In 1906 *Architectural Record* devoted another issue to the firm. This time the commentary praised the work in effusive terms, and its authors, Harry Desmond and Herbert Croly, explicitly noted a kinship between the ideals and arts of the Renaissance and McKim, Mead & White's accomplishments.[9]

The selection shown in the *Monograph* reflects the recognition of, and the historical perspective on, an American Renaissance as it had developed in the firm's office by 1914, when the Architectural Book Publishing Company approached the partners with the idea of a book devoted to the firm's work. By then William Mead had largely withdrawn, and the newer partners, unsurprisingly, tended to select designs that confirmed current directions. These buildings reaffirmed the prevailing conception of a Renaissance: a belief that America in its arts and its culture was experiencing a rebirth akin to that which had swept Europe in the fifteenth century and had led to the discovery of the New World. The American colonial mansions were, after all, the progeny of buildings erected in Florence in the 1420s. In the firm's view, the "nightmare" of the period from about 1830 to 1880, during which the arts and culture had fallen into lawless disorder and anarchy, had ended with a rediscovery of classicism in the 1880s and '90s, which, from the perspective of 1914-20, seemed to have a continuing and glowing future. The World's Columbian Exposition of 1893 in Chicago (pls. 41–44) had firmly established the American Renaissance, and the recent Panama-Pacific Exposition in San Francisco (pls. 384–387) indicated its enduring reign.[10]

The *Monograph* had several purposes. First, like most publications in which architects have had a hand, it would tend to confirm their own importance. Second, it would help attract clients, serving as a promotional aid in a profession that disdained the salesman's hustle. Third, it would serve an educational function in the drafting rooms and the architectural schools. In all these capacities it would spread the word of American classicism.

The firm produced new presentation drawings of plans, elevations and sections of all the buildings chosen for inclusion. (Interestingly, the partners chose not to use the many original perspective drawings still available.) As a special feature, large-scale drawings were done of ornament, moldings and details. New photographs of almost all the buildings were also commissioned, with the consequence that automobiles appear in front of structures like the Russell and Erwin Building and the Boston Public Library (pls. 100–109) that had been completed years before. Only in several early works like the casinos at Newport and Narragansett Pier (pls. 1, 6) and the Osborn house (pls. 12, 13) were original early photographs used. But even for these buildings new drawings were made.

The result was that, with the minor exception of a few early works, the *Monograph* presented the firm's work as a seamless whole, a continuity that had existed for nearly forty years. The prominence of some early buildings, such as the casinos and the Charles L. Tiffany mansion in New York (pls. 5, 5A), meant they could not be ignored; however, the concentration is on the classical designs and work of the 1890s and later. Well over half of the plates are devoted to buildings completed after 1900. The observant reader could note the vast differences between the early rough-faced stone of the Osborn house and the more suave Edgar house (pl. 14), but there is no reference to the missing hundred or more shingled structures from 1879 through the early 1880s with which the firm initially made its reputation.[11] As later students have shown, the firm's styles went through decided transformations in its early years, from the picturesque Queen Anne and Modernized Colonial of the shingled houses in Newport and in Elberon, New Jersey, to the more settled and consolidated forms of the Osborn and Edgar houses, and finally by the late 1880s to a high-classic expression.[12] Experiments with medieval imagery, such as Saint Paul's Church in Stockbridge (pl. 4) and St. Peter's Church in Morristown (pl. 23), appear in the *Monograph* as well, and these and other early works—such as the experiments with the François Ier style in the Winans and Whittier houses (pls. 2, 3)—indicate McKim, Mead & White's involvement in the so-called "battle of the styles" as they searched for an appropriate expression for American architecture and civilization. In many ways their classicism won the battle. It was cut from many pieces; Roman, Florentine and Venetian Renaissance, French eighteenth-century, English Georgian, American Colonial and other styles contributed to the vision of this modern American Renaissance.

The *Monograph* project was conceived of as 400 plates, to be bound eventually in four massive volumes. They were originally published in installments; the first group of 20 plates appeared in 1915. They were not issued in numerical order and quickly became confused as further drawings were published, resulting in the missing plate numbers and the addition of other plates (5A, 19A, etc). America's entry into the war slowed both the production of new drawings and their publication, and the final plates were not issued until 1920. A "Student's Edition" of 136 selected plates of drawings from the *Monograph* came out in 1925.

Though the *Monograph* had its predecessors—Van Rensselaer's *Henry Hobson Richardson* of 1888 was one, and some similar foreign folios had been published—its scale and availability made this publication unique. It set a pattern for the *œuvres complètes* and vanity books on individual architects and firms that would grow to a flood in the years to come. *A Monograph of the Work of McKim Mead & White* offered an ideal and a reality. Along with buildings it presented triumphal arches, pedestals for statues and memorials, layouts for campuses and large groups of buildings, gates and other elements, all of which indicated a new level of aspiration for American civilization. The *Monograph* represents a stunning achievement both purely as a publication and as a record of the preeminent American architectural partnership.

RICHARD GUY WILSON

NOTES

1. Robert Kerr, "Supplement," in James Fergusson, *History of the Modern Styles of Architecture*, 3rd ed. (New York: Dodd, Mead, 1891), p. 351. Fergusson's original commentary is on pp. 327-42.

2. Charles H. Reilly, "The Modern Renaissance in American Architecture," *Journal of the Royal Institute of British Architects*, ser. 3, vol. 17 (June 25, 1910), p. 635. See also Stanley D. Adshead, "A Comparison of Modern American Architecture with That of European Cities," *Architectural Record* 29 (February 1911), pp. 113-25.

3. Charles H. Reilly, *McKim, Mead & White* (London: Ernest Benn, 1924).

4. Standard studies of McKim are Alfred H. Granger, *Charles Follen McKim: A Study of His Life and Work* (Boston: Houghton Mifflin, 1913), and Charles Moore, *The Life and Times of Charles Follen McKim* (Boston: Houghton Mifflin, 1929).

5. Studies include Charles Baldwin, *Stanford White* (New York: Dodd, Mead, 1931), and Paul R. Baker, *Stanny: The Gilded Life of Stanford White* (New York: Free Press, 1989).

6. "Correction," *Art Age* 3 (January 1886), p. 100.

7. C. Howard Walker, "Joseph Wells, Architect, 1853-1890," *Architectural Record* 66 (July 1929), pp. 14-18, and William Mitchell Kendall, "Letter to Royal Cortissoz," same issue, p. 18.

8. Russell Sturgis, "The Work of McKim, Mead & White," Great American Architects Series, *Architectural Record*, special issue (May 1895).

9. Henry W. Desmond and Herbert Croly, "The Work of Messrs. McKim, Mead & White," *Architectural Record* 20 (September 1906), pp. 153-246.

10. Richard Guy Wilson, Dianne H. Pilgrim and Richard Murray, *The American Renaissance, 1876-1917* (Brooklyn and New York: The Brooklyn Museum and Pantheon, 1979).

11. Vincent Scully, Jr., *The Shingle Style: Architectural Theory and Design from Richardson to the Origins of Wright* (New Haven: Yale University Press, 1955).

12. For surveys see Richard Guy Wilson, *McKim, Mead & White, Architects* (New York: Rizzoli, 1983), and Leland Roth, *McKim, Mead & White, Architects* (New York: Harper & Row, 1983) and *The Architecture of McKim, Mead & White, 1870-1920* (New York: Garland, 1978).

A MONOGRAPH

OF THE WORK OF

McKIM MEAD & WHITE

1879 – 1915

·VOLUME·ONE·

·PUBLISHED·BY·

THE ARCHITECTURAL BOOK PUBLISHING CO

PAUL WENZEL & MAURICE KRAKOW

31 EAST 12TH STREET

NEW YORK

(Original title page)

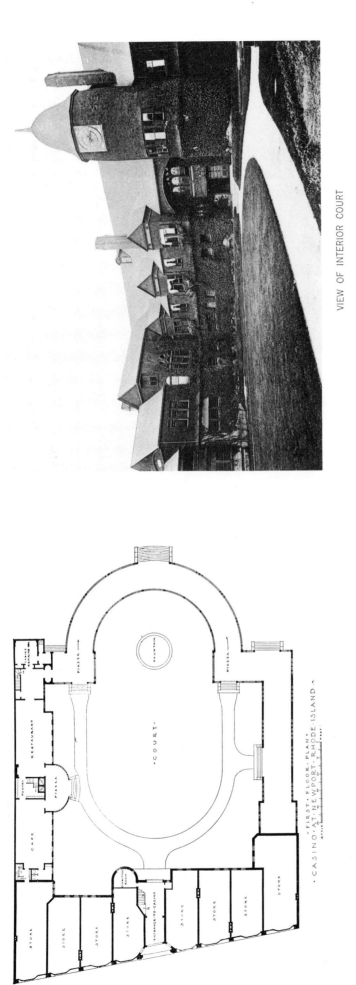

VIEW OF INTERIOR COURT

· FIRST · FLOOR · PLAN ·
· CASINO · AT · NEWPORT · RHODE · ISLAND ·

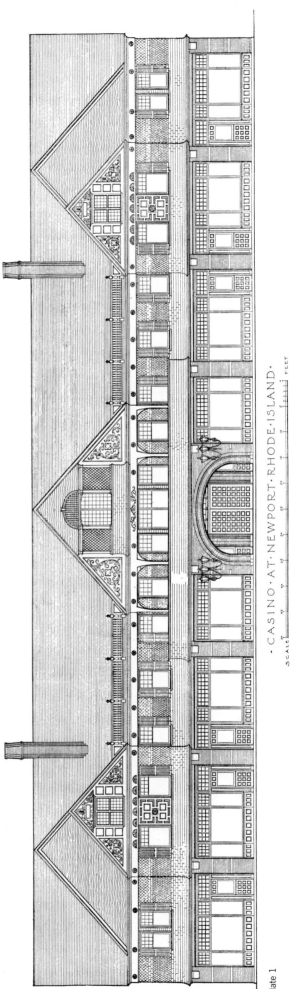

· CASINO · AT · NEWPORT · RHODE · ISLAND ·
SCALE   FEET

1881

Plate 1

ROSS WINANS, RESIDENCE, BALTIMORE, MD.

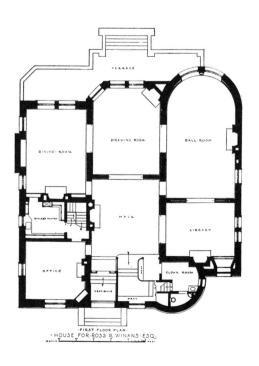

FIRST FLOOR PLAN
HOUSE FOR ROSS R WINANS ESQ

Plate 2   ENTRANCE DETAIL

1882

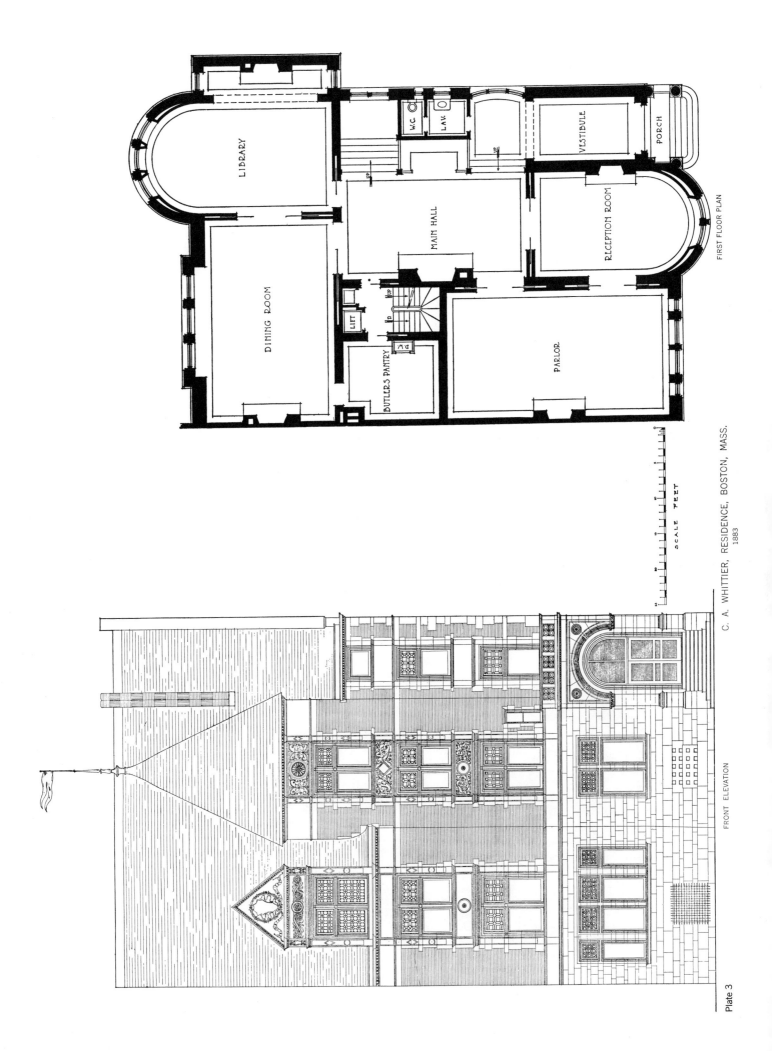

LIBRARY

DINING ROOM

MAIN HALL

W.C.

LAV.

VESTIBULE

PORCH

RECEPTION ROOM

LIFT

BUTLERS PANTRY

PARLOR

FIRST FLOOR PLAN

SCALE FEET

C. A. WHITTIER, RESIDENCE, BOSTON, MASS.
1883

FRONT ELEVATION

Plate 3

ST·PAUL'S·CHURCH·I·STOCKBRIDGE·MASS·
SCALE   FEET·

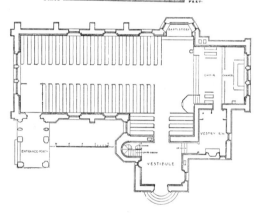

Plate 4   ST. PAUL'S CHURCH · STOCKBRIDGE, MASS.
1883

CHARLES L. TIFFANY, RESIDENCE, NEW YORK CITY.
1884

Plate 5

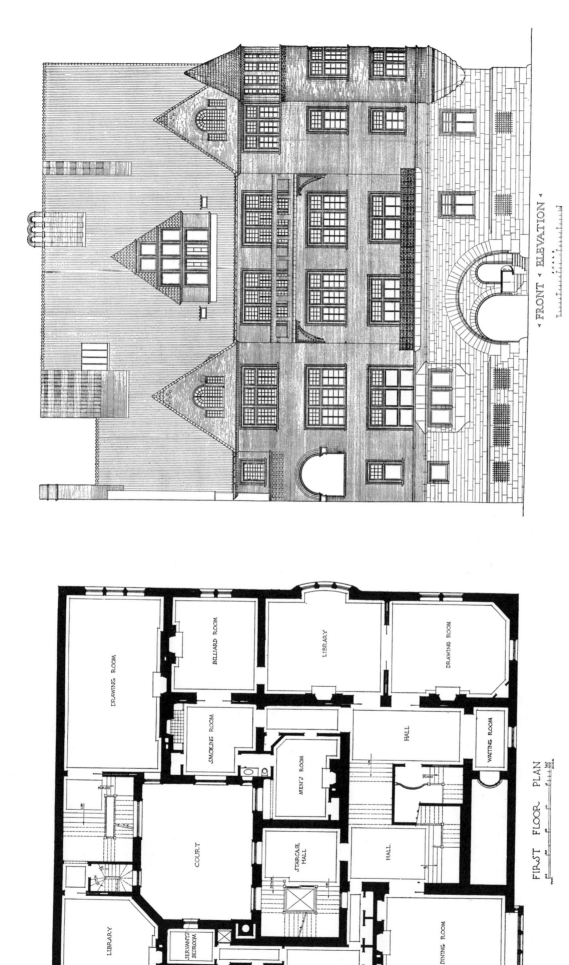

FRONT ELEVATION
SCALE

FIRST FLOOR PLAN
SCALE

DRAWING ROOM

BILLIARD ROOM

LIBRARY

DRAWING ROOM

SMOKING ROOM

HALL

WAITING ROOM

CLOS.

COURT

MEN'S ROOM

LIBRARY

STAIRCASE HALL

HALL

SERVANT'S BEDROOM

SERVANT'S BEDROOM

KITCHEN

DINING ROOM

CHARLES L. TIFFANY, RESIDENCE, NEW YORK CITY.
1884

Plate 5A

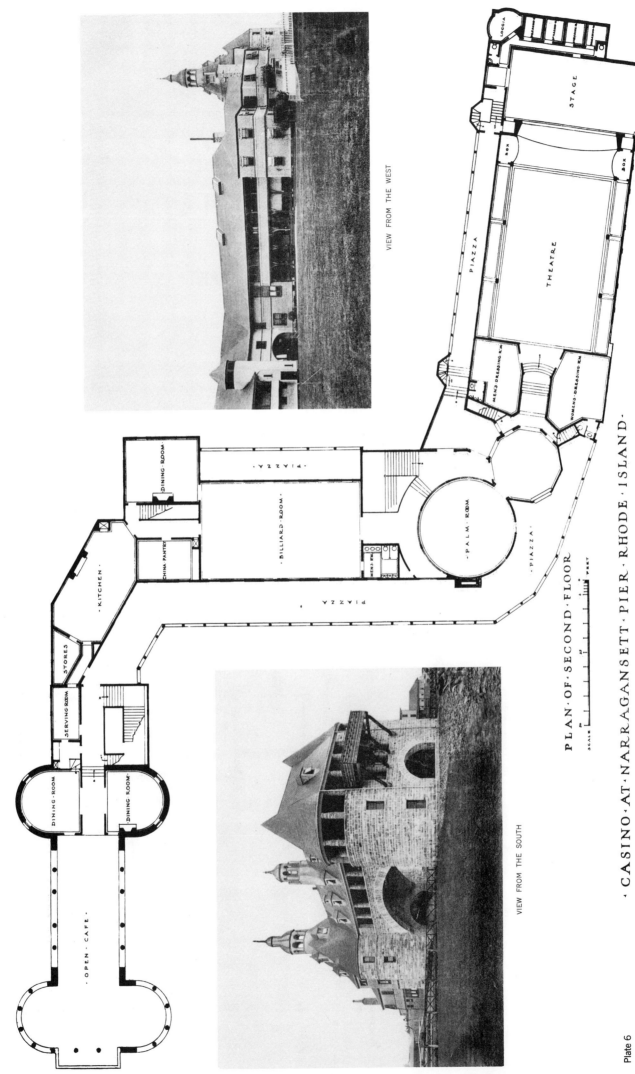

VIEW FROM THE WEST

VIEW FROM THE SOUTH

·PLAN·OF·SECOND·FLOOR·

1884

SCALE

·CASINO·AT·NARRAGANSETT·PIER·RHODE·ISLAND·

STAGE

BOX

BOX

THEATRE

PIAZZA

PIAZZA

MEN'S DRESSING RM

WOMEN'S DRESSING RM

LOGGIA

·PIAZZA·

·PALM·ROOM·

MEN'S RM

·BILLIARD·ROOM·

·PIAZZA·

·PIAZZA·

·DINING·ROOM·

·KITCHEN·

CHINA PANTRY

STORES

SERVING ROOM

·DINING·ROOM·

·DINING·ROOM·

·OPEN·CAFE·

Plate 6

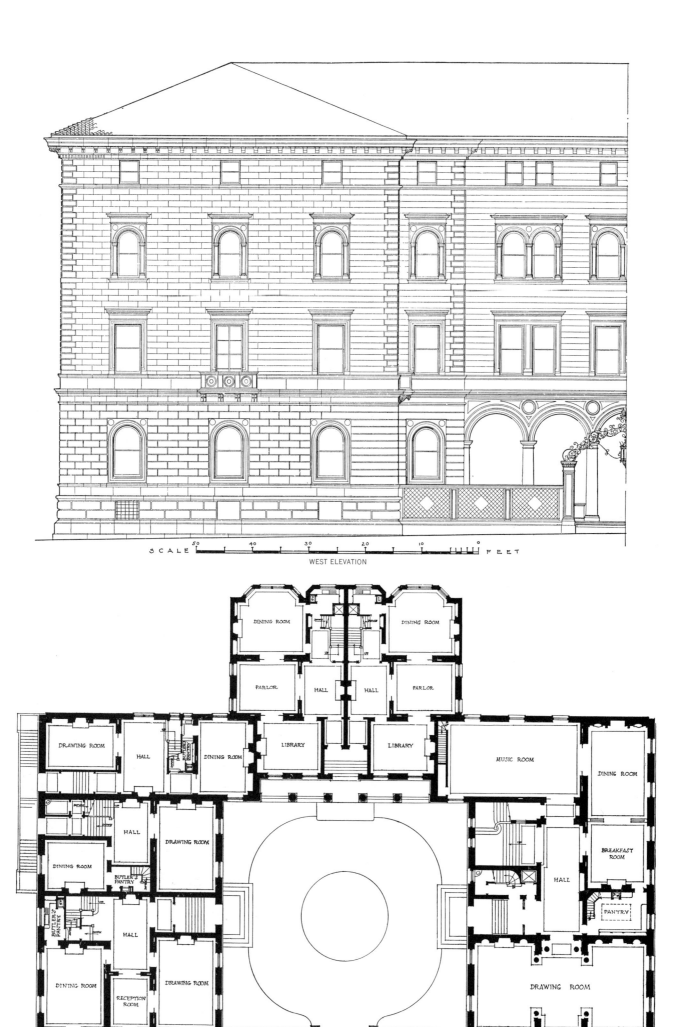

SCALE 50 40 30 20 10 0 FEET

WEST ELEVATION

DINING ROOM   DINING ROOM

PARLOR   HALL   HALL   PARLOR

DRAWING ROOM   HALL   BUTLER'S PANTRY   DINING ROOM   LIBRARY   LIBRARY   MUSIC ROOM   DINING ROOM

HALL   DRAWING ROOM   HALL   BREAKFAST ROOM

DINING ROOM   BUTLER'S PANTRY   BUTLER'S PANTRY   HALL   PANTRY

DINING ROOM   HALL   DRAWING ROOM   DRAWING ROOM

RECEPTION ROOM

FEET   SCALE

FIRST FLOOR PLAN

Plate 7   HENRY VILLARD, RESIDENCE, NEW YORK CITY.
1885

MADISON AVENUE FACADE

ENTRANCE GATEWAY

HENRY VILLARD, RESIDENCE, NEW YORK CITY.
1885

Plate 8

DOOR TO DINING ROOM

MANTEL IN ENTRANCE HALL

HENRY VILLARD, RESIDENCE, NEW YORK CITY.
1885

Plate 9

LUNETTE OVER MANTEL

ENTRANCE HALL

HENRY VILLARD, RESIDENCE, NEW YORK CITY.
1885

Plate 10

MANTEL IN DINING ROOM

DINING ROOM

HENRY VILLARD, RESIDENCE, NEW YORK CITY
1885

Plate 11

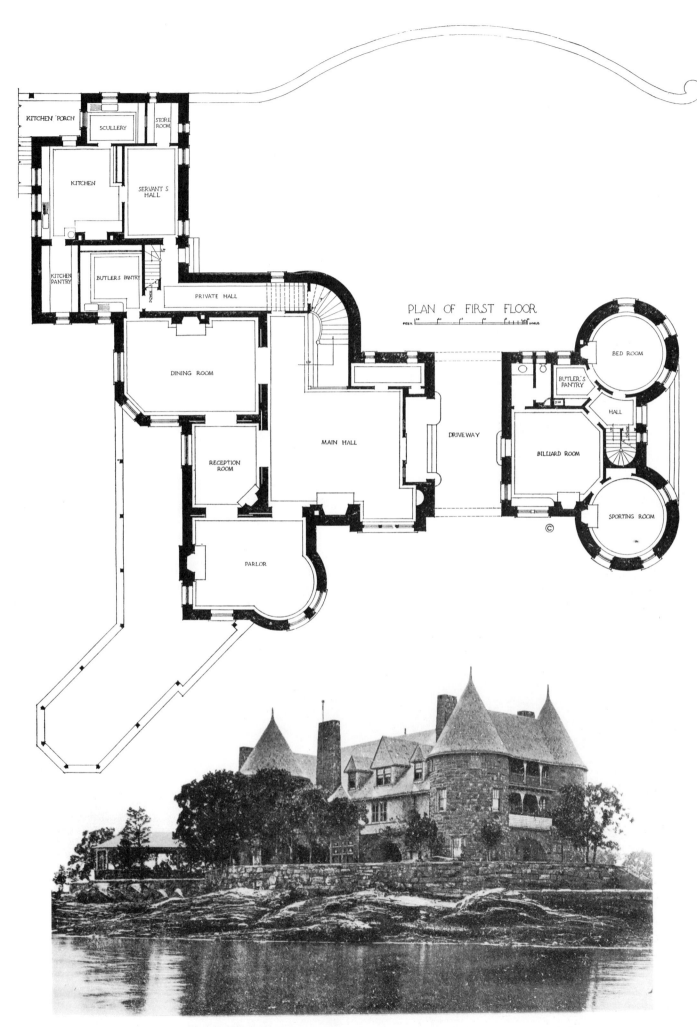

PLAN OF FIRST FLOOR

FEET   SCALE

KITCHEN PORCH

SCULLERY

STORE ROOM

KITCHEN

SERVANT'S HALL

KITCHEN PANTRY

BUTLER'S PANTRY

PRIVATE HALL

DINING ROOM

RECEPTION ROOM

PARLOR

MAIN HALL

DRIVEWAY

BUTLER'S PANTRY

BED ROOM

HALL

BILLIARD ROOM

SPORTING ROOM

RESIDENCE OF CHARLES J. OSBORN, MAMARONECK, N. Y.
1885

Plate 12

RESIDENCE OF CHARLES J. OSBORN, MAMARONECK, N. Y.
1885

Plate 13   CHARLES J. OSBORN, MAMARONECK, N. Y. GATE LODGE.
1885

RESIDENCE OF MRS. WILLIAM EDGAR, NEWPORT, R. I.
1886

CHARLES J. OSBORN, MAMARONECK, N. Y. - THE STABLE.
1885

Plate 14

PETER COOPER MONUMENT
1897

SCULPTURE BY AUGUSTUS ST. GAUDENS

DAVID GLASGOW FARRAGUT MONUMENT
1881

Plate 15

H. A. C. TAYLOR, RESIDENCE, NEWPORT, R. I.

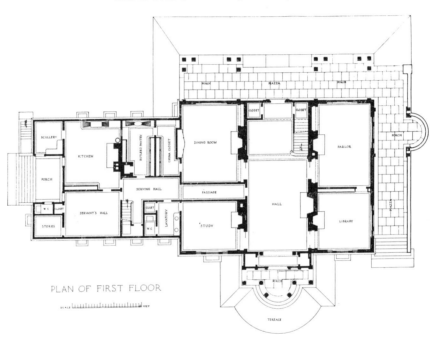

PLAN OF FIRST FLOOR

H. A. C. TAYLOR, RESIDENCE, NEWPORT, R. I.
1886

Plate 16

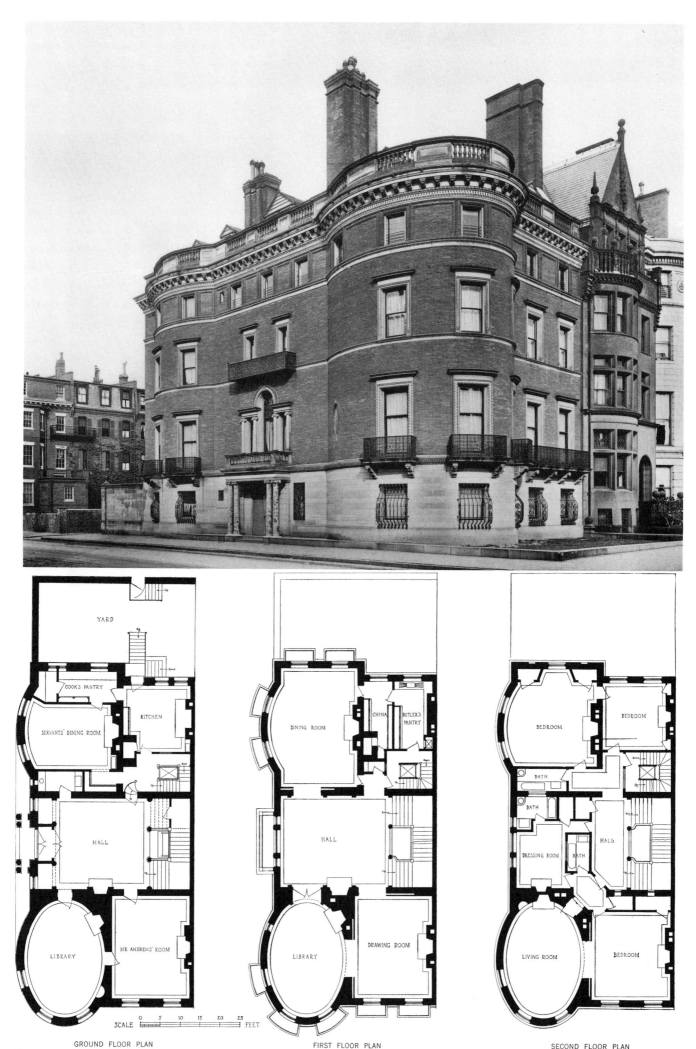

YARD

COOK'S PANTRY

KITCHEN

SERVANTS' DINING ROOM

HALL

LIBRARY

MR ANDREWS' ROOM

DINING ROOM

CHINA

BUTLER'S PANTRY

HALL

LIBRARY

DRAWING ROOM

BEDROOM

BEDROOM

BATH

BATH

DRESSING ROOM

BATH

HALL

LIVING ROOM

BEDROOM

SCALE 0 5 10 15 20 25 FEET

GROUND FLOOR PLAN

FIRST FLOOR PLAN

SECOND FLOOR PLAN

Plate 17

JOHN F. ANDREWS, RESIDENCE, BOSTON, MASS.

1886

ALGONQUIN CLUB, BOSTON, MASS.
1889

RUSSELL AND ERWIN BUILDING, NEW BRITAIN, CONN.
1885

Plate 18

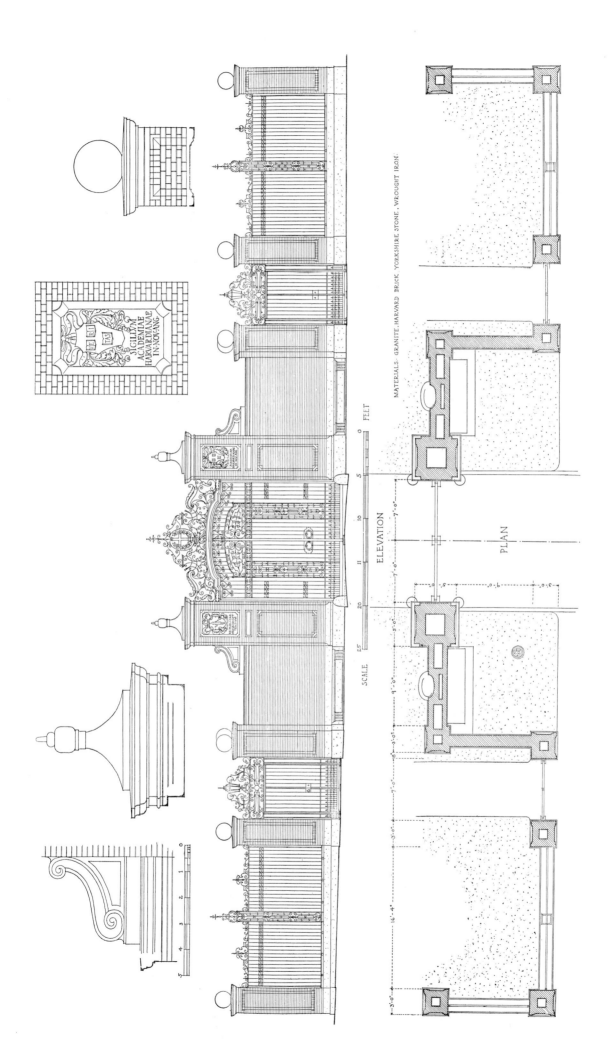

MATERIALS: GRANITE, HARVARD BRICK, YORKSHIRE STONE, WROUGHT IRON.

SIGILLVM
ACADEMIAE
HARVARDIANAE
IN·NOV·ANG.

FEET

SCALE

ELEVATION

PLAN

JOHNSTON GATES, MAIN ENTRANCE HARVARD UNIVERSITY, CAMBRIDGE MASS.
1894

Plate 19

JOHNSTON GATES, HARVARD UNIVERSITY, CAMBRIDGE MASS.
1890

Plate 19A

SHELTER AT CONEY ISLAND AVENUE ENTRANCE

SHELTER AT EASTERN PARKWAY ENTRANCE

Plate 20

ENTRANCES TO PROSPECT PARK, BROOKLYN, N. Y.
1890 - 1894

DETAIL AT CONEY ISLAND AVENUE ENTRANCE

PEDESTAL AND SEAT AT CONEY ISLAND AVENUE ENTRANCE, BRONZE GROUP BY FREDERICK MAC MONNIES.

ENTRANCES TO PROSPECT PARK BROOKLYN, N. Y.
1890

Plate 21

ELEVATION

Plate 22   NEW YORK LIFE INSURANCE COMPANY, BUILDING, KANSAS CITY, MO.

1890

CHANCEL AND CHOIR SCREEN

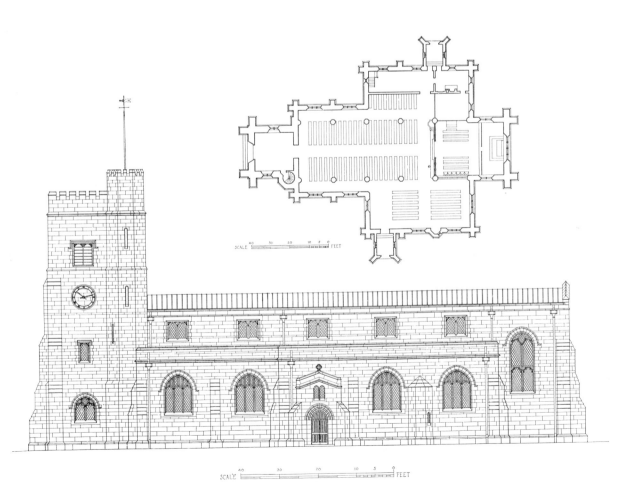

SCALE 40 30 20 10 5 0 FEET

SCALE 40 30 20 10 5 0 FEET

PLAN AND ELEVATION OF ORIGINAL SCHEME

ST. PETER'S CHURCH, MORRISTOWN, N. J.
1890

Plate 23

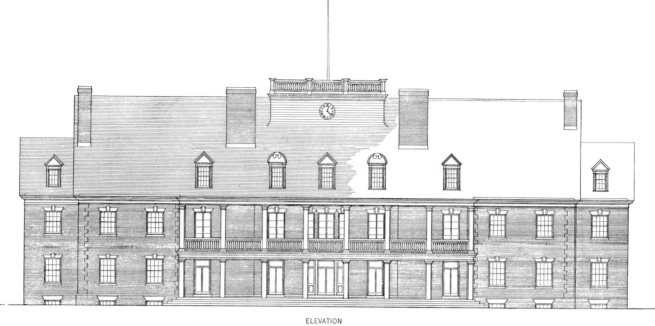

ELEVATION

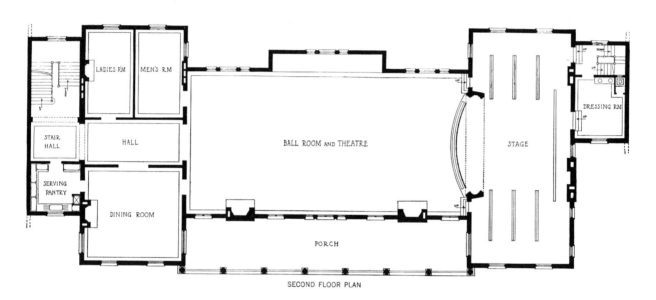

LADIES RM	MEN'S RM
STAIR HALL	HALL
SERVING PANTRY	DINING ROOM

BALL ROOM and THEATRE

STAGE

DRESSING RM

PORCH

SECOND FLOOR PLAN

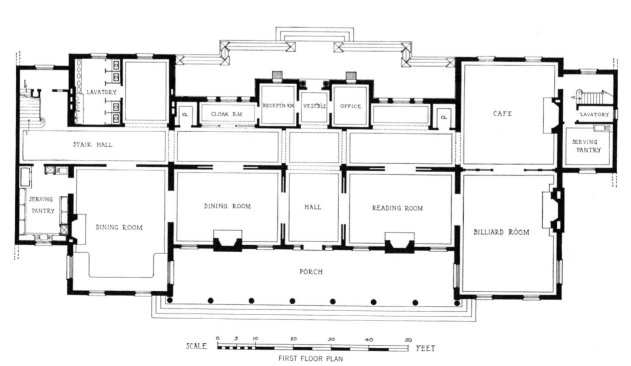

LAVATORY	CLOAK RM	RECEPT'N RM	VESTBLE	OFFICE	CAFE	LAVATORY
STAIR HALL						SERVING PANTRY
SERVING PANTRY	DINING ROOM	DINING ROOM	HALL	READING ROOM	BILLIARD ROOM

PORCH

SCALE ⊢ 0 5 10 20 30 40 50 ⊣ FEET

FIRST FLOOR PLAN

Plate 24

GERMANTOWN CRICKET CLUB, PHILADELPHIA, PA.
1891

FACADE TOWARD PLAYING FIELD

MAIN ENTRANCE GATES

GERMANTOWN CRICKET CLUB, PHILADELPHIA, PA.
1891

Plate 25

DETAIL OF ENTRANCE

MANTEL IN DINING ROOM

GERMANTOWN CRICKET CLUB, PHILADELPHIA, PA.
1891

Plate 26

CENTURY CLUB, NEW YORK CITY.
1891

Plate 27

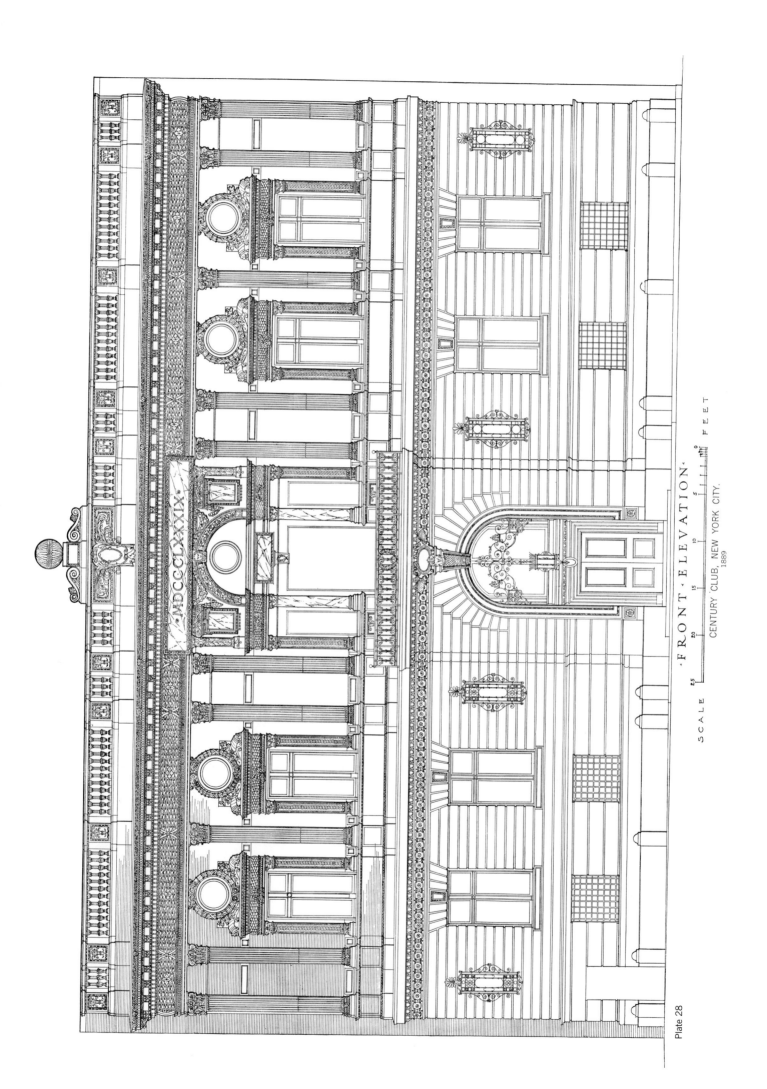

·FRONT·ELEVATION·

CENTURY CLUB, NEW YORK CITY.

1889

SCALE

FEET

MDCCCLXXXIX.

Plate 28

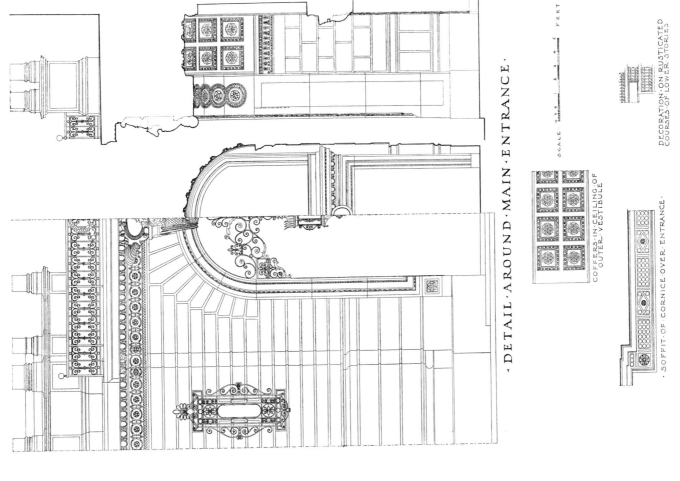

· DETAIL · AROUND · MAIN · ENTRANCE ·

SCALE   1   2   3   4   5   FEET

· COFFERS · IN · CEILING · OF ·
· OUTER · VESTIBULE ·

· DECORATION · ON · RUSTICATED ·
· COURSES · OF · LOWER · STORIES ·

· SOFFIT · OF · CORNICE · OVER · ENTRANCE ·

CENTURY CLUB, NEW YORK CITY.
1889

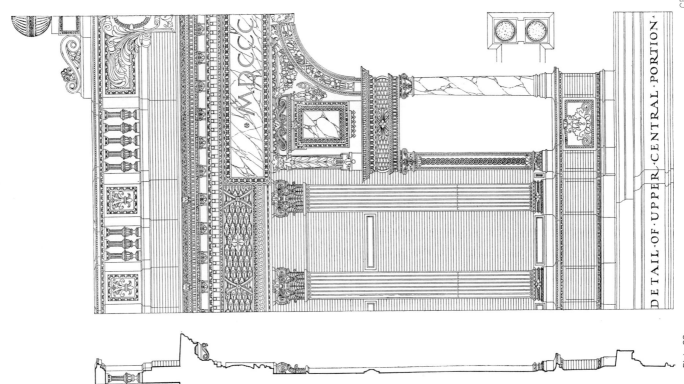

· DETAIL · OF · UPPER · CENTRAL · PORTION ·

Plate 29

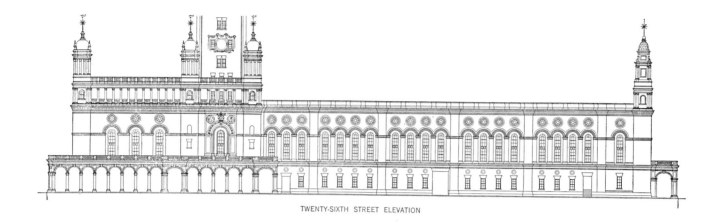

TWENTY-SIXTH STREET ELEVATION

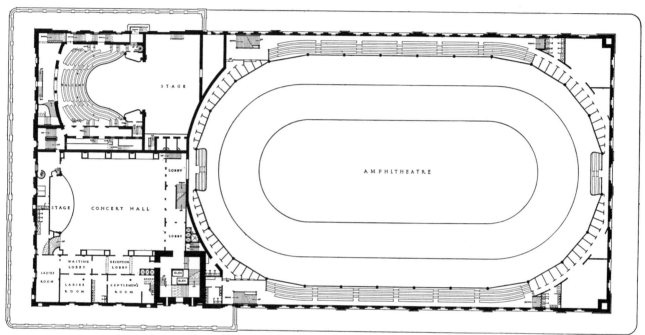

BALCONY FLOOR PLAN

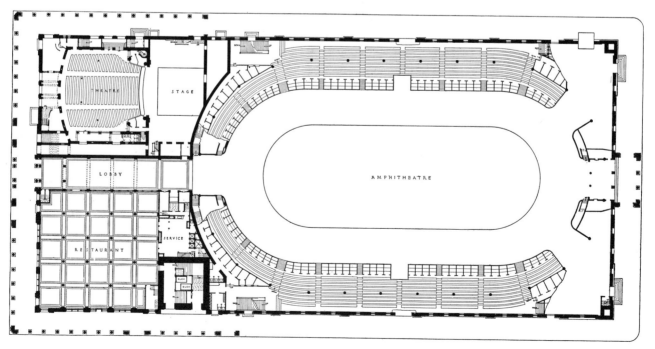

SCALE ⊢━━━━━━━━━━━━━┤ FEET

GROUND FLOOR PLAN

Plate 30

MADISON SQUARE GARDEN, NEW YORK CITY.
1891

SOUTHWEST ANGLE FROM MADISON SQUARE

MADISON SQUARE GARDEN, NEW YORK CITY.

1891

Plate 32

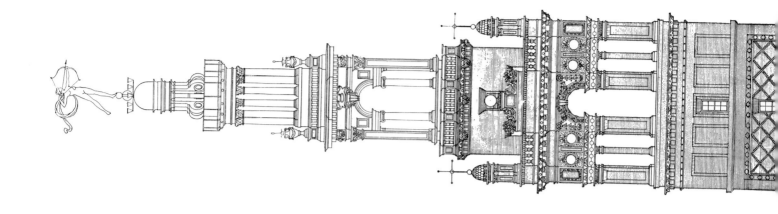

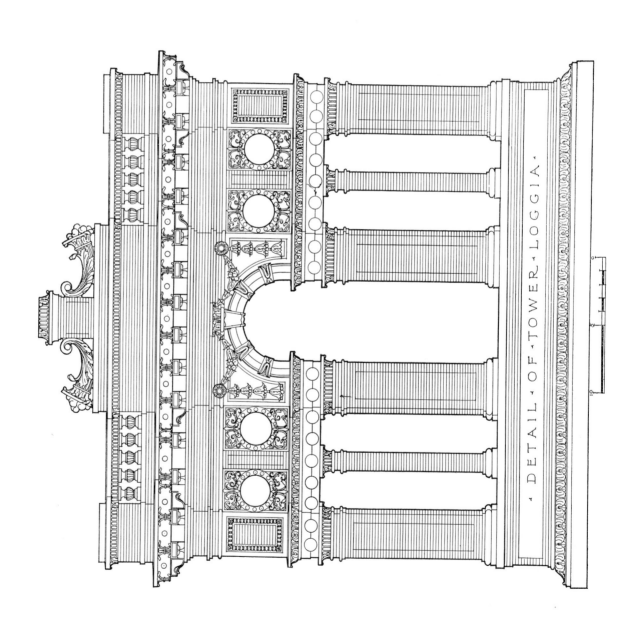

· DETAIL · OF · TOWER · LOGGIA ·

MADISON AVENUE ELEVATION

MADISON SQUARE GARDEN, NEW YORK CITY.
1891

SCALE FEET

Plate 31-31A

ARCADE AT MAIN ENTRANCE

MADISON SQUARE GARDEN, NEW YORK CITY.

CENTRAL MOTIVE ON MADISON AVENUE ABOVE ENTRANCE

Plate 33

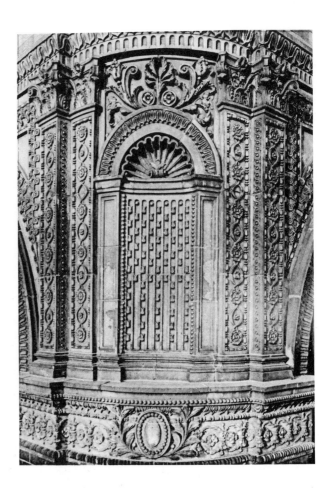

TERRA COTTA DETAILS OF LOWER ARCADE

MADISON SQUARE GARDEN, NEW YORK CITY.
1891

Plate 34

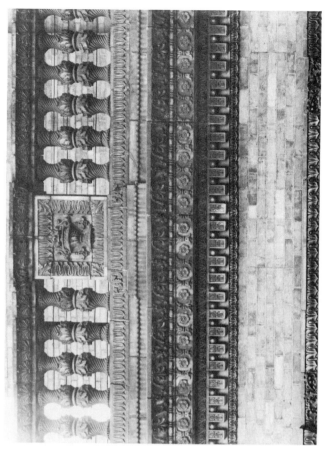

DETAILS CF LOWER ARCADE

LOWER ARCADE

MADISON SQUARE GARDEN, NEW YORK CITY.
1891

Plate 35

COLONNADE OF ROOF GARDEN

UPPER PART OF TOWER

MADISON SQUARE GARDEN, NEW YORK CITY.
1891

Plate 36

DETAILS OF TERRA COTTA AND BRICKWORK ON TOWER

Plate 37

MADISON SQUARE GARDEN, NEW YORK CITY.
1891

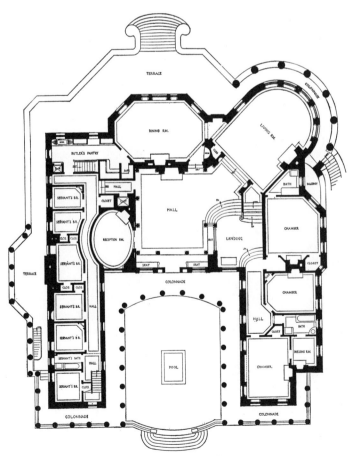

PLAN OF FIRST FLOOR

E. D. MORGAN RESIDENCE, NEWPORT, R. I.
1891

Plate 38

Plate 39

THE WASHINGTON ARCH, NEW YORK CITY.
1892

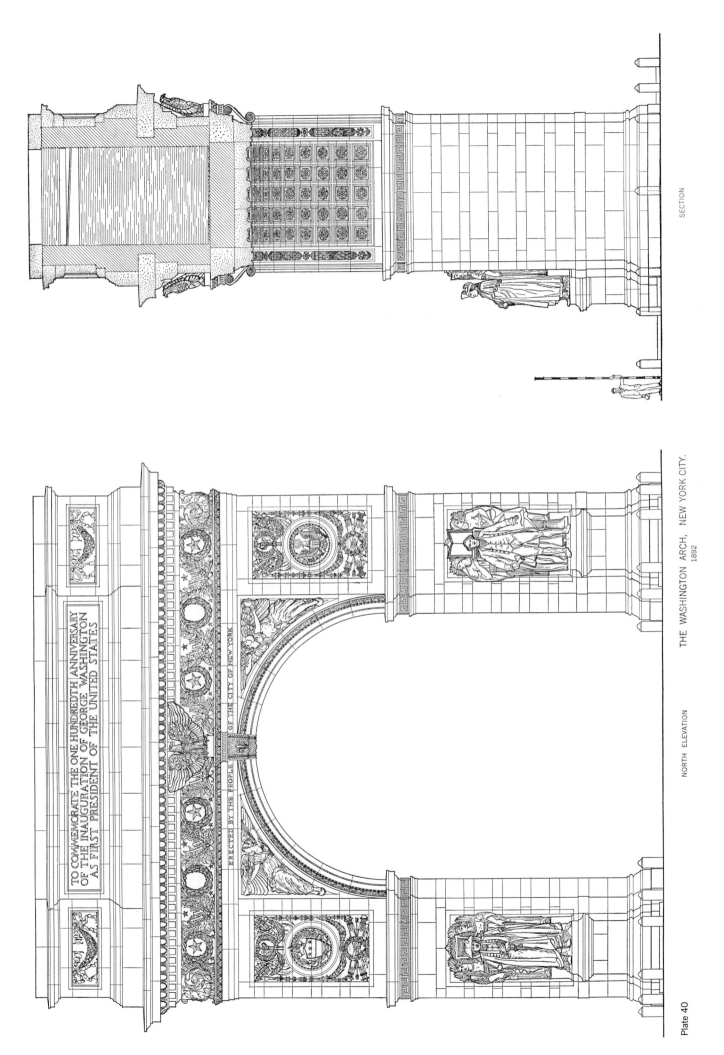

TO COMMEMORATE THE ONE HUNDREDTH ANNIVERSARY
OF THE INAUGURATION OF GEORGE WASHINGTON
AS FIRST PRESIDENT OF THE UNITED STATES

ERECTED BY THE PEOPLE OF THE CITY OF NEW YORK

SECTION

NORTH ELEVATION

THE WASHINGTON ARCH, NEW YORK CITY.
1892

Plate 40

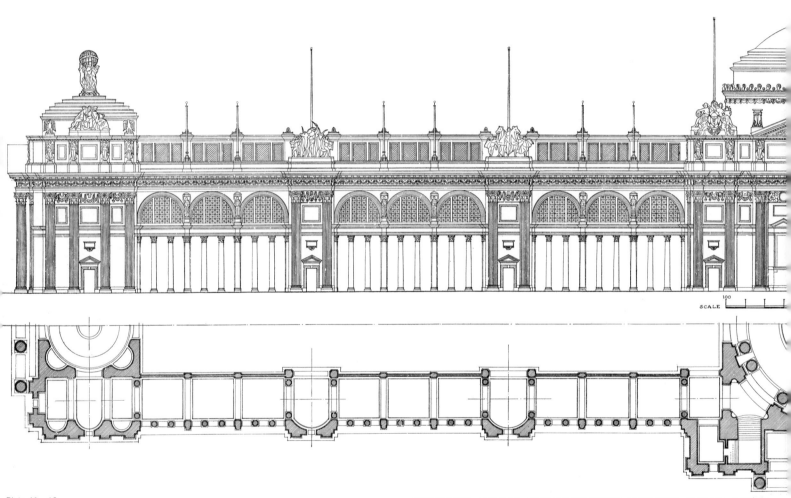

SCALE

Plate 41 - 42

AGRICULTURAL BUILDING, WORLD'S COLUMBIAN EXPOSITION, CHICAGO, ILLINOIS.
1893

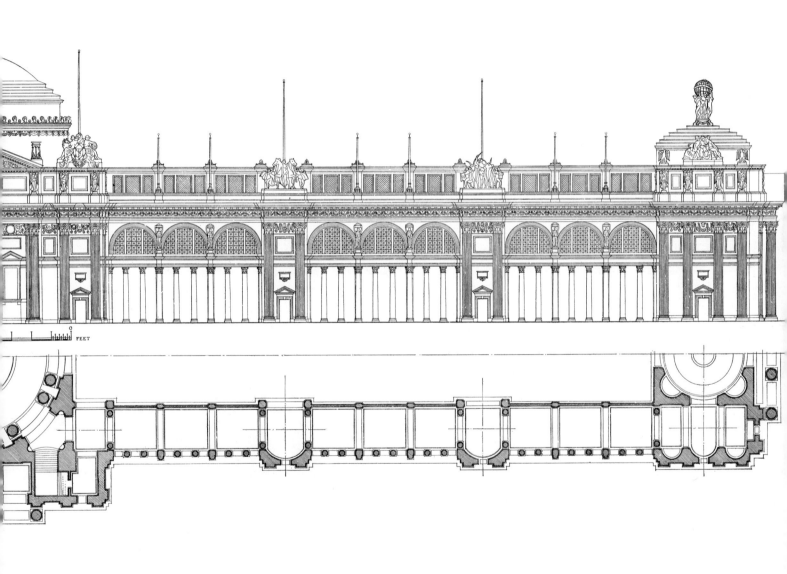

FEET

NEW YORK STATE BUILDING, WORLD'S COLUMBIAN EXPOSITION, CHICAGO, ILLINOIS.
1893

Plate 43

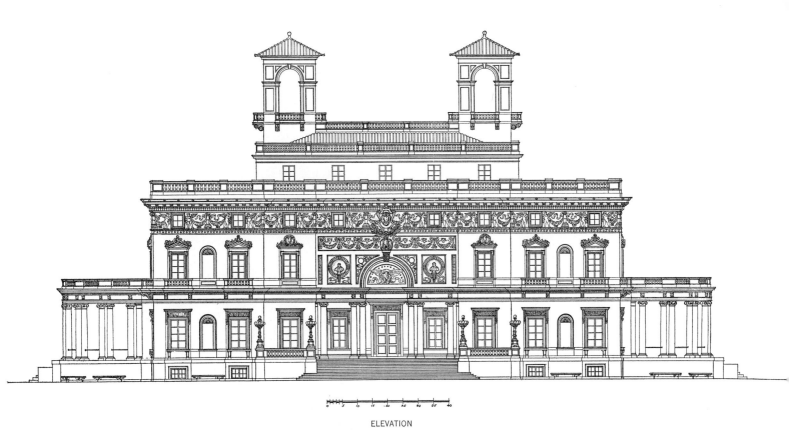

ELEVATION

LADIES ROOM

SMOKING ROOM

COAT ROOM

RECEPTION ROOM

MAIN HALL

RECEPTION ROOM

LADIES PARLOR

GENTLEMENS PARLOR

RECEPTION-RM.

VESTIBULE

POST-OFFICE AND INFORMATION RM.

FIRST FLOOR PLAN

NEW YORK STATE BUILDING, WORLD'S FAIR, CHICAGO, ILLINOIS.
1893

Plate 44

Plate 45   WALKER ART BUILDING BOWDOIN COLLEGE, BRUNSWICK, ME.
1893

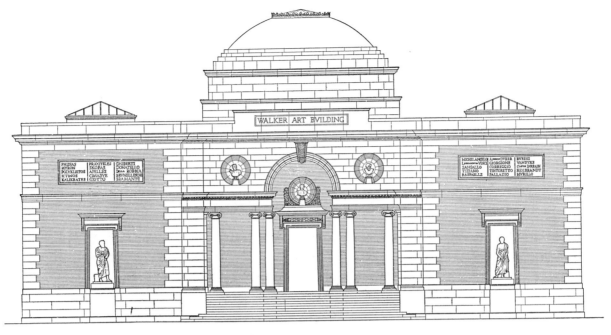

SCALE |___|___|___|___|___|___|___|FEET

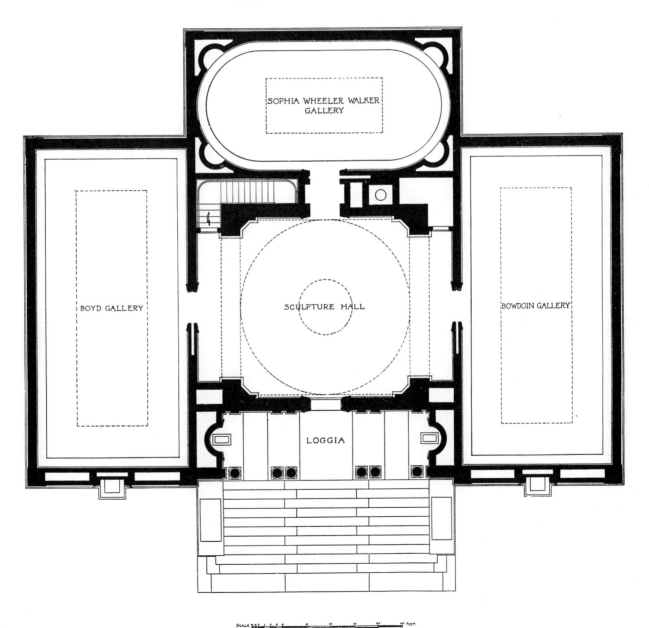

SCALE |___|___|___|___|___|___|___|___|___|FEET

WALKER ART GALLERY, BOWDOIN COLLEGE, BRUNSWICK, MAINE.
1893

Plate 46

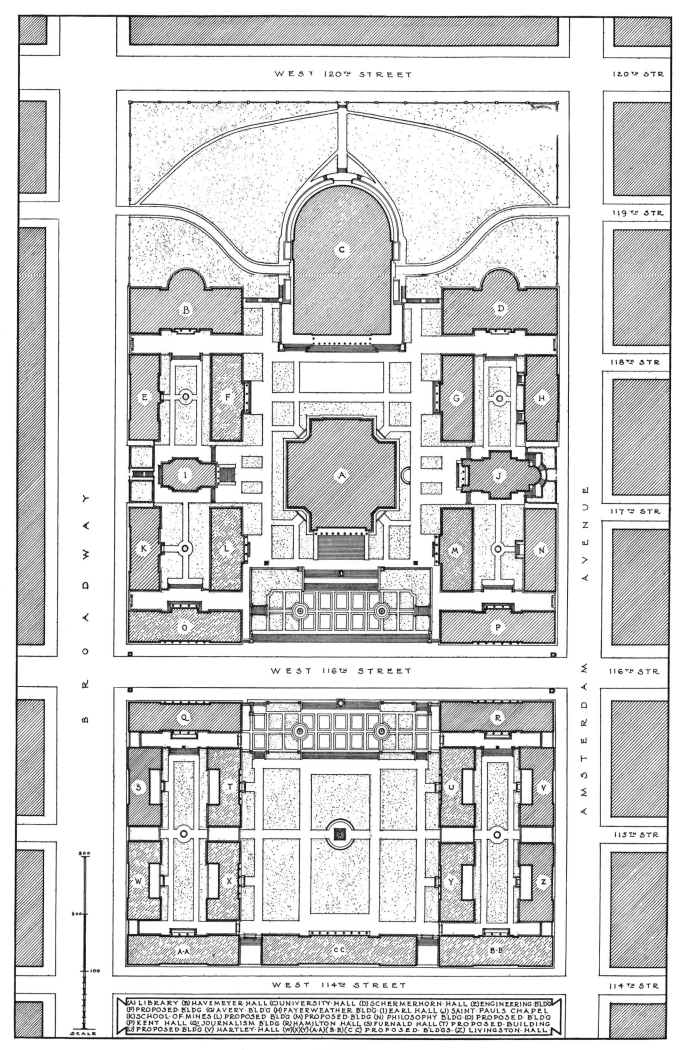

WEST 120TH STREET

120TH STR

119TH STR

C

118TH STR

B   D

E   F   G   H

117TH STR

I   A   J

K   L   M   N

O   P

WEST 116TH STREET

116TH STR

Q   R

S   T   U   V

115TH STR

W   X   Y   Z

A·A   C·C   B·B

WEST 114TH STREET

114TH STR

B R O A D W A Y

A M S T E R D A M   A V E N U E

500

200

100

SCALE

(A) LIBRARY (B) HAVEMEYER HALL (C) UNIVERSITY HALL (D) SCHERMERHORN HALL (E) ENGINEERING BLD'G
(F) PROPOSED BLDG (G) AVERY BLD'G (H) FAYERWEATHER BLDG (I) EARL HALL (J) SAINT PAULS CHAPEL
(K) SCHOOL OF MINES (L) PROPOSED BLDG (M) PROPOSED BLDG (N) PHILOSOPHY BLDG (O) PROPOSED BLD'G
(P) KENT HALL (Q) JOURNALISM BLDG (R) HAMILTON HALL (S) FURNALD HALL (T) PROPOSED BUILDING
(U) PROPOSED BLDG (V) HARTLEY HALL (W)(X)(Y)(A·A)(B·B)(C·C) PROPOSED B'LDG'S. (Z) LIVINGSTON HALL

Plate 47

BLOCK PLAN
COLUMBIA UNIVERSITY, NEW YORK CITY.
1893

COLUMBIA UNIVERSITY LIBRARY, NEW YORK CITY.
1893

Plate 48

Plate 49

KING'S·COLLEGE·FOUNDED·IN·THE·PROVINCE·OF·NEW·YORK
BY·ROYAL·CHARTER·IN·THE·REIGN·OF·GEORGE·II
PERPETUATED·AS·COLUMBIA·COLLEGE·BY·THE·PEOPLE·OF·THE·STATE·OF·NEW·YORK
WHEN·THEY·BECAME·FREE·AND·INDEPENDENT·MAINTAINED·AND·CHERISHED·FROM·GENERATION·TO·GENERATION
FOR·THE·ADVANCEMENT·OF·THE·PUBLIC·GOOD·AND·THE·GLORY·OF·ALMIGHTY·GOD

THE·LIBRARY·OF·COLUMBIA·UNIVERSITY

MDCCLIV

MDCCCXCVII

4'-10" 9'-8" 8'-10" 25'-0" 18'-0"

SCALE   50   40   30   20   10   0   FEET

SOUTH ELEVATION

COLUMBIA UNIVERSITY LIBRARY, NEW YORK CITY.
1893

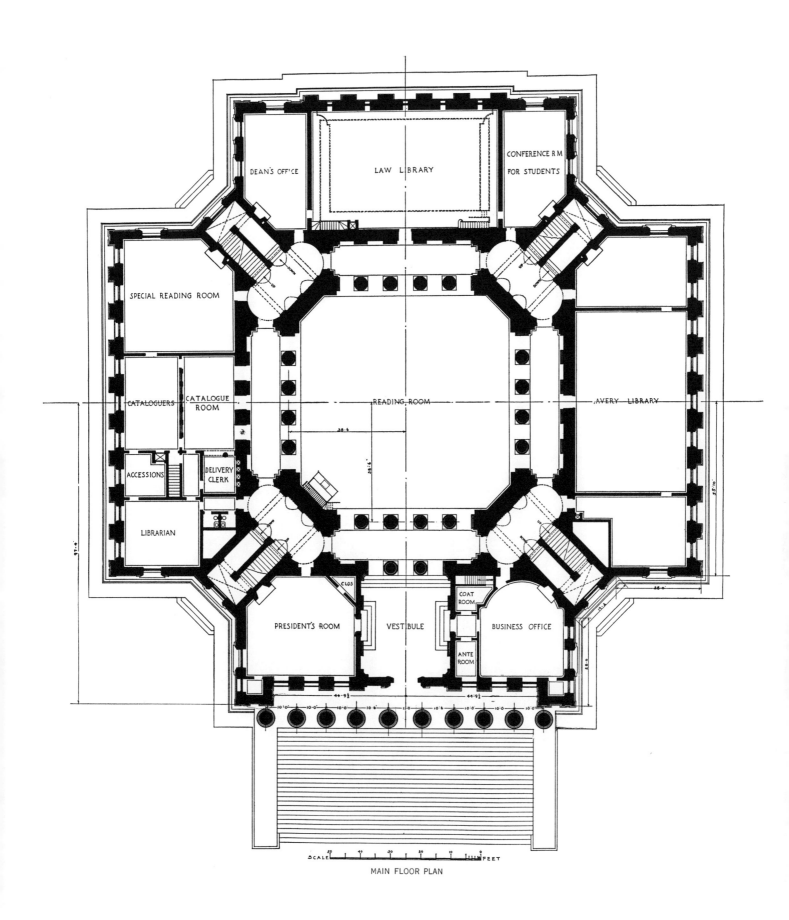

DEAN'S OFFICE LAW LIBRARY CONFERENCE R M FOR STUDENTS

SPECIAL READING ROOM

CATALOGUERS CATALOGUE ROOM

READING ROOM AVERY LIBRARY

ACCESSIONS DELIVERY CLERK

LIBRARIAN

CLOS COAT ROOM

PRESIDENT'S ROOM VESTIBULE BUSINESS OFFICE

ANTE ROOM

SCALE 50 40 30 20 10 0 FEET

MAIN FLOOR PLAN

COLUMBIA UNIVERSITY LIBRARY, NEW YORK CITY.
1893

Plate 50

UPPER·CHENEAU

DETAILS
OF·THE
SOUTH
PORTICO

SIDE·WINDOWS
FIRST·STORY

Plate 51   COLUMBIA UNIVERSITY LIBRARY, NEW YORK CITY.
                                                1893

VESTIBULE

GENERAL VIEW READING ROOM

COLUMBIA UNIVERSITY LIBRARY, NEW YORK CITY.
1893

Plate 52

TRUSTEES ROOM

Plate 53 COLUMBIA UNIVERSITY LIBRARY, NEW YORK CITY.
1893

FEET
10

5

ORNAMENT →

LIMESTONE

BRONZE·CAPITALS

29'-0"

CONTINUE

ORNAMENT →

ORNAMENT →

ASCUTNEY·GREEN·GRANITE·SHAFTS

OPEN

OPEN

CENTRE·OF·ROOM

7'-10"

9'-7"

WROUGHT
IRON·GATES

BELGIAN·BLACK
MARBLE·BASE

BROWN·NUMIDIAN·MARBLE

BRONZE

FLOOR LINE.

DETAILS OF READING ROOM
COLUMBIA UNIVERSITY LIBRARY. NEW YORK CITY.
1893

Plate 54

ENTRANCE DOORWAY

Plate 55   JUDSON MEMORIAL CHURCH, WASHINGTON SQUARE, NEW YORK CITY.

1893

‹DETAIL OF MAIN ENTRANCE‹   ‹SECTION‹

SCALE |‑‑‑‑‑‑‑‑‑‑‑‑‑‑‑‑‑‑‑‑| FEET

JUDSON MEMORIAL CHURCH, WASHINGTON SQUARE, NEW YORK CITY.
1893

Plate 56

THE METROPOLITAN CLUB, NEW YORK CITY.
1894

Plate 57

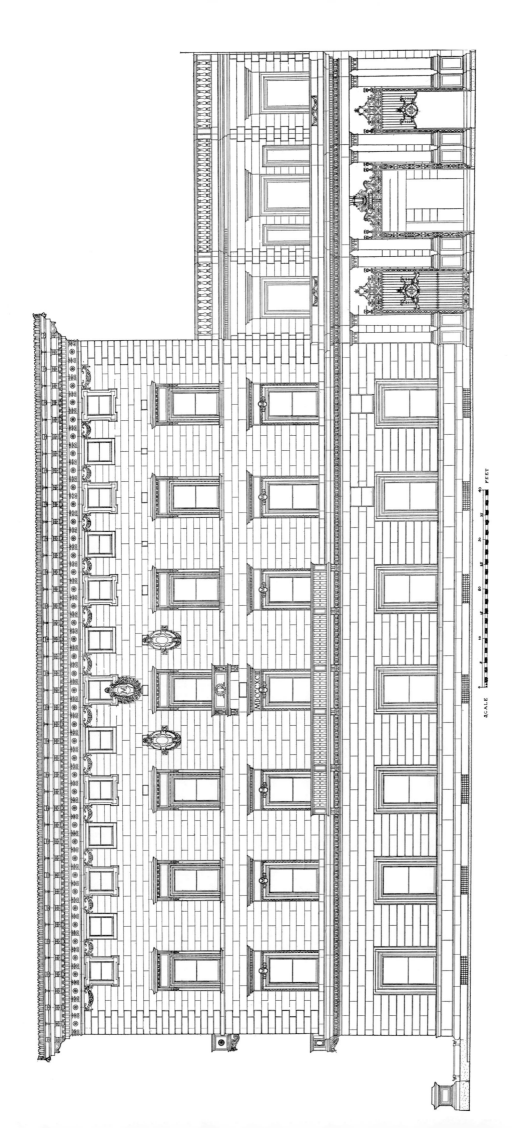

SIXTIETH STREET ELEVATION
METROPOLITAN CLUB, NEW YORK CITY.
1894

SCALE

FEET

Plate 58

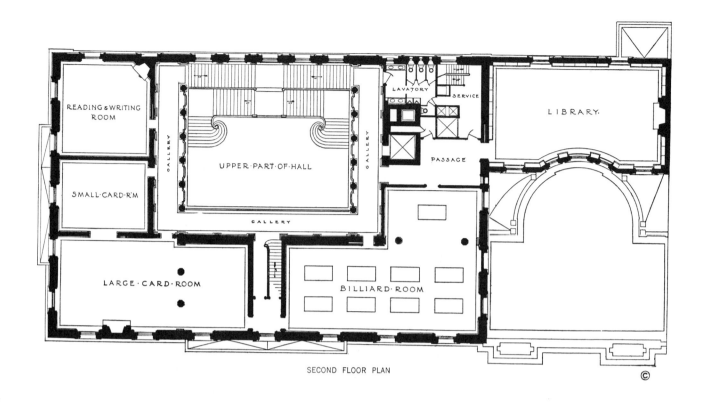

READING & WRITING ROOM

SMALL · CARD · R'M

UPPER · PART · OF · HALL

GALLERY

GALLERY

GALLERY

LAVATORY

SERVICE

PASSAGE

LIBRARY.

LARGE · CARD · ROOM

BILLIARD · ROOM

SECOND FLOOR PLAN

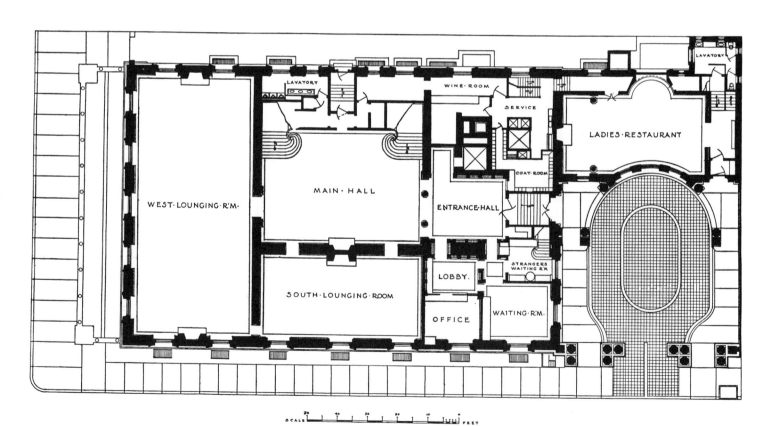

WEST · LOUNGING · R'M

MAIN · HALL

SOUTH · LOUNGING · ROOM

LAVATORY

WINE · ROOM

SERVICE

COAT · ROOM

ENTRANCE · HALL

LOBBY.

STRANGERS WAITING · R'M

OFFICE

WAITING · R'M

LADIES · RESTAURANT

LAVATORY

SCALE · · · · · · · · FEET

FIRST FLOOR PLAN

Plate 59

METROPOLITAN CLUB, NEW YORK CITY.
1894

COPPER CHENEAU

DETAILS OF
GROUND FLOOR

CENTER

SIDEWALK

THIRD FLOOR

MATERIALS

THE ENTIRE FIRST STORY,
AND ALL QUOINS, STRING
COURSES, WINDOW TRIMS
AND MAIN CORNICE IN THE
UPPER STORIES ARE OF
TOOLED ROCKY CREEK, MD.
WHITE MARBLE.
THE ASHLAR WALL SURFACE
IN UPPER STORIES IS OF
RUBBED VERMONT WHITE
MARBLE.

DETAIL OF ORDER AT ENTRANCE.

SECOND FLOOR

DETAILS OF FIFTH AVENUE AND SIXTIETH STREET FACADES

DRAWING SHOWS SOUTHWEST CORNER
OF BUILDING, FACING FIFTH AVENUE.

SCALE   FEET.

METROPOLITAN CLUB, NEW YORK CITY.
1894

Plate 60

ENTRANCE GATEWAY

MAIN HALL

Plate 61

METROPOLITAN CLUB, NEW YORK CITY.
1894

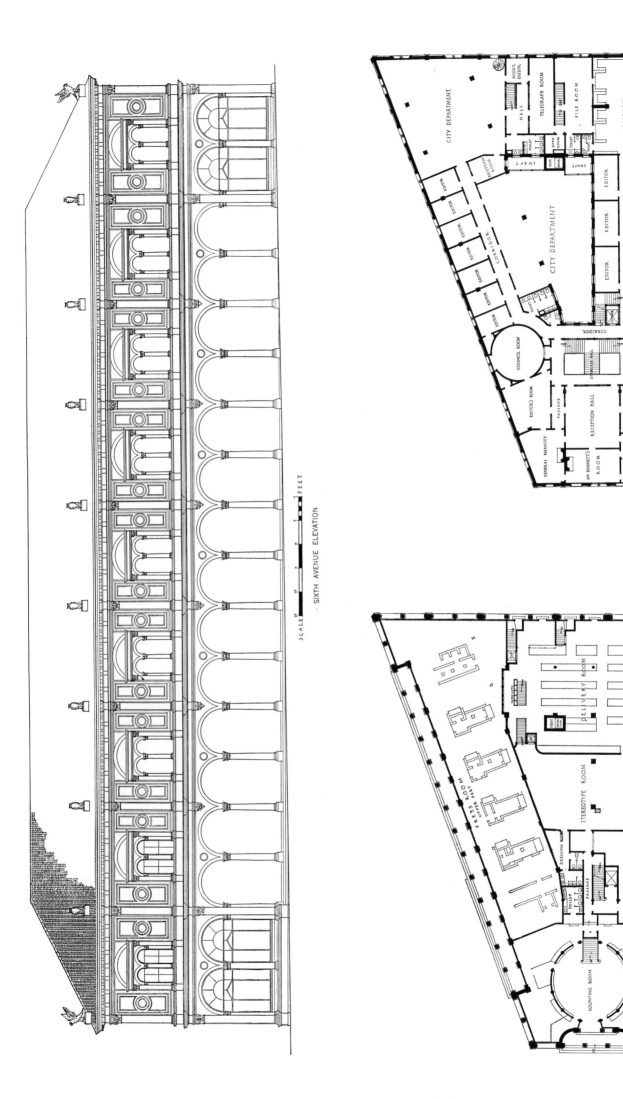

SIXTH AVENUE ELEVATION

SCALE FEET

SECOND FLOOR PLAN

FIRST FLOOR PLAN

NEW YORK HERALD BUILDING, NEW YORK CITY.
1894

SCALE

Plate 62

SOUTH ELEVATION

SCALE |_____|_____|_____| FEET

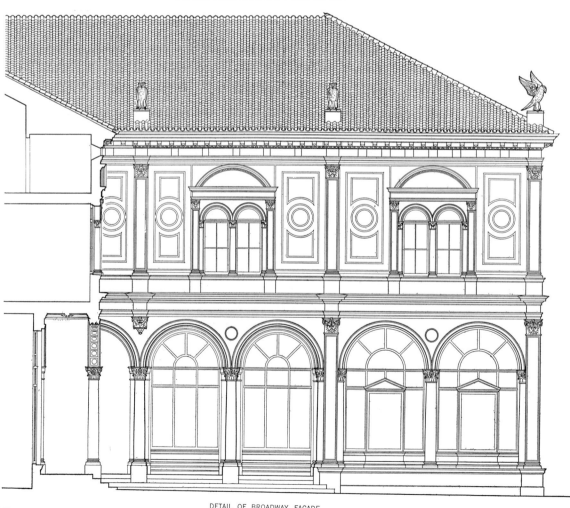

DETAIL OF BROADWAY FACADE
NEW YORK HERALD BUILDING, NEW YORK CITY.
1894

Plate 63

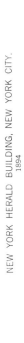

NEW YORK HERALD BUILDING, NEW YORK CITY.
1894

Plate 64

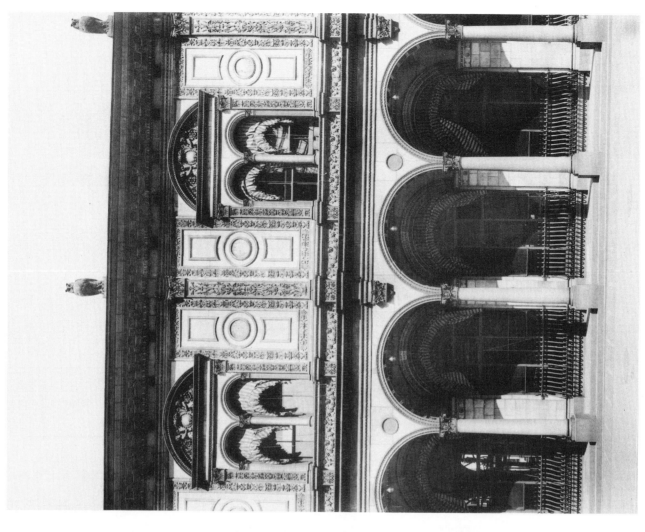

DETAIL OF BROADWAY FACADE

NEW YORK HERALD BUILDING, NEW YORK CITY.
1894

DETAIL OF ENTRANCE

Plate 64A

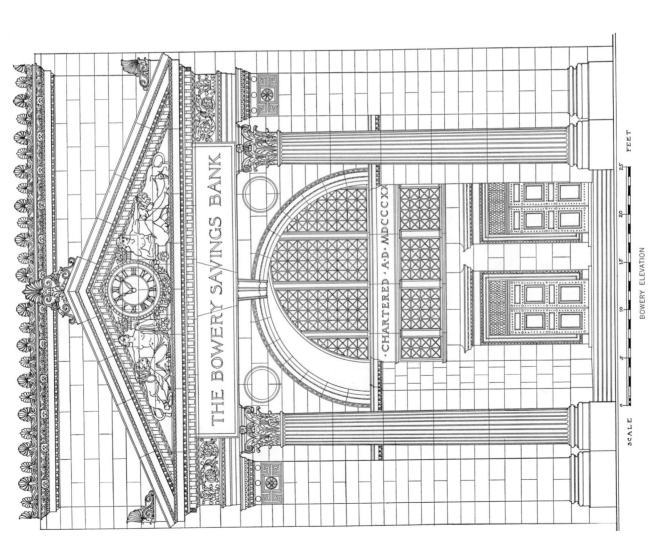

PLAN

BOWERY

GRAND STREET

SCALE

FEET

BOWERY ELEVATION

THE BOWERY SAVINGS BANK, NEW YORK CITY.
1895

Plate 66

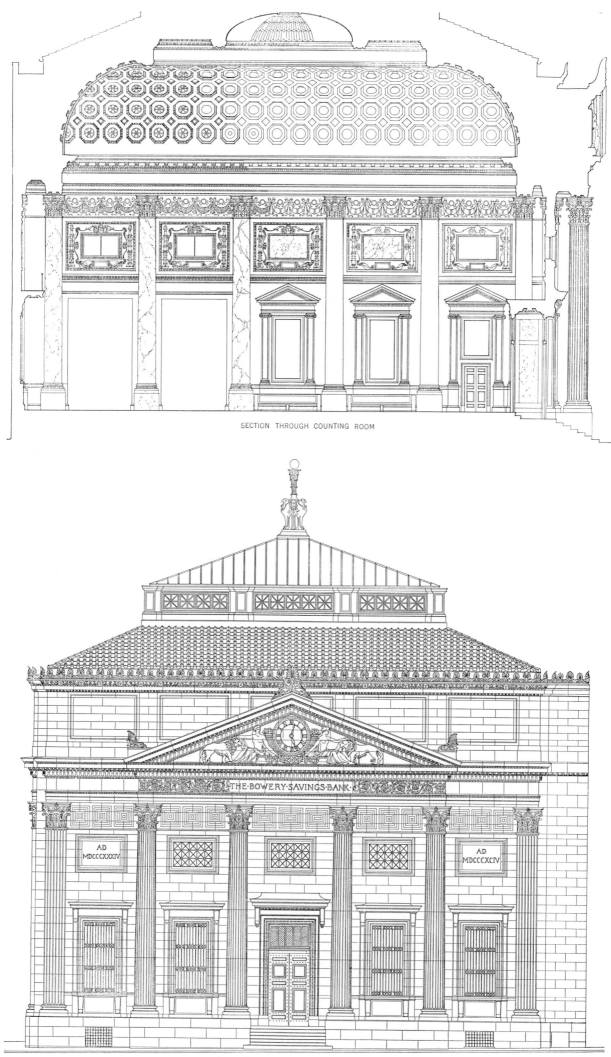

SECTION THROUGH COUNTING ROOM

THE·BOWERY·SAVINGS·BANK·

AD
MDCCCXXXIV

AD
MDCCCXCIV

SCALE 0 5 10 15 20 25 FEET.

GRAND STREET ELEVATION
THE BOWERY SAVINGS BANK, NEW YORK CITY.
1895.

Plate 67

GRAND STREET FACADE

THE BOWERY SAVINGS BANK, NEW YORK CITY.

Plate 68

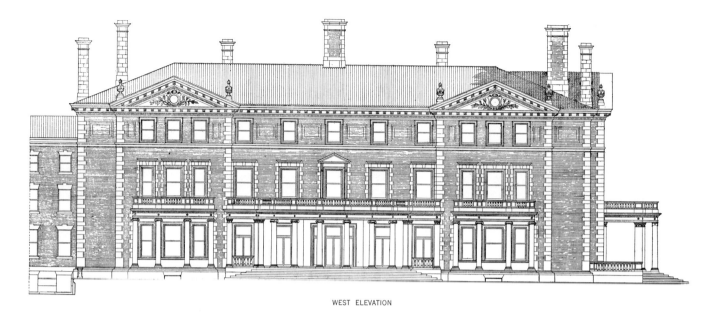

WEST ELEVATION

SECOND FLOOR PLAN

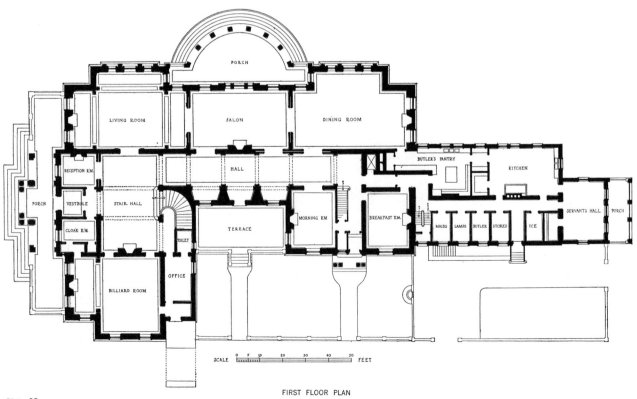

FIRST FLOOR PLAN

Plate 69

ELLIOTT F. SHEPARD RESIDENCE, SCARBOROUGH, N. Y.
1895

GENERAL VIEW FROM NORTHWEST

FACADE TOWARD HUDSON RIVER

ELLIOTT F. SHEPARD RESIDENCE, SCARBOROUGH, N. Y.
1895

Plate 70

VIEWS AND DETAILS IN GARDEN

ELLIOTT F. SHEPARD RESIDENCE, SCARBOROUGH, N. Y.
1895

Plate 71

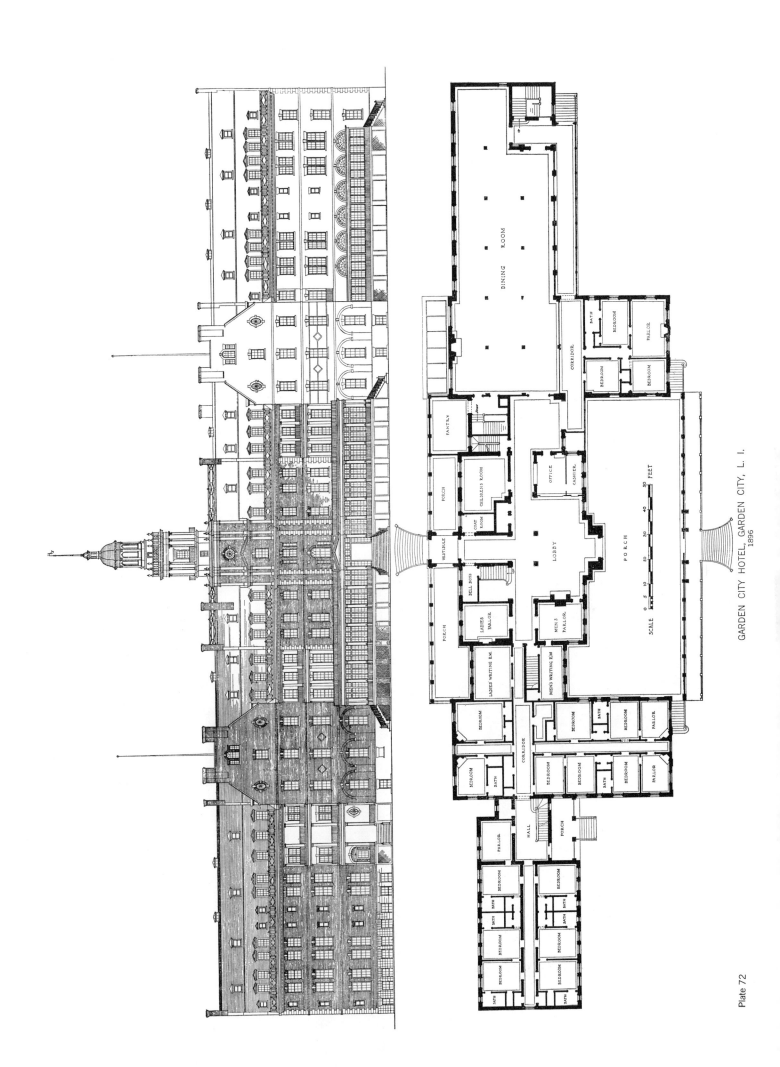

GARDEN CITY HOTEL, GARDEN CITY, L. I.
1896

DINING ROOM

CORRIDOR

BATH
BEDROOM
PARLOR
BEDROOM
BEDROOM

PANTRY

PORCH

CHILDREN'S ROOM

OFFICE
CASHIER

COAT ROOM

VESTIBULE

BELL BOYS

LOBBY

MEN'S PARLOR

PORCH

LADIES PARLOR

LADIES WRITING R.M.

MEN'S WRITING R.M.

PORCH

BEDROOM
BEDROOM
BATH
BEDROOM
PARLOR

BEDROOM

CORRIDOR

BEDROOM
BEDROOM
BATH
BEDROOM
PARLOR

HALL
PORCH

PARLOR

BEDROOM
BATH
BEDROOM

BEDROOM
BATH
BEDROOM

PARLOR

BEDROOM
BATH
BEDROOM

BEDROOM
BATH
BEDROOM

BATH
BATH

SCALE

0 5 10 20 30 40 50 FEET

Plate 72

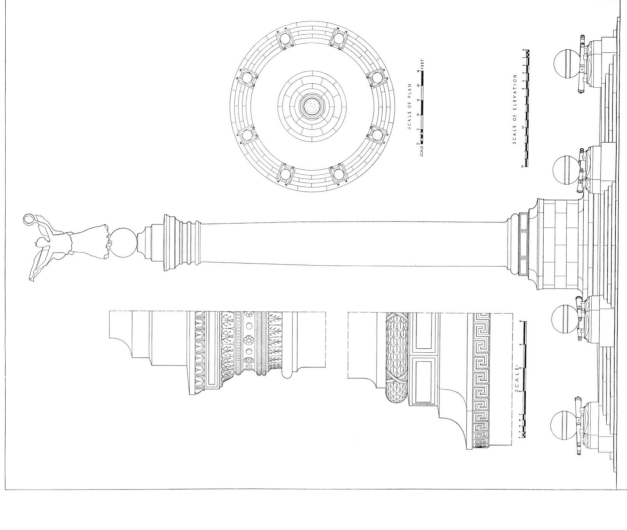

SCALE OF PLAN

SCALE OF ELEVATION

SCALE

THE BATTLE MONUMENT, WEST POINT, N. Y.
1896

Plate 73

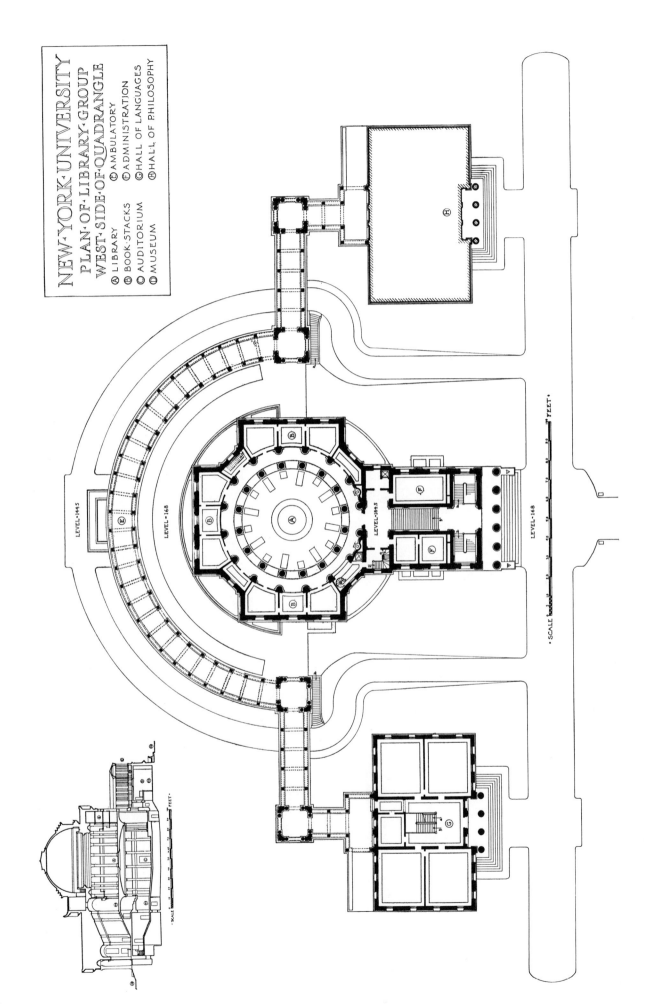

NEW·YORK·UNIVERSITY
PLAN·OF·LIBRARY·GROUP
WEST·SIDE·OF·QUADRANGLE

Ⓐ LIBRARY   Ⓔ AMBULATORY
Ⓑ BOOK·STACKS   Ⓕ ADMINISTRATION
Ⓒ AUDITORIUM   Ⓖ HALL OF LANGUAGES
Ⓓ MUSEUM   Ⓗ HALL OF PHILOSOPHY

LEVEL·144·5

LEVEL·168

LEVEL·168·5

LEVEL·168

· SCALE ·   · FEET ·

· SCALE ·   · FEET ·

NEW YORK UNIVERSITY, NEW YORK CITY.
1896

Plate 74

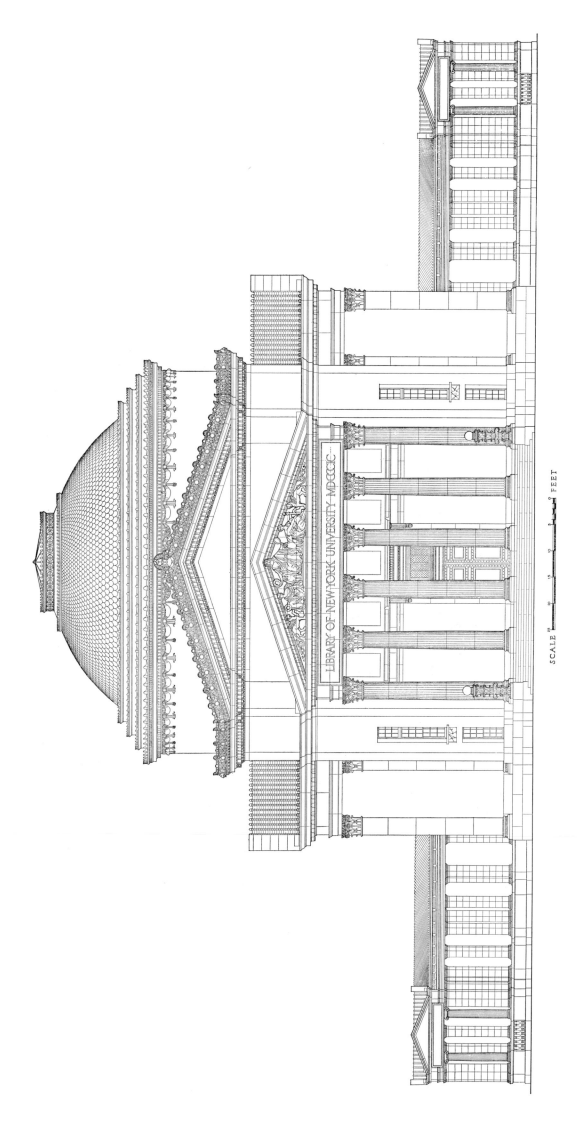

LIBRARY OF NEW YORK UNIVERSITY · MDCCCC ·

SCALE FEET

NEW YORK UNIVERSITY, NEW YORK CITY.
1896

Plate 75

LIBRARY AND HALL OF LANGUAGES.

LIBRARY AND AMBULATORY FROM REAR.

NEW YORK UNIVERSITY, NEW YORK CITY.
1896

Plate 76

PORTICO OF LIBRARY

READING ROOM IN LIBRARY

NEW YORK UNIVERSITY, NEW YORK CITY.
1896

Plate 77

FACADE TOWARD GARDEN

ENTRANCE FRONT

ROBERT W. CUMMING RESIDENCE, NEWARK, N. J.
1896

Plate 79

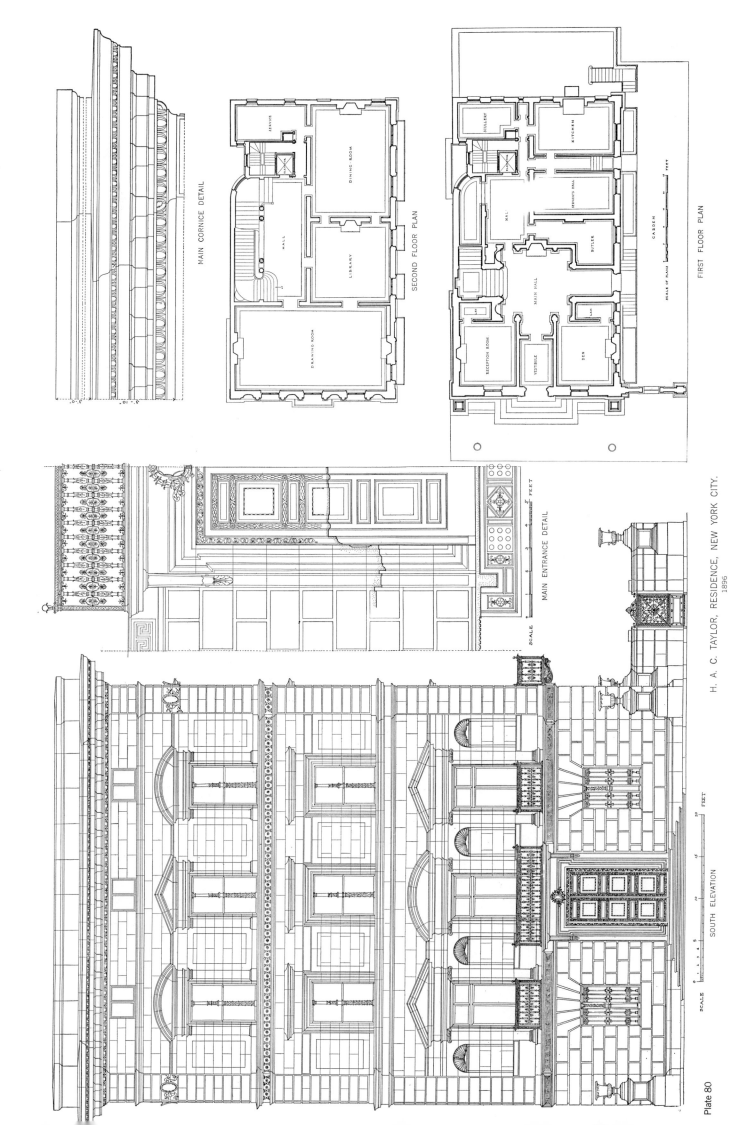

MAIN CORNICE DETAIL

SECOND FLOOR PLAN

DRAWING ROOM

LIBRARY

HALL

DINING ROOM

SERVICE

FIRST FLOOR PLAN

RECEPTION ROOM

VESTIBULE

DEN

LAV.

MAIN HALL

HALL

LAV.

BUTLER

SERVANT'S HALL

KITCHEN

SCULLERY

GARDEN

SCALE OF PLANS

MAIN ENTRANCE DETAIL

SCALE

SOUTH ELEVATION

SCALE

FEET

H. A. C. TAYLOR, RESIDENCE, NEW YORK CITY.
1896

Plate 80

SECOND STORY HALL

FACADE ON 71ST STREET

H. A. C. TAYLOR RESIDENCE, NEW YORK CITY.
1896

Plate 81

DINING ROOM

Plate 82
H. A. C. TAYLOR RESIDENCE, NEW YORK CITY.
1896

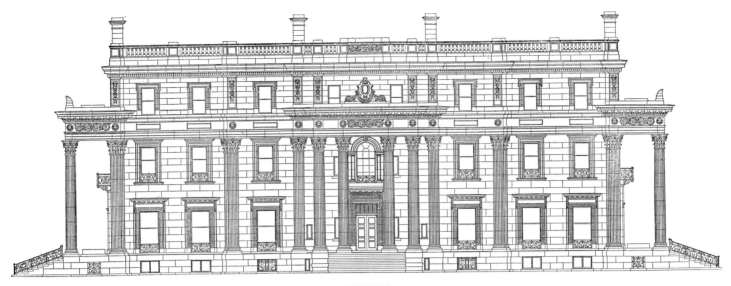

ELEVATION

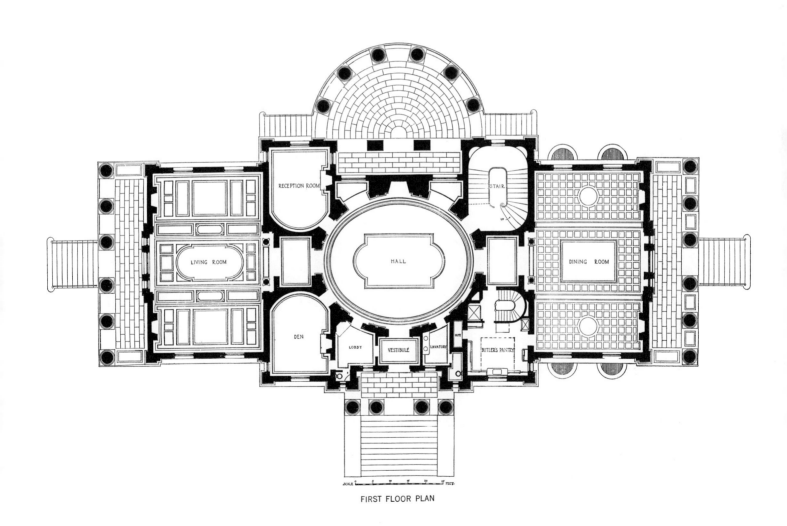

FIRST FLOOR PLAN

FREDERICK W. VANDERBILT RESIDENCE
HYDE PARK, N. Y.
1896

Plate 83

EAST FACADE

VIEW FROM NORTHWEST

Plate 84   F. W. VANDERBILT RESIDENCE, HYDE PARK, N. Y.
1896

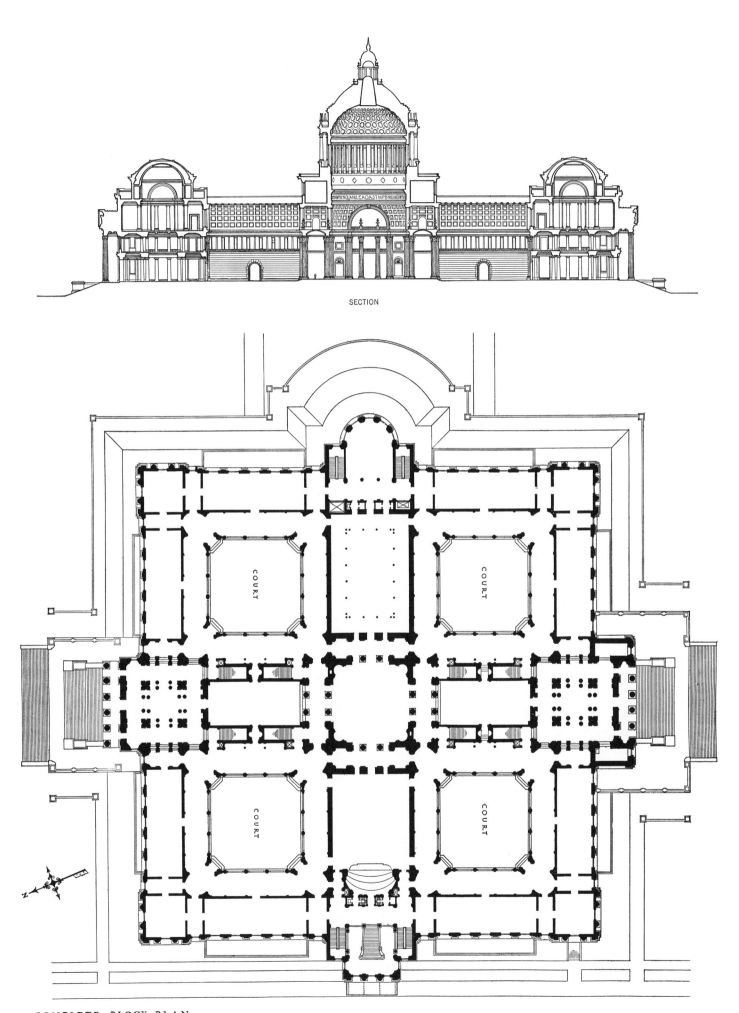

SECTION

COMPLETE BLOCK PLAN

SCALE

0   20   40   60   80   100

THE BROOKLYN INSTITUTE OF ARTS AND SCIENCES.
BEGUN 1897

Plate 85

COURT

COURT

COURT

COURT

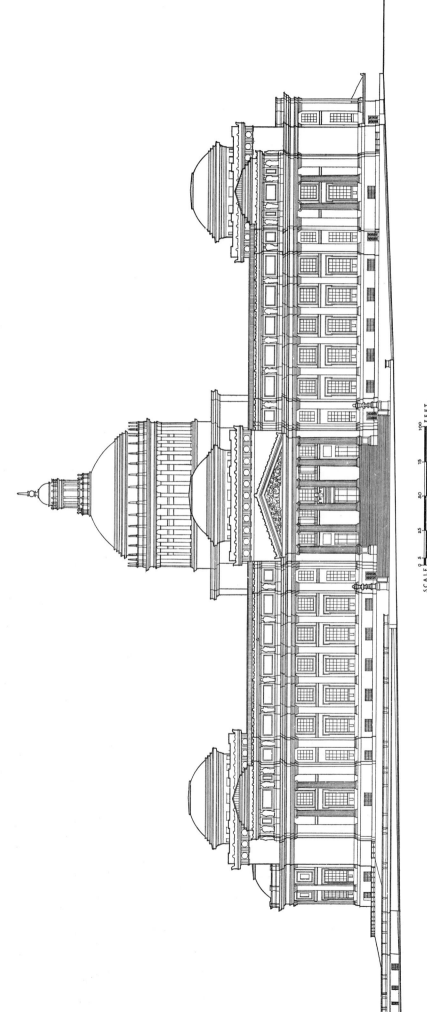

NORTH ELEVATION OF COMPLETED SCHEME

BROOKLYN INSTITUTE OF ARTS & SCIENCES.
BEGUN 1897

SCALE 0 5   25   50   75   100
                              FEET.

Plate 86

NORTH FACADE
THE BROOKLYN INSTITUTE OF ARTS AND SCIENCES.
BEGUN 1897

Plate 87

DETAIL OF NORTH FACADE

CENTRAL PORTICO, NORTH ELEVATION

THE BROOKLYN INSTITUTE OF ARTS & SCIENCES.
1897

Plate 88

ACROTERION
AT APEX
OF PEDIMENT

BASE OF DOME

UPPER CORNICE
CENTRAL PORTION

SOFFIT OF ABOVE CORNICE

MAIN ENTRANCE
DOORWAY

BRONZE

GRANITE

4'-3"

2'-9"

3'-4"

47'-3"

14'-2"

4'-6

DETAILS OF
NORTH PORTICO
SCALE
5 4 3 2 1 0
MATERIAL ~ INDIANA LIMESTONE

5'-6

5'-0"

EXTERIOR DETAILS
BROOKLYN INSTITUTE OF ARTS & SCIENCES.
1897

Plate 89

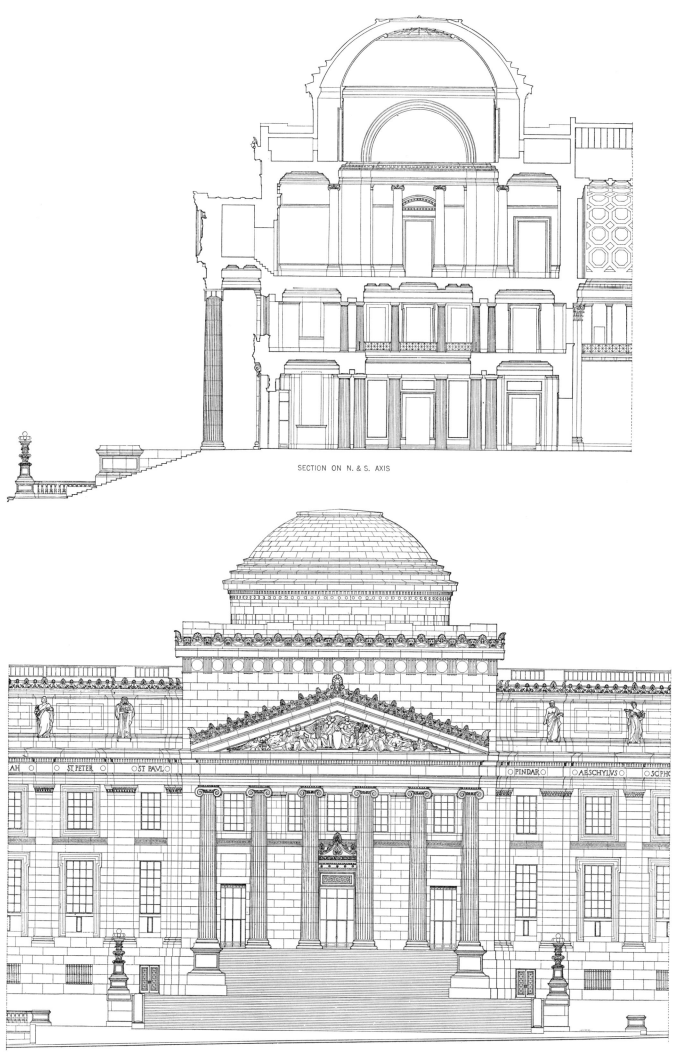

SECTION ON N. & S. AXIS

SCALE 50 40 30 20 10 0 FEET

Plate 90

CENTRAL PORTION, NORTH ELEVATION
THE BROOKLYN INSTITUTE OF ARTS AND SCIENCES.
BEGUN 1897

HALL OF RENAISSANCE SCULPTURE, THIRD FLOOR

CORRIDOR OF ANTIQUE SCULPTURE FIRST FLOOR

THE BROOKLYN INSTITUTE OF ARTS & SCIENCES.
BEGUN 1897

Plate 91

DIRECTORS' ROOM

BANKING ROOM

Plate 93

NEW YORK LIFE INSURANCE CO., NEW YORK CITY.
1897

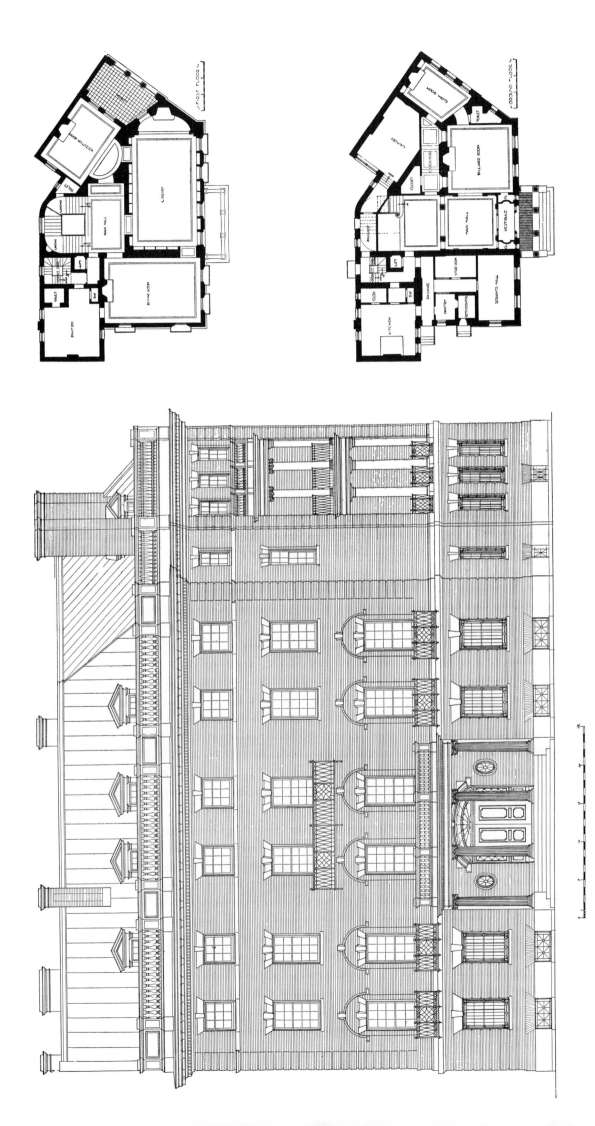

THOMAS NELSON PAGE RESIDENCE, WASHINGTON, D. C.
1897

Plate 94

Plate 95   THOMAS NELSON PAGE, RESIDENCE, WASHINGTON, D. C.
1897

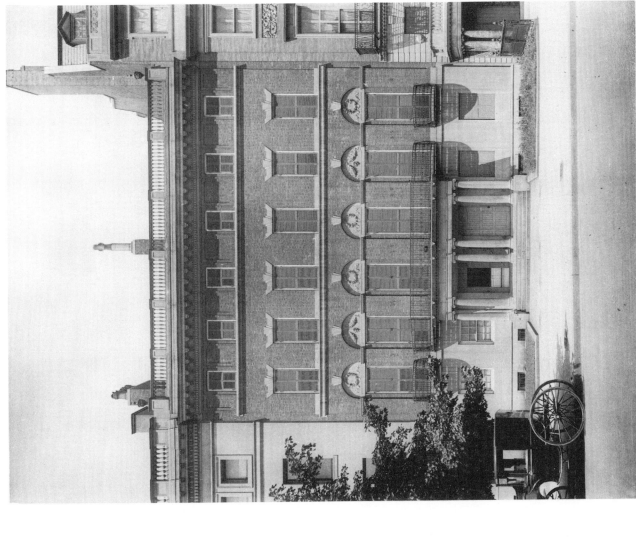

1892

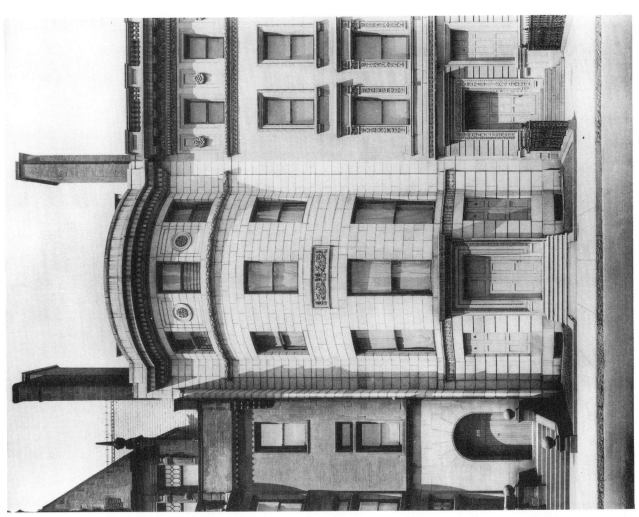

1897

HOUSES ON COMMONWEALTH AVE., BOSTON, MASS.

Plate 96

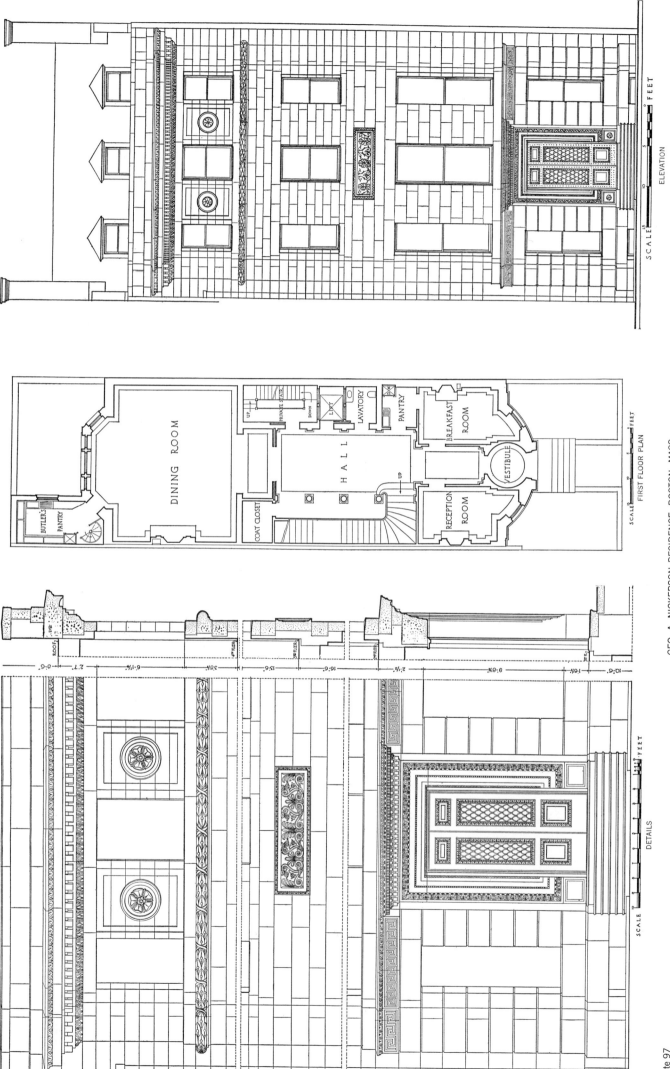

SCALE ⊢⊢⊢⊢⊢⊢ FEET
ELEVATION

SCALE ⊢⊢⊢⊢ FEET
FIRST FLOOR PLAN

SCALE ⊢⊢⊢⊢ FEET
DETAILS

DINING ROOM

BUTLER'S PANTRY

HALL

COAT CLOSET

UP

PRIVATE STAIR

DOWN

LIFT

LAVATORY

PANTRY

BREAKFAST ROOM

RECEPTION ROOM

VESTIBULE

UP

GEO. A. NICKERSON RESIDENCE, BOSTON, MASS.
1897

Plate 97

SHERRY'S HOTEL, NEW YORK CITY.
1898

Plate 98

BALL ROOM

DINING ROOM

SHERRY'S HOTEL, NEW YORK CITY.
1898

Plate 99

THE BOSTON PUBLIC LIBRARY, BOSTON, MASS.
FACADE FACING COPLEY SQUARE
1898

Plate 100

THE BOSTON PUBLIC LIBRARY, BOSTON, MASS.
DARTMOUTH STREET ELEVATION
1898

SCALE

Plate 101

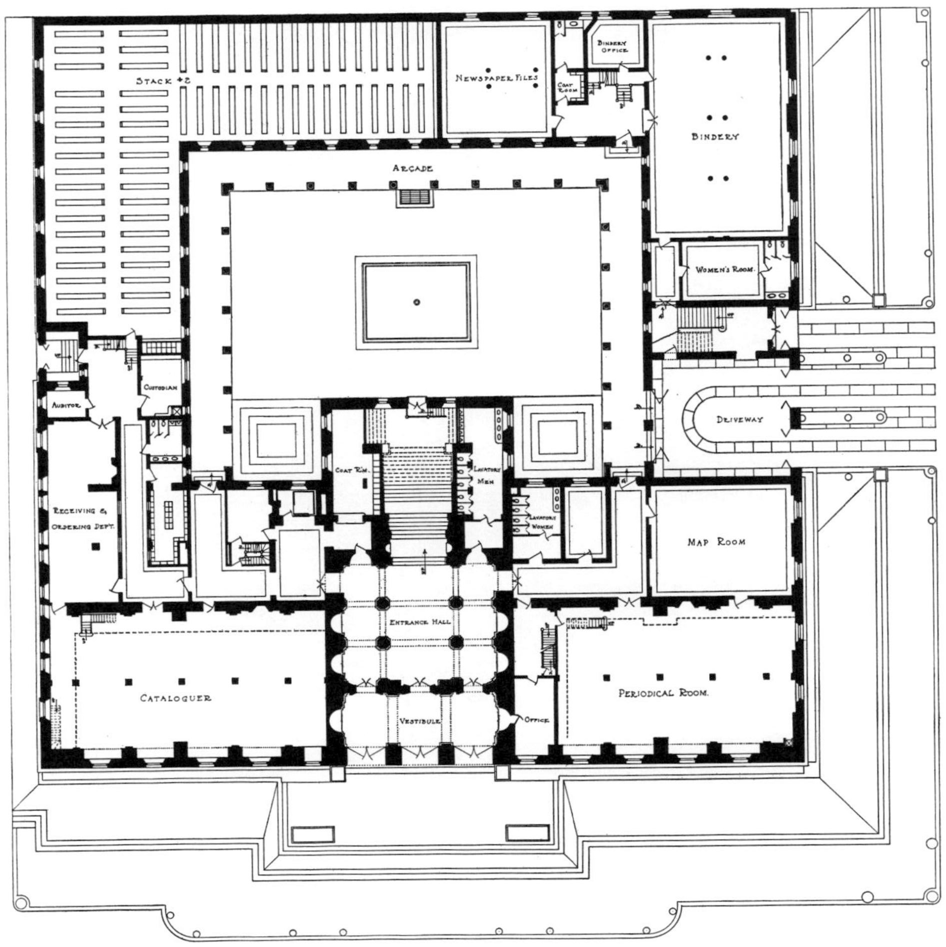

SECOND FLOOR PLAN

FIRST FLOOR PLAN

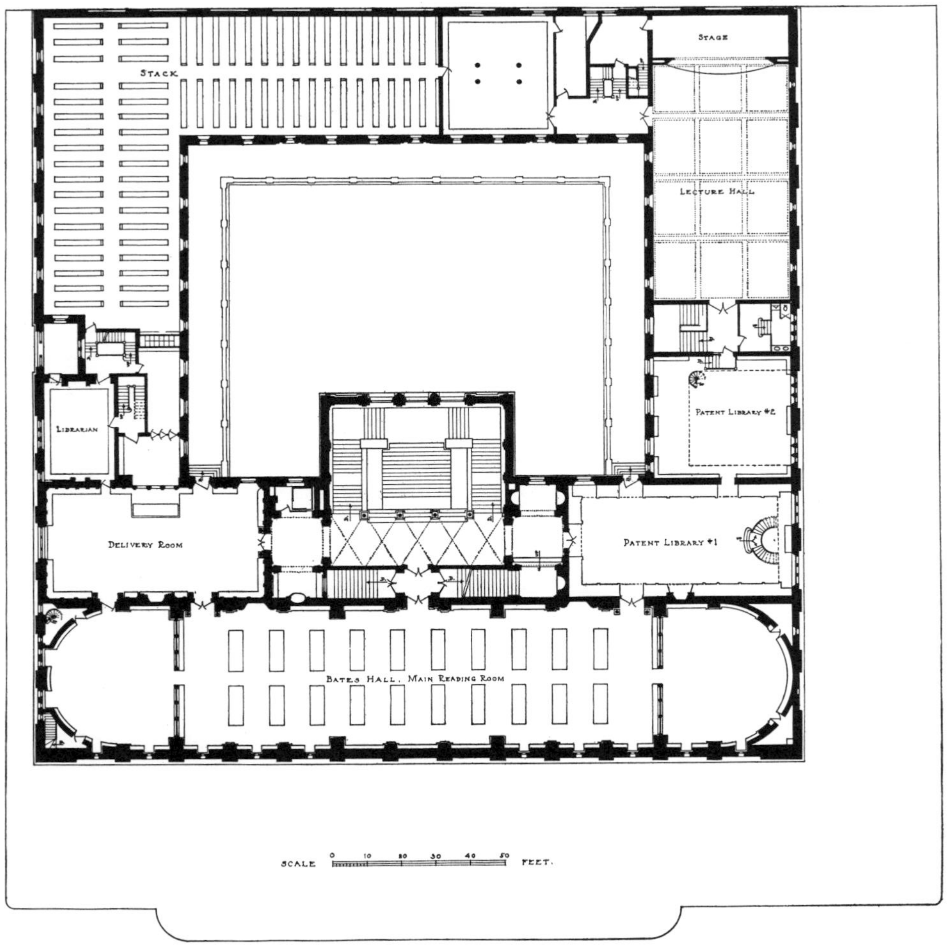

THE BOSTON PUBLIC LIBRARY, BOSTON, MASS.
1898

Plate 102

VIEW IN COURT

BOSTON PUBLIC LIBRARY, BOSTON, MASS.
1898

Plate 103

START OF MAIN STAIR

STAIR HALL, FROM LANDING

THE BOSTON PUBLIC LIBRARY, BOSTON, MASS.
1898

Plate 104

STAIR HALL WITH DECORATION BY PUVIS DE CHAVANNES

DELIVERY ROOM WITH FRIEZE BY E. A. ABBEY - THE HOLY GRAIL

THE BOSTON PUBLIC LIBRARY, BOSTON, MASS.
1898

DOORWAY IN BATES HALL

BATES HALL, MAIN READING ROOM

BOSTON PUBLIC LIBRARY, BOSTON, MASS.
1898

Plate 106

DETAIL OF MAIN ENTRANCE

BOSTON PUBLIC LIBRARY, BOSTON, MASS.
1898

DETAIL IN COURT

Plate 107

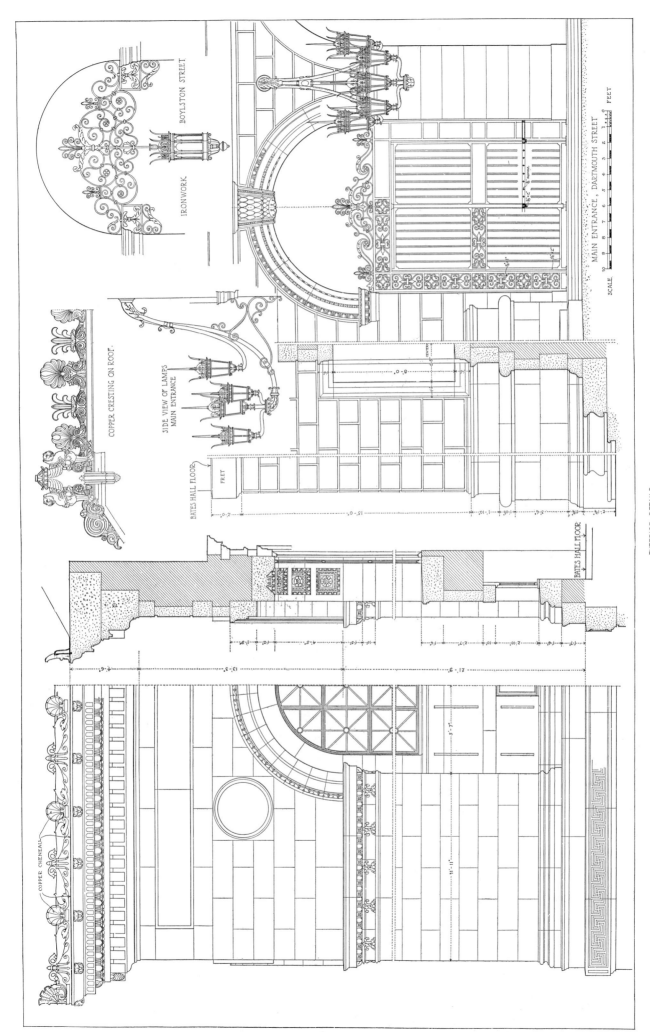

BOYLSTON STREET

IRONWORK

COPPER CRESTING ON ROOF.

SIDE VIEW OF LAMPS
MAIN ENTRANCE

BATES HALL FLOOR

FRET

BATES HALL FLOOR

COPPER CHENEAU

MAIN ENTRANCE, DARTMOUTH STREET

SCALE.   FEET

EXTERIOR DETAILS
BOSTON PUBLIC LIBRARY, BOSTON, MASS.
1898

Plate 108

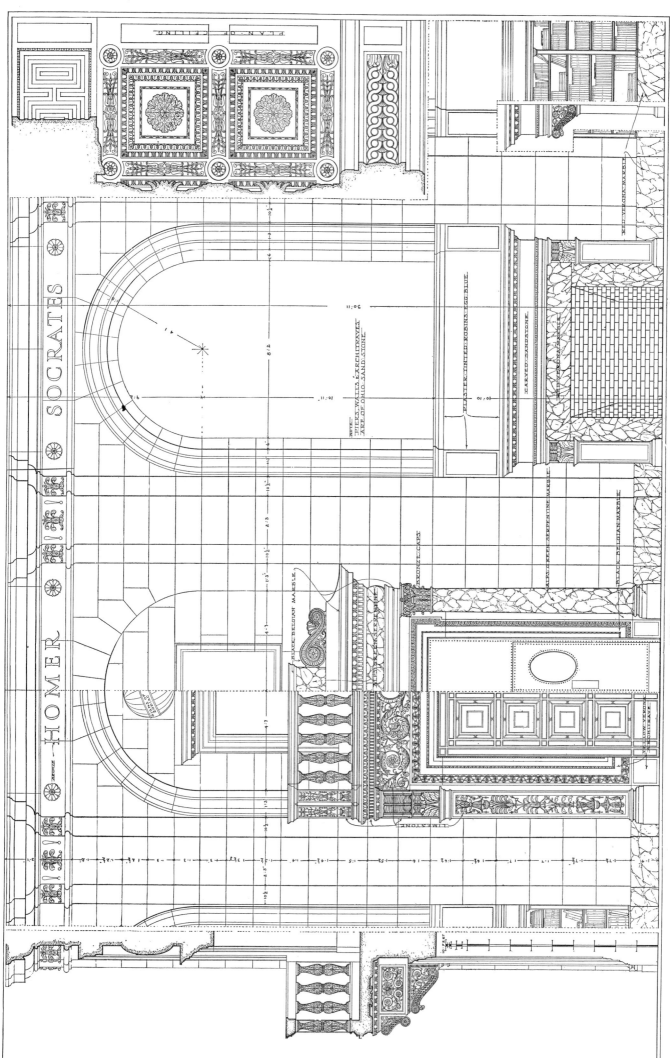

INTERIOR DETAILS, BATES HALL MAIN READING ROOM
BOSTON PUBLIC LIBRARY, BOSTON MASS.
1898

Plate 109

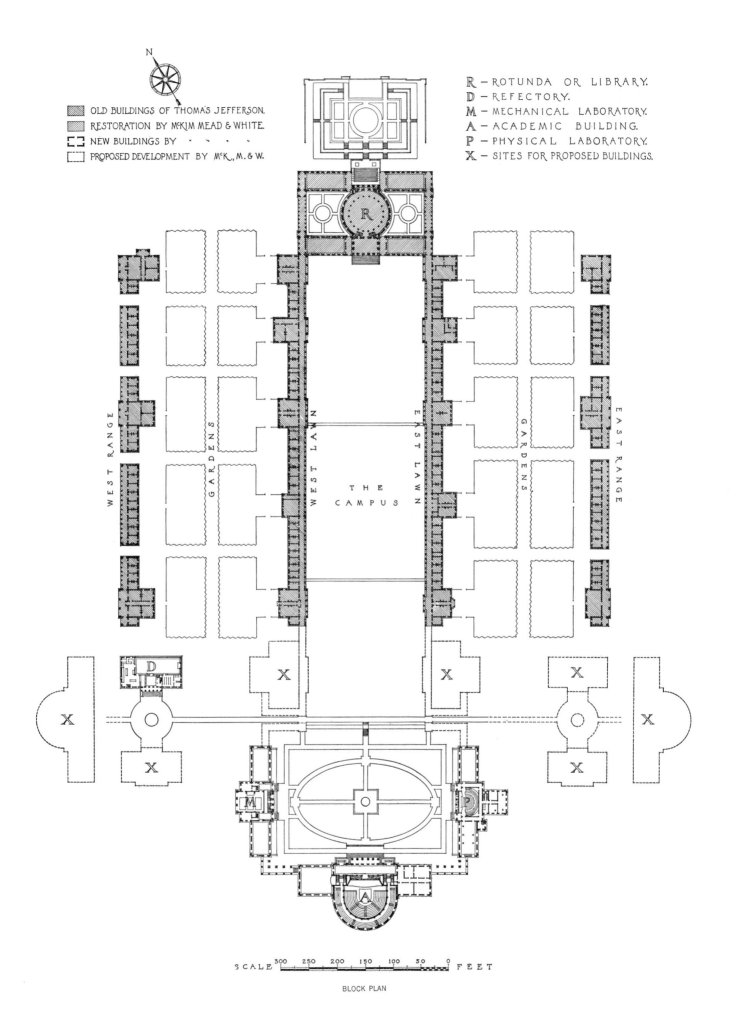

N

OLD BUILDINGS OF THOMAS JEFFERSON.
RESTORATION BY McKIM MEAD & WHITE.
NEW BUILDINGS BY " " "
PROPOSED DEVELOPMENT BY McK., M. & W.

R — ROTUNDA OR LIBRARY.
D — REFECTORY.
M — MECHANICAL LABORATORY.
A — ACADEMIC BUILDING.
P — PHYSICAL LABORATORY.
X — SITES FOR PROPOSED BUILDINGS.

WEST RANGE

GARDENS

WEST LAWN

EAST LAWN

THE CAMPUS

GARDENS

EAST RANGE

SCALE 300 250 200 150 100 50 0 FEET

BLOCK PLAN

UNIVERSITY OF VIRGINIA, CHARLOTTESVILLE, VA.
1898

Plate 110

MECHANICAL LABORATORY ELEVATION

ACADEMIC BUILDING ELEVATION

MATERIALS, WALLS, RED BRICK; COLUMNS, PILASTERS, CORNICES,
DOOR AND WINDOW TRIMS, PORTLAND CEMENT STUCCO; STEPS, BLUESTONE.

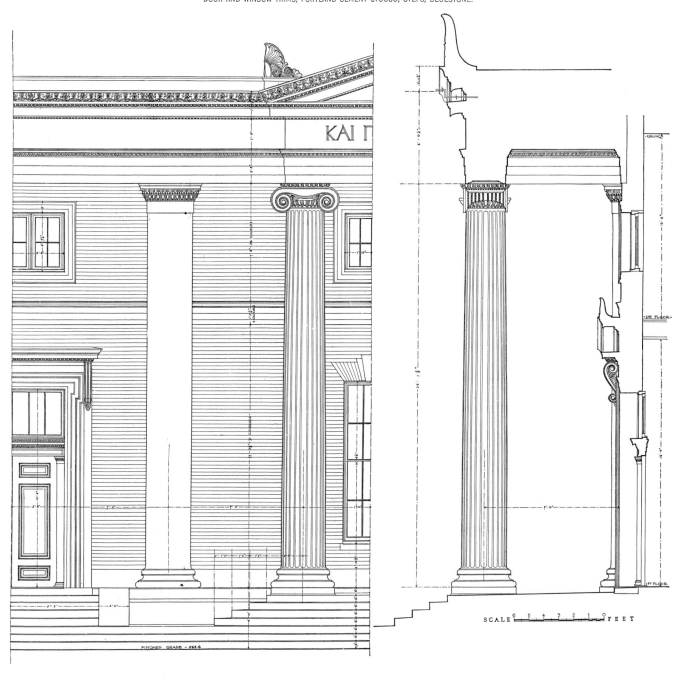

SCALE 6 5 4 3 2 1 0 FEET

DETAIL CENTRAL PORTION, ACADEMIC BUILDING
UNIVERSITY OF VIRGINIA, CHARLOTTESVILLE, VA.
1898

Plate 111

ACADEMIC BUILDING

MECHANICAL LABORATORY

RESTORATION OF ROTUNDA & TERRACES ACCORDING TO THE ORIGINAL SCHEME OF THOMAS JEFFERSON, ARCHITECT.

COURT AT SIDE OF ROTUNDA

Plate 112A   THE UNIVERSITY OF VIRGINIA, RESTORATIONS & ADDITIONS, CHARLOTTESVILLE, VA.
1898

MAIN FACADE

TENNIS COURT   SWIMMING POOL

CASINO OF JOHN JACOB ASTOR, RHINEBECK, N. Y.   Plate 113
1898

LOUNGING ROOM

SWIMMING POOL

Plate 114   CASINO OF JOHN JACOB ASTOR, RHINEBECK, N. Y.
1898

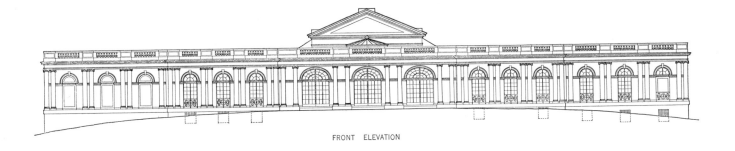

FRONT ELEVATION

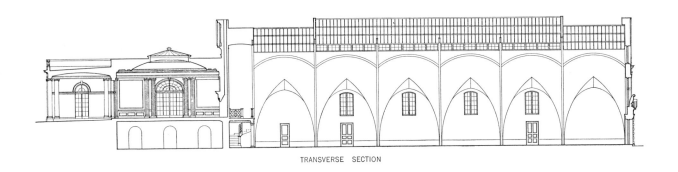

TRANSVERSE SECTION

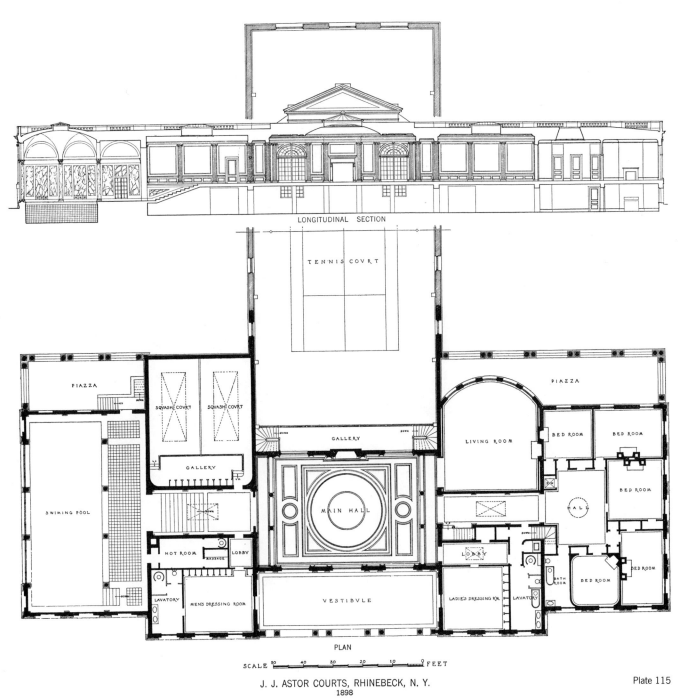

LONGITUDINAL SECTION

TENNIS COVRT

PIAZZA

SQVASH COVRT   SQVASH COVRT

GALLERY

LIVING ROOM

BED ROOM   BED ROOM

PIAZZA

GALLERY

BED ROOM

SWIMING POOL

MAIN HALL

HALL

HOT ROOM   MASSAGE   LOBBY

LOBBY

BED ROOM

BED ROOM

BATH ROOM

LAVATORY

MEN'S DRESSING ROOM

VESTIBVLE

LADIE'S DRESSING RM.   LAVATORY

PLAN

SCALE 50 40 30 20 10 0 FEET

J. J. ASTOR COURTS, RHINEBECK, N. Y.
1898

Plate 115

Plate 116

THE CULLUM MEMORIAL, WEST POINT, N. Y.
1898

ASSEMBLY HALL, SECOND FLOOR

DETAIL OF ASSEMBLY HALL   DETAIL OF ENTRANCE

THE CULLUM MEMORIAL, WEST POINT, N. Y.
1898

Plate 117

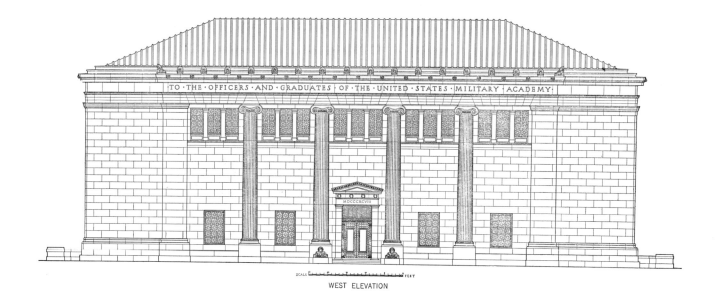

TO·THE·OFFICERS·AND·GRADUATES·OF·THE·UNITED·STATES·MILITARY·ACADEMY

MDCCCXCVIII

SCALE ⊢┴┴┴┴┼┴┴┴┴┼┴┴┴┴┤ FEET

WEST ELEVATION

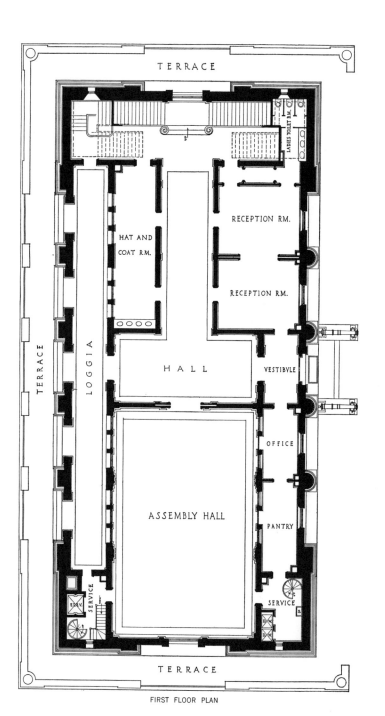

TERRACE

RECEPTION RM.

HAT AND
COAT RM.

LADIES TOILET R.M.

RECEPTION RM.

LOGGIA

TERRACE

HALL

VESTIBVLE

OFFICE

ASSEMBLY HALL

PANTRY

SERVICE

ELEV.

SERVICE

TERRACE

FIRST FLOOR PLAN

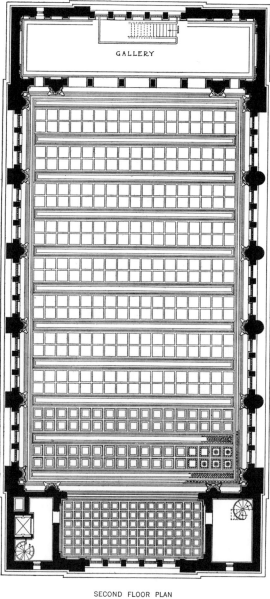

GALLERY

SECOND FLOOR PLAN

Plate 118

CULLUM MEMORIAL, WEST POINT, N. Y.
1898

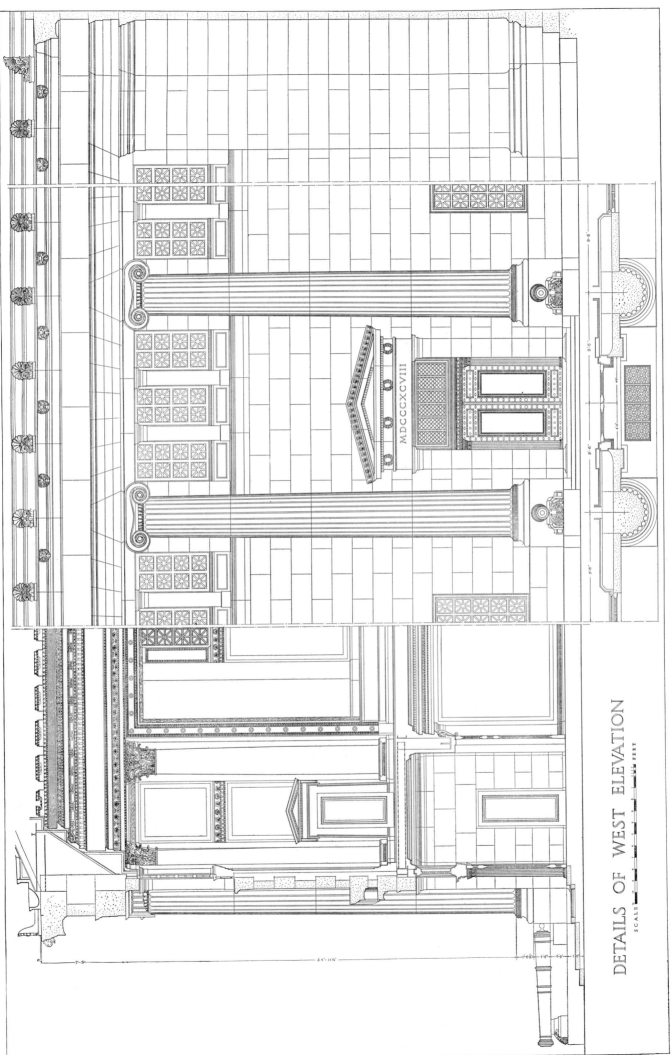

DETAILS OF WEST ELEVATION

SCALE ░░░░░ FEET

MDCCCXCVIII

CULLUM MEMORIAL, WEST POINT, N. Y.

1898

Plate 119

SCALE |⊢⊢⊢⊢⊢⊢⊢⊢⊢⊢⊢⊢⊢⊢⊢⊢⊢⊢⊢⊢⊢⊢⊢⊢⊢| FEET
0   5   10   15   20   25

 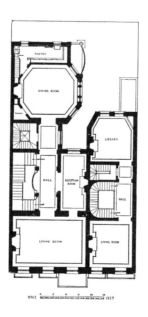 

Plate 120   HOUSES FOR JAMES J. GOODWIN, NEW YORK CITY.

HOUSES FOR H. A. C. TAYLOR, NEW YORK CITY.
1898

HOUSES FOR JAS. J. GOODWIN, NEW YORK CITY.
1898

Plate 121

FACADE

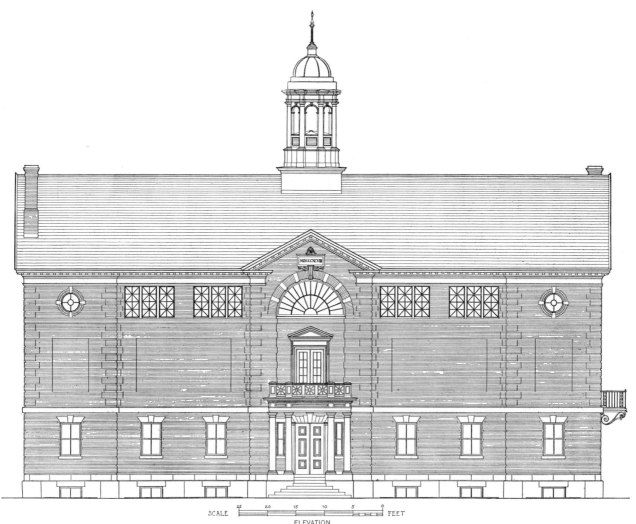

SCALE 25 20 15 10 5 0 FEET

ELEVATION

Plate 122   RADCLIFFE COLLEGE GYMNASIUM, CAMBRIDGE, MASS.

1899

GYMNASIUM FLOOR

RUNNING TRACK

SCALE

FEET

SECOND FLOOR PLAN

LAVATORY

BATH ATTENDANT

LOCKER ROOM

CORRIDOR

ANTHROPOMETRIC DEP'T

HALL

VESTIBULE

CORRIDOR

MEDICAL GYMNASTICS

DIRECTOR'S ROOM

FIRST FLOOR PLAN

RADCLIFFE COLLEGE GYMNASIUM, CAMBRIDGE, MASS.
1899

DETAIL OF ENTRANCE

Plate 123

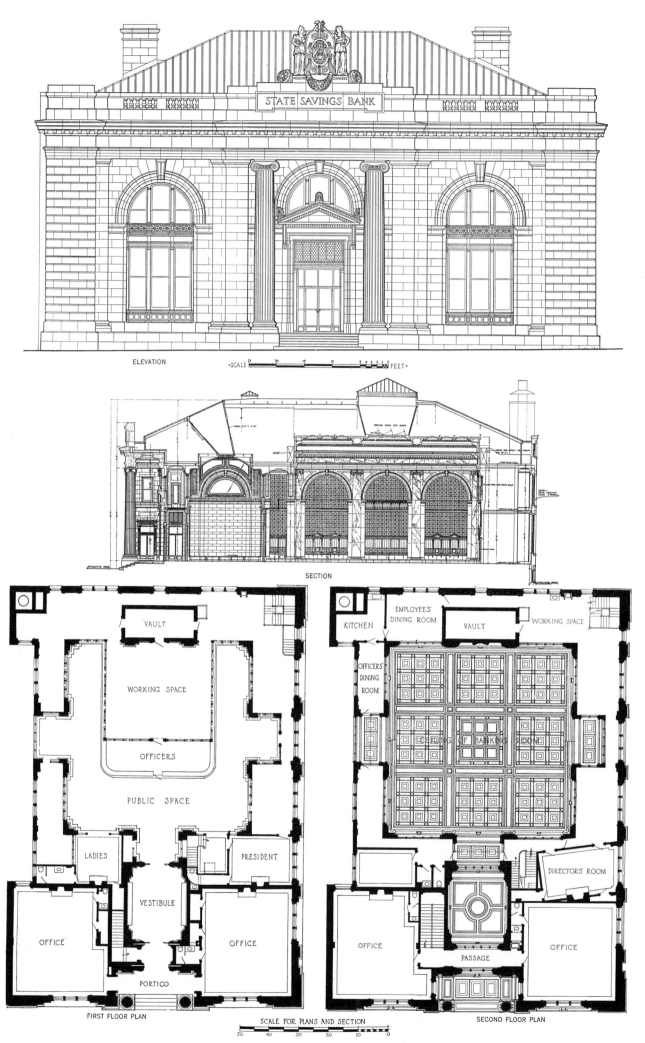

ELEVATION

·SCALE· FEET·

STATE SAVINGS BANK

SECTION

FIRST FLOOR PLAN

VAULT

WORKING SPACE

OFFICERS

PUBLIC SPACE

LADIES

PRESIDENT

VESTIBULE

OFFICE

OFFICE

PORTICO

SECOND FLOOR PLAN

KITCHEN

EMPLOYEES' DINING ROOM

VAULT

WORKING SPACE

OFFICERS' DINING ROOM

CEILING OF BANKING ROOM

DIRECTORS' ROOM

OFFICE

PASSAGE

OFFICE

SCALE FOR PLANS AND SECTION

50 40 30 20 10

Plate 124

THE STATE SAVINGS BANK, DETROIT, MICHIGAN

1900

GENERAL VIEW OF EXTERIOR

MAIN ENTRANCE DOORWAY

DETAIL OF COUNTER SCREEN

STATE SAVINGS BANK, DETROIT, MICHIGAN.
NOW THE PEOPLES STATE BANK
1900

Plate 125

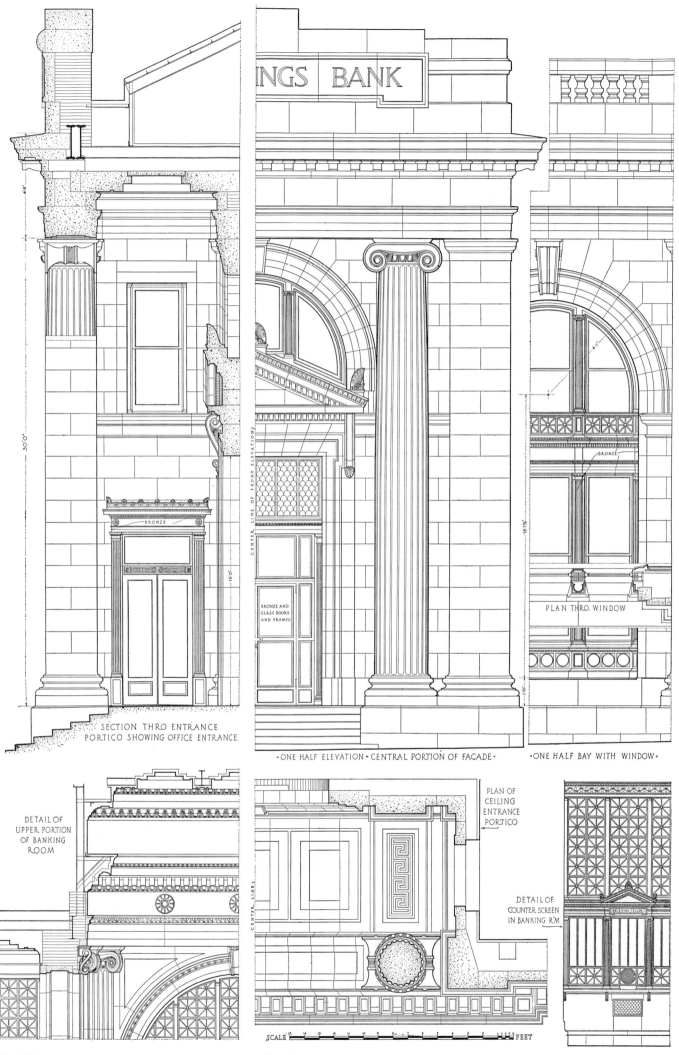

SAVINGS BANK

SECTION THRO ENTRANCE
PORTICO SHOWING OFFICE ENTRANCE.

BRONZE

·ONE HALF ELEVATION· CENTRAL PORTION OF FACADE·

BRONZE AND
GLASS DOORS
AND FRAMES

CENTER LINE OF FRONT ELEVATION

PLAN THRO. WINDOW

BRONZE

·ONE HALF BAY WITH WINDOW·

DETAIL OF
UPPER PORTION
OF BANKING
ROOM

CENTER LINE

PLAN OF
CEILING
ENTRANCE
PORTICO

DETAIL OF
COUNTER SCREEN
IN BANKING R'M

RECEIVING TELLER

SCALE ⊢━━━━━━━━━━━━━━━━━━┤ FEET

Plate 126

THE STATE SAVINGS BANK, DETROIT, MICH.
EXTERIOR AND INTERIOR DETAILS
1900

THE UNIVERSITY CLUB, NEW YORK CITY.
1900

Plate 130

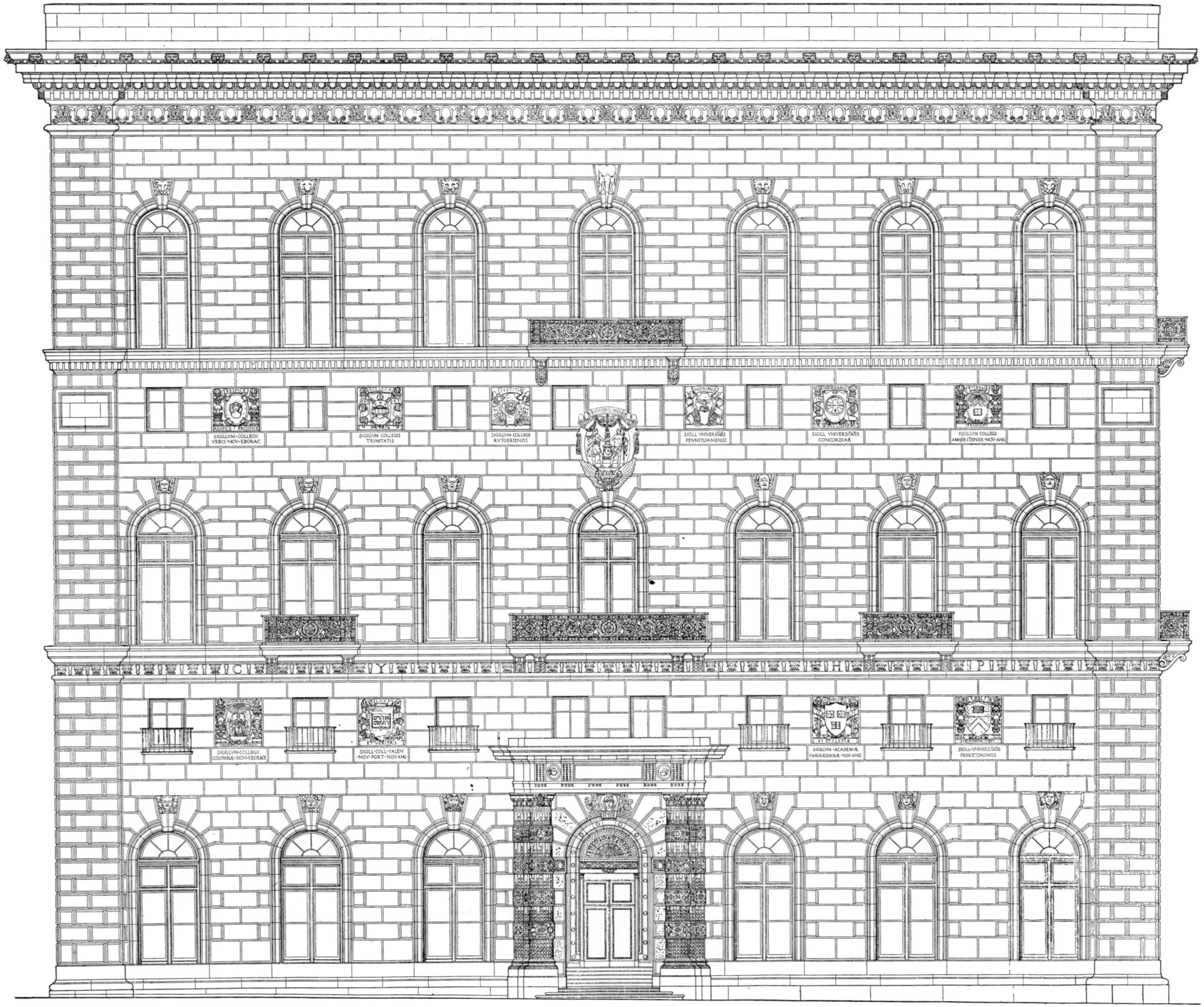

ELEVATION FIFTY-FOURTH STREET
UNIVERSITY CLUB, NEW YORK CITY.
1900

SCALE 0 5 10 15 20 25 FEET

Plate 131

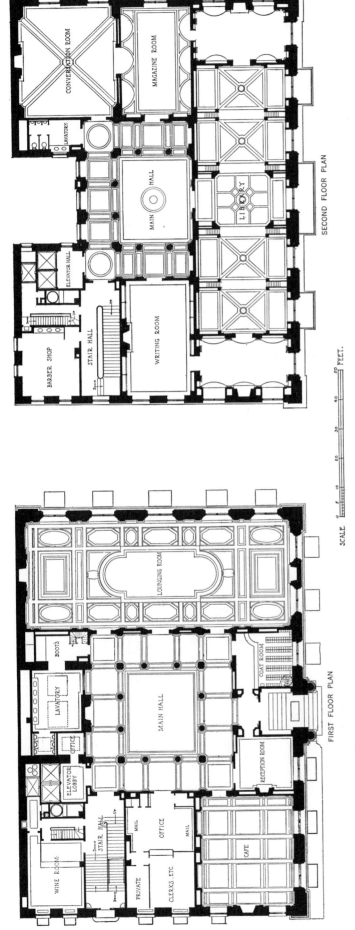

CONVERSATION ROOM

MAGAZINE ROOM

LAVATORY

MAIN HALL

LIBRARY

ELEVATOR HALL

STAIR HALL

BARBER SHOP

WRITING ROOM

SECOND FLOOR PLAN

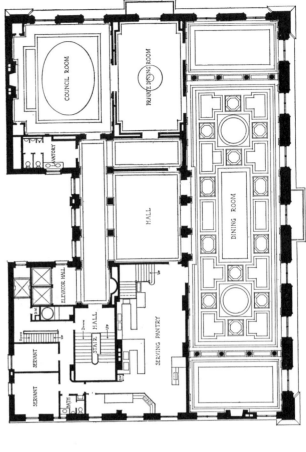

COUNCIL ROOM

PRIVATE DINING ROOM

LAVATORY

HALL

ELEVATOR HALL

STAIR HALL

SERVANT

SERVANT

BATH

SERVING PANTRY

DINING ROOM

THIRD FLOOR PLAN

SCALE

FEET.

FIRST FLOOR PLAN

LOUNGING ROOM

BOOT'S

LAVATORY

OFFICE

ELEVATOR LOBBY

MAIN HALL

COAT ROOM

RECEPTION ROOM

WINE ROOM

STAIR HALL

MAIL

PRIVATE OFFICE

MAIL

CLERKS. ETC

CAFE

FIRST BEDROOM FLOOR PLAN

PARLOR

BED ROOM

BED ROOM

BATH

BED ROOM

PARLOR

BATH

BATH

BED ROOM

BED ROOM

VALET'S ROOM

BATH

BED ROOM

BED ROOM

BED ROOM

MEMBER'S LOCKERS

LAVATORY

BATHS

CORRIDOR

BATH

BED ROOM

BED ROOM

BATH

BED ROOM

VALET'S ROOM

BED ROOM

BATH

LINEN

BED ROOM

STAIR HALL

BED ROOM

BED ROOM

BATH

PARLOR

UNIVERSITY CLUB, NEW YORK CITY.
1900

Plate 132

DETAIL OF FACADE

ENTRANCE DOORWAY

UNIVERSITY CLUB, NEW YORK CITY.
1900

Plate 133

CHRISTO
VE RI TAS
ET ECCLESIÆ

TERRAS
IRRADIENT

SECTION THRO' ENTRANCE

·PLAN·

SCALE ⊢⊢⊢⊢⊢⊢⊢⊢⊢⊢⊢⊢⊢⊢⊢ FEET

·SECTION·   ·FIFTH AVE ELEVATION·   ·MAIN ENTRANCE·

DETAILS OF EXTERIOR STONEWORK

UNIVERSITY CLUB, NEW YORK CITY.
1900

Plate 134

SECOND FLOOR HALL

FIRST FLOOR HALL

Plate 135

THE UNIVERSITY CLUB, NEW YORK CITY.

1900

MAIN DINING ROOM

LOUNGING ROOM, FIRST FLOOR

THE UNIVERSITY CLUB, NEW YORK CITY.
1900

Plate 136

DETAIL OF LIBRARY

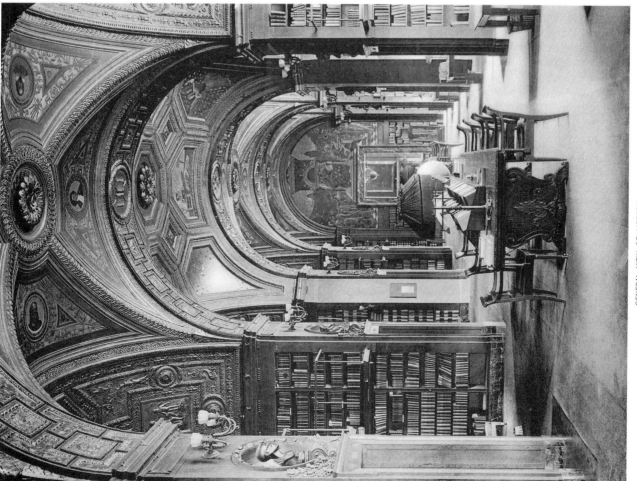

GENERAL VIEW OF LIBRARY

UNIVERSITY CLUB, NEW YORK CITY.
DECORATIONS BY H. SIDDONS MOWBRAY, 1904.

Plate 137

MAGAZINE ROOM

UNIVERSITY CLUB, NEW YORK CITY.
1900

Plate 138

CEILING DECORATION BY H. SIDDONS MOWBRAY

COUNCIL ROOM

Plate 139

UNIVERSITY CLUB, NEW YORK CITY.
1900

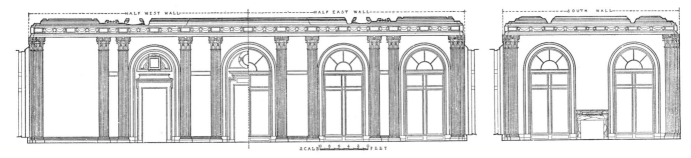

HALF WEST WALL — HALF EAST WALL — SOUTH WALL

SCALE 0 9 9 4 3 FEET

ELEVATIONS

UPPER CORNICE AND CEILING PLASTER
WITH INSERTS OF MARBLE.

WOOD WORK
OF ITALIAN WALNUT
CARVED AND GILDED

HALF ELEVATION
OF WINDOW

HALF ELEVATION
OF DOOR WAY
TO HALL

WALLS
RED VELVET

DOOR WAY ON AXIS
OF MAIN HALL

MARBLE DOOR TRIMS
AND MANTELS
BROWN NUMIDIAN

WOOD — WOOD — WOOD

SECTION THRO.
WINDOW.

PLAN AT WINDOW   PLAN AT DOOR.   PLAN AT DOOR

SCALE 10 9 8 7 6 5 4 3 2 1 0 FEET

DETAIL OF WALL AND ONE FOURTH OF CEILING

DETAILS OF LOUNGING ROOM

THE UNIVERSITY CLUB, NEW YORK CITY.
1900

Plate 140

SCALE [feet] FEET

HALF ELEVATION OF NORTH WALL, AND DETAIL OF PORTION OF CEILING, MAIN DINING ROOM

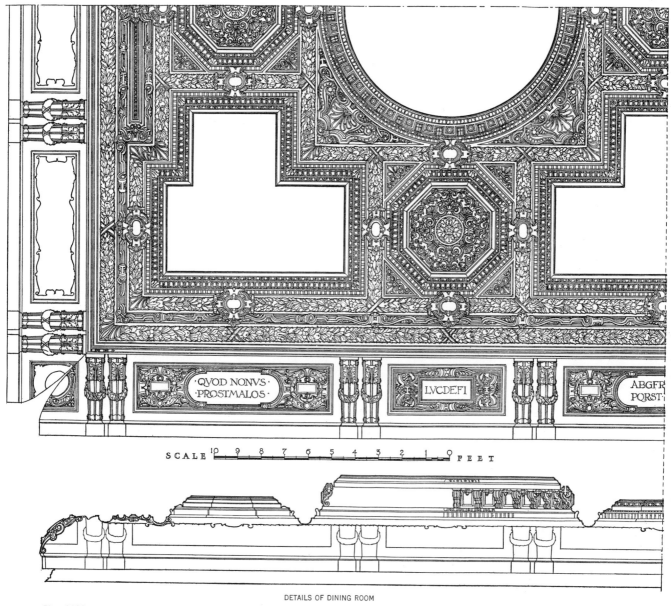

·QVOD NONVS· ·PROSTMALOS·

LVCDEFI

ABGFR PQRST

SCALE 10 9 8 7 6 5 4 3 2 1 0 FEET

DETAILS OF DINING ROOM

THE UNIVERSITY CLUB, NEW YORK CITY.

1900

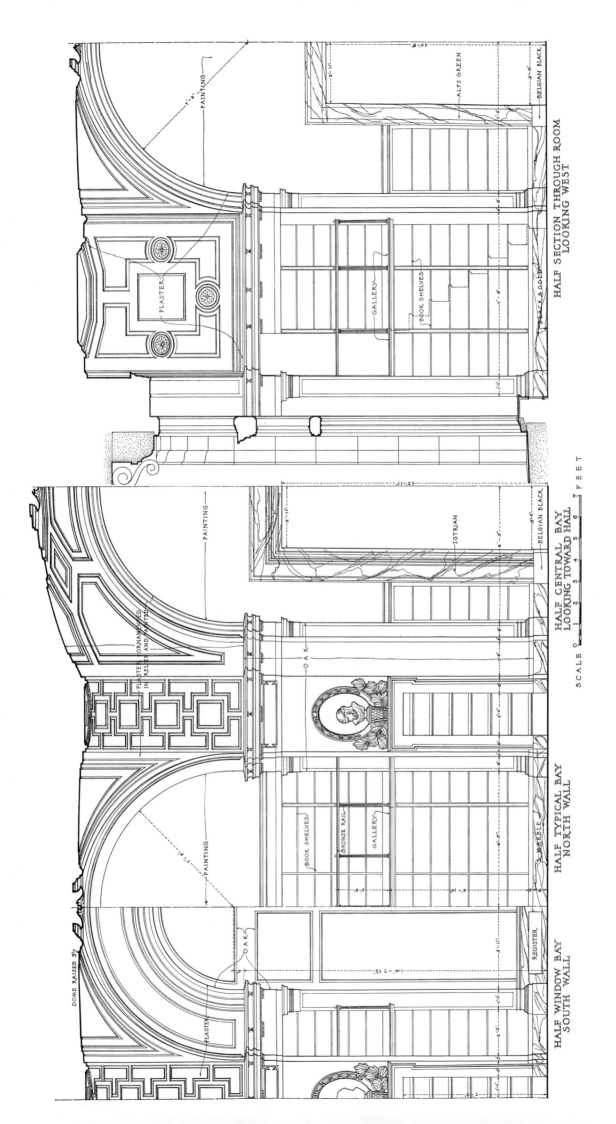

HALF SECTION THROUGH ROOM
LOOKING WEST

PAINTING

PLASTER

GALLERY

BOOK SHELVES

ALPS GREEN

BELGIAN BLACK

BLACK & GOLD

PAINTING

PLASTER ORNAMENTED
IN RELIEF AND PAINTED

OAK

BOOK SHELVES

BRONZE RAIL

GALLERY

MARBLE

BELGIAN BLACK

ISTRIAN

HALF CENTRAL BAY
LOOKING TOWARD HALL

SCALE 0 1 2 3 4 5 6 7 FEET

DOME RAISED 3½

PAINTING

PLASTER

OAK

REGISTER

HALF WINDOW BAY
SOUTH WALL

HALF TYPICAL BAY
NORTH WALL

UNIVERSITY CLUB, NEW YORK CITY
DETAILS OF THE LIBRARY
1900

Plate 140B

UPPER PART OF CORNICE AND VAULTED CEILING, PLASTER.

WHITE NORWEGIAN MARBLE

BRONZE CAPITALS

TERRAZZO

SIENA MARBLE

TERRAZZO
3-COLORS

WHITE MARBLE INLAY

SHAFTS OF
COLUMNS AND
PILASTERS
CONNEMARA
MARBLE

CARVED PANEL ABOVE
WHITE STATUARY MARBLE

BRICK LINING
ISTRIAN STONE MANTEL

WHITE NORWEGIAN MARBLE

MANTEL IN 1ST STORY HALL

4 3 2 1 0
SCALE

Plate 140C

UNIVERSITY CLUB, NEW YORK CITY.
1900

EXTERIOR

THE BOSTON SYMPHONY MUSIC HALL, BOSTON, MASS.
1900

Plate 141

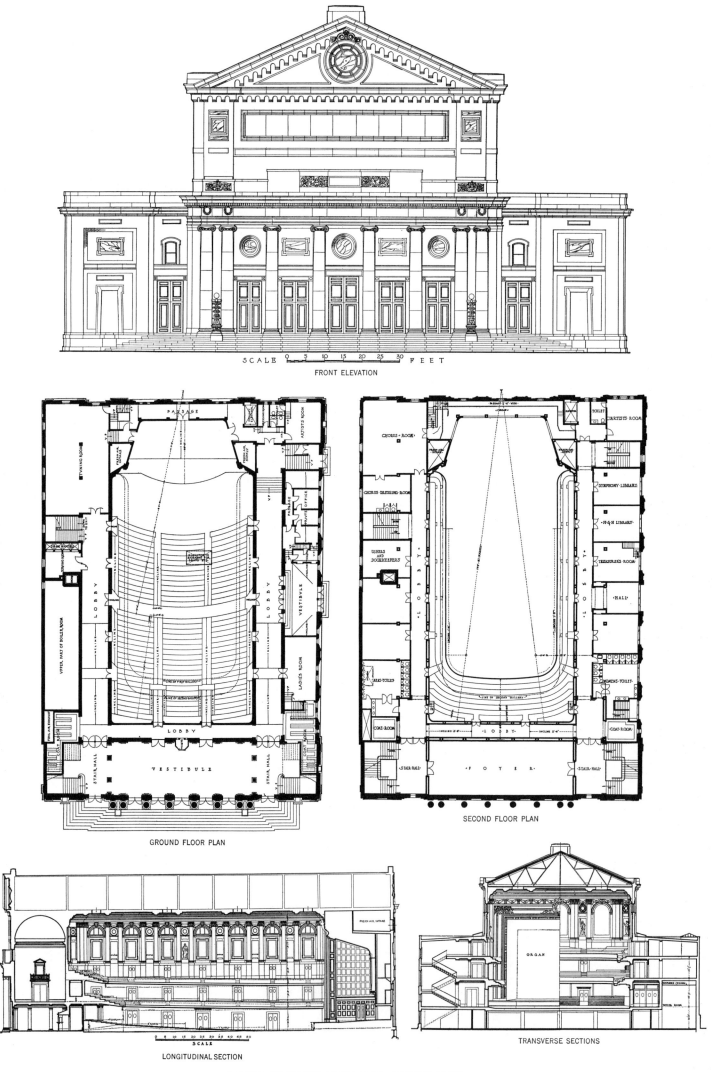

SCALE 0 5 10 15 20 25 30 FEET

FRONT ELEVATION

GROUND FLOOR PLAN

SECOND FLOOR PLAN

SCALE 0 5 10 15 20 25 30 35 40 45 50

LONGITUDINAL SECTION

TRANSVERSE SECTIONS

Plate 142

BOSTON SYMPHONY MUSIC HALL, BOSTON MASS.

1900

SECTION THROUGH
GABLE CORNICE
ON LINE B-B'

CORNER OF CLEAR STORY GABLE

CENTRAL PORTION OF CLEAR STORY GABLE

SECTION ON
LINE A-A' ABOVE

SECTION ON LINE C-C'

LEVANTO
MARBLE
INSERTS

GLASS

GLASS

GLASS

GLASS

CENTER LINE OF FACADE

SECTION ON CENTER LINE

SCALE

THE BOSTON SYMPHONY MUSIC HALL, BOSTON, MASS.
EXTERIOR DETAILS, FRONT ELEVATION
1900

Plate 143

ENTRANCE HALL

STAIR HALL

Plate 144   WM. C. WHITNEY RESIDENCE, NEW YORK CITY.
1900

DINING ROOM

BALL ROOM

WM. C. WHITNEY RESIDENCE, NEW YORK CITY.
1900

Plate 145

FRONT ELEVATION

FIRST FLOOR PLAN

0 5 10 15 20 25 30 35 40 45 50
·SCALE·

Plate 146

A. A. POPE RESIDENCE, FARMINGTON, CONN.
1900

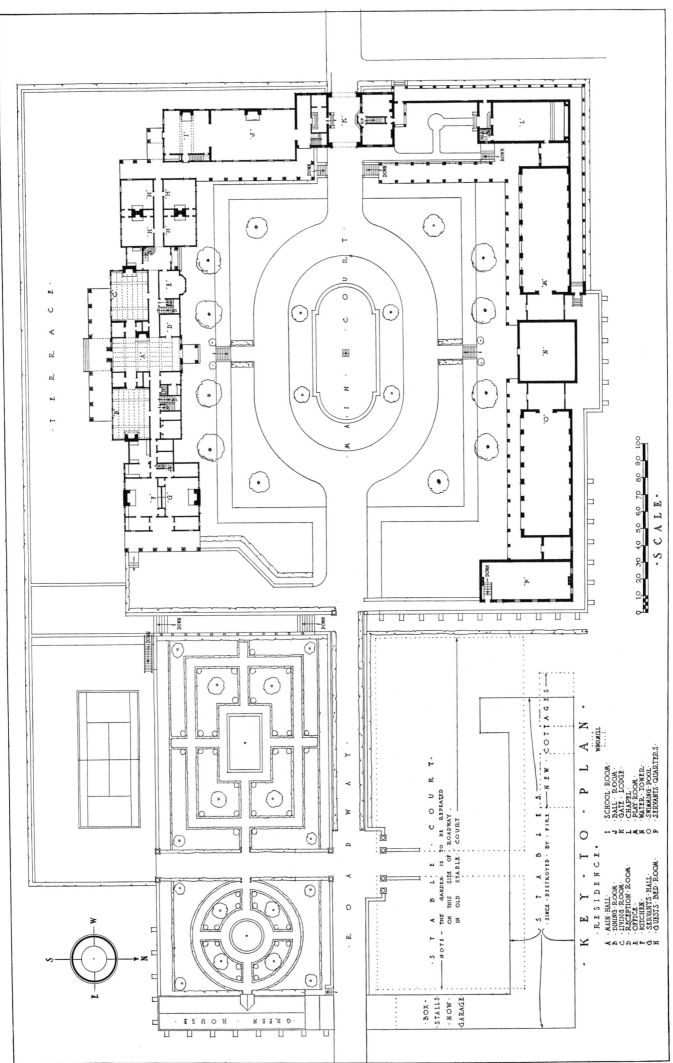

S C A L E ·

0 10 20 30 40 50 60 70 80 90 100

ESTATE OF E. D. MORGAN, WHEATLEY HILLS, L. I.
BEGUN 1900

· K E Y · T O · P L A N ·

· R E S I D E N C E ·

A · MAIN · HALL.
B · DINING · ROOM.
C · LIVING · ROOM.
D · RECEPTION · ROOM.
E · OFFICE.
F · KITCHEN.
G · SERVANT'S · HALL.
H · GUEST'S · BED · ROOM.

I · SCHOOL · ROOM.
J · BALL · ROOM.
K · GATE · LODGE.
L · CHAPEL.
M · PLAY · ROOM.
N · WATER · TOWER.
O · SWIMMING · POOL.
P · SERVANTS · QUARTERS.

· S T A B L E · C O U R T ·

NOTE — THE STABLE IS TO BE REPLACED
ON THIS SIDE OF ROADWAY
IN OLD STABLE COURT

· S T A B L E S · N E W · C O T T A G E S

SINCE · DESTROYED · BY · FIRE

· WINDMILL ·

· BOX ·
· STALLS ·
· NOW ·
· GARAGE ·

· G R E E N · H O U S E ·

Plate 147

GENERAL VIEW OF BUILDINGS

VIEW IN GARDEN

ENTRANCE DRIVEWAY

Plate 148

ESTATE OF E. D. MORGAN, WHEATLEY HILLS, L. I.
1901

THE HOUSE

THE CHAPEL

THE WATER TOWER

ESTATE OF E. D. MORGAN, WHEATLEY HILLS, L. I.
1901

Plate 149

ENTRANCE COURT

GENERAL VIEW OF GARDEN

Plate 150   ESTATE OF E. D. MORGAN, WHEATLEY HILLS, L. I.
1901

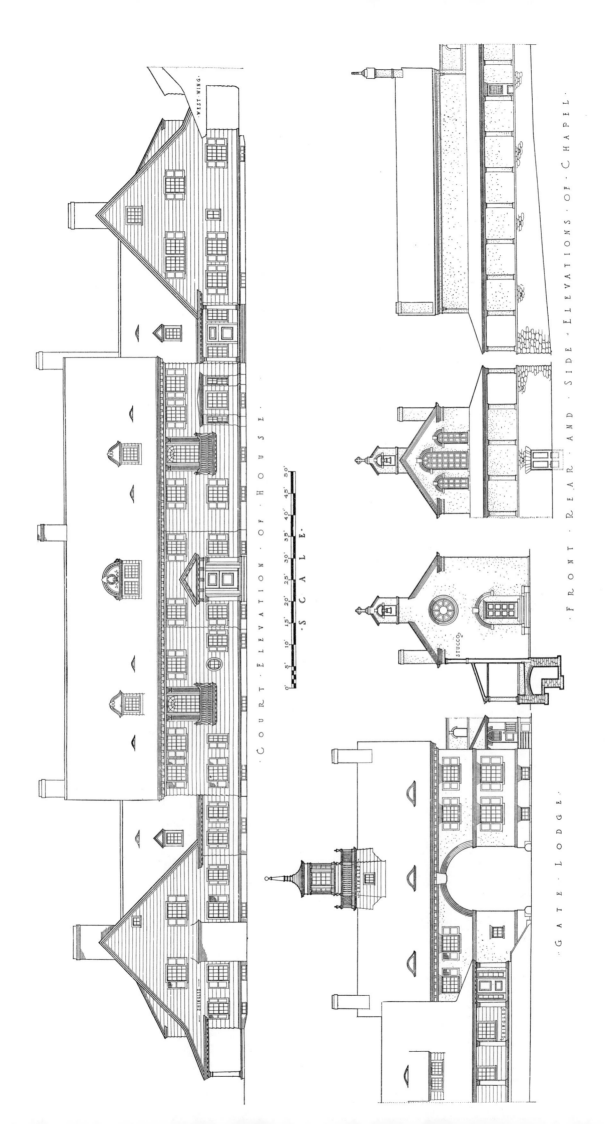

· C O U R T · E L E V A T I O N · O F · H O U S E ·

· W E S T · W I N G ·

· S C A L E ·

0'   5'   10'   15'   20'   25'   30'   35'   40'   45'   50'

· G A T E · L O D G E ·

STUCCO

· F R O N T · R E A R · A N D · S I D E · E L E V A T I O N S · O F · C H A P E L ·

ESTATE OF E. D. MORGAN, WHEATLEY HILLS, L. I.
1901

Plate 151

THE "PORCELLIAN" GATE OR THE McKEAN MEMORIAL GATE.

CLASS OF 1875

CLASS OF 1877

CLASS OF 1857

MEMORIAL GATEWAYS, HARVARD UNIVERSITY, CAMBRIDGE, MASS.
1900 - 1901

Plate 152

CLASS OF 1880

CLASS OF 1887-88

CLASS OF 1890

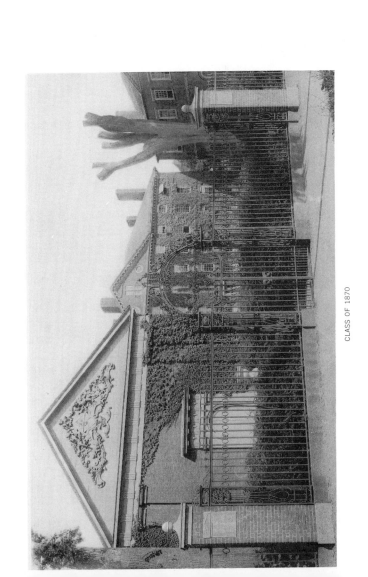

CLASS OF 1870

MEMORIAL GATEWAYS, HARVARD UNIVERSITY, CAMBRIDGE, MASS.

1901 TO 1905

Plate 153

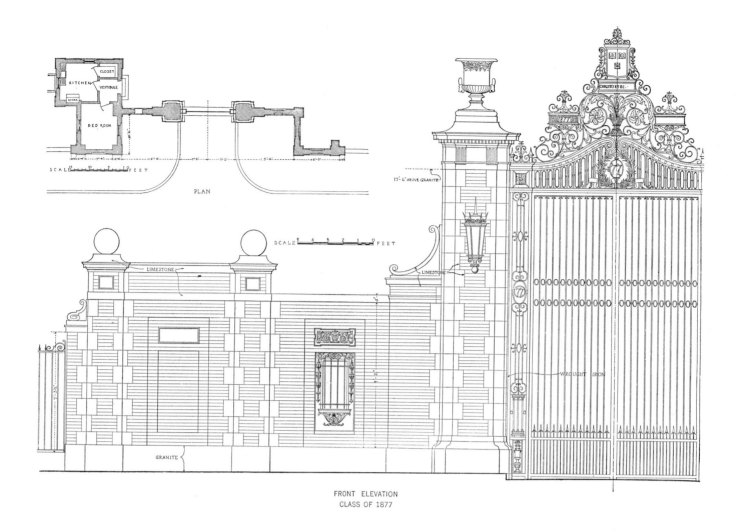

PLAN

SCALE ___ FEET

SCALE _____ FEET

17'-6" ABOVE GRANITE

LIMESTONE

LIMESTONE

GRANITE

WROUGHT IRON

FRONT ELEVATION
CLASS OF 1877

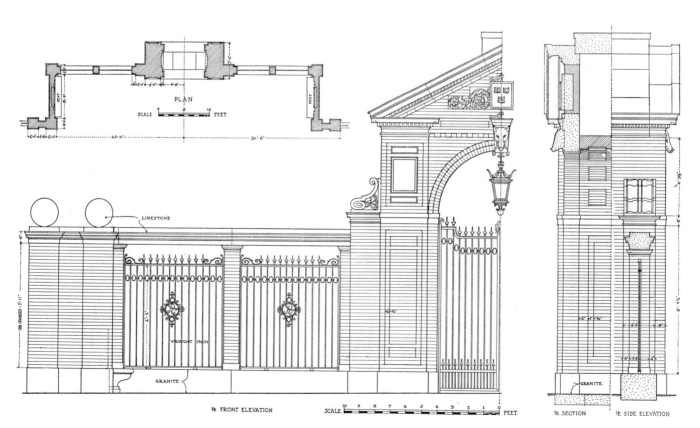

PLAN

SCALE _____ FEET

LIMESTONE

WROUGHT IRON

GRANITE

½ FRONT ELEVATION

SCALE _____ FEET

GRANITE

½ SECTION   ½ SIDE ELEVATION

THE "PORCELLIAN" GATE OR THE McKEAN MEMORIAL GATE

Plate 154

MEMORIAL GATEWAYS, HARVARD UNIVERSITY, CAMBRIDGE, MASS.
1900 - 1901

SECOND STORY HALL

FIRST STORY HALL

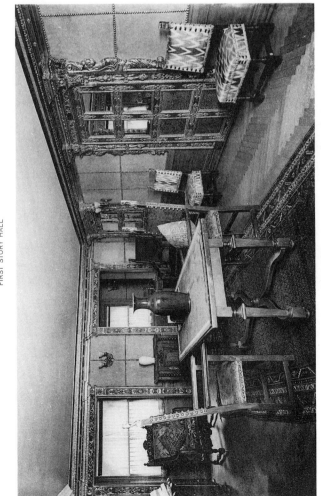

RECEPTION ROOM

RESIDENCE OF HENRY W. POORE, NEW YORK CITY
1900

Plate 155

LIBRARY

DINING ROOM

Plate 156 RESIDENCE OF HENRY W. POORE, NEW YORK CITY

EXTERIOR VIEW

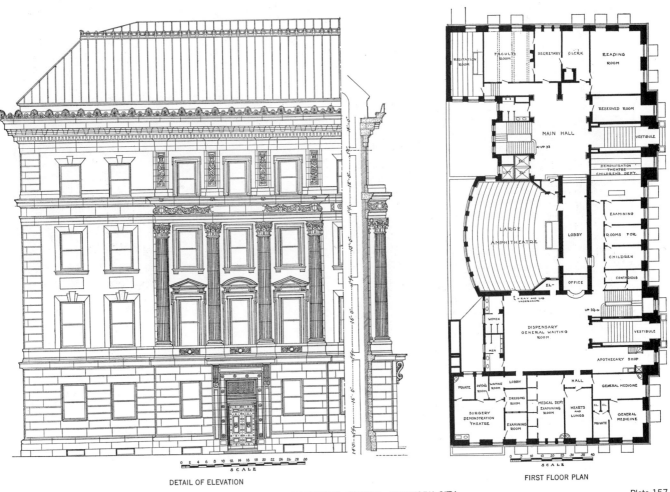

DETAIL OF ELEVATION

FIRST FLOOR PLAN

CORNELL UNIVERSITY MEDICAL SCHOOL, NEW YORK CITY.
1901

Plate 157

THE HARVARD UNION

CLASS OF 1879 MEMORIAL GATEWAY

Plate 158

HARVARD UNIVERSITY, CAMBRIDGE, MASS.

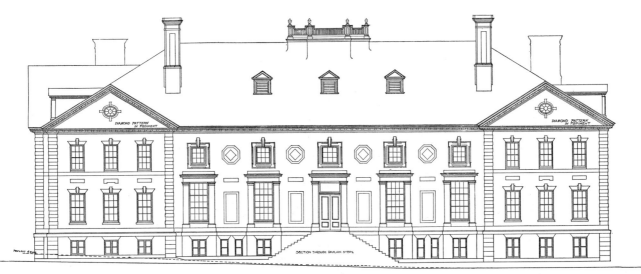

0 5 10 15 20 25 30 35 40 45 50
·SCALE·

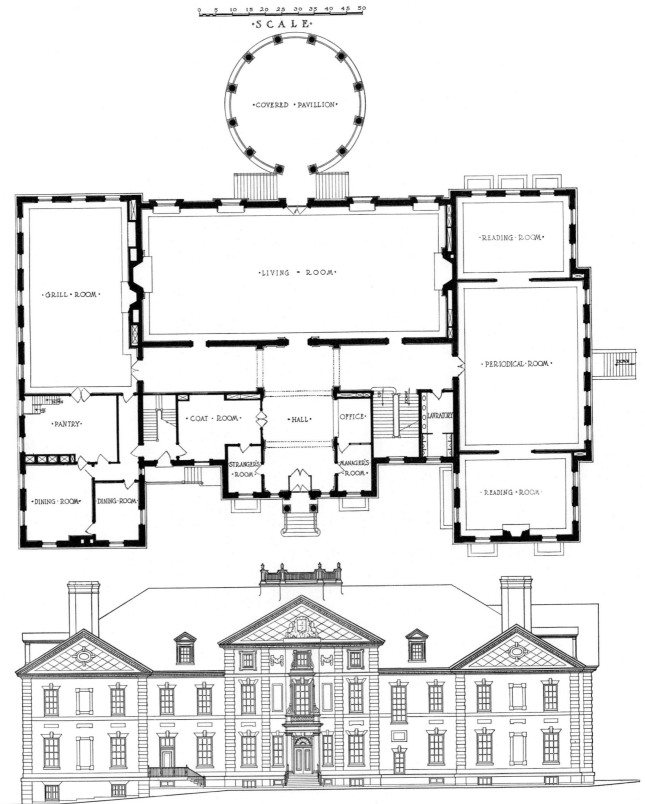

·COVERED·PAVILLION·

·GRILL·ROOM·

·LIVING·ROOM·

·READING·ROOM·

·PERIODICAL·ROOM·

·PANTRY·

·COAT·ROOM·

·HALL·

·OFFICE·

·LAVRATORY·

·STRANGER'S ROOM·

·MANAGER'S ROOM·

·DINING·ROOM·

·DINING·ROOM·

·READING·ROOM·

THE HARVARD UNION, CAMBRIDGE, MASS.
1902

Plate 159

MANTEL IN DINING HALL

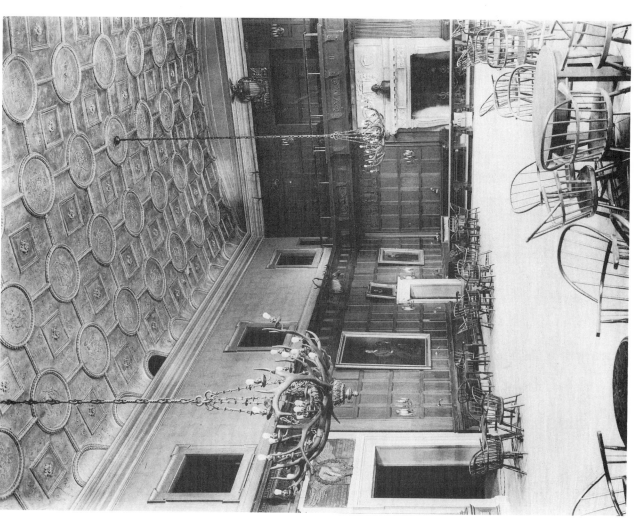

DINING HALL

THE HARVARD UNION, CAMBRIDGE, MASS.
1902

Plate 160

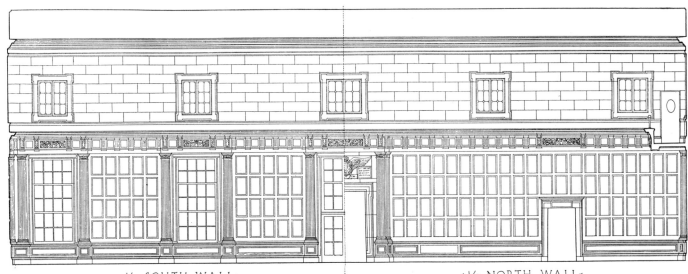

·½ SOUTH WALL·   ·½ NORTH WALL·

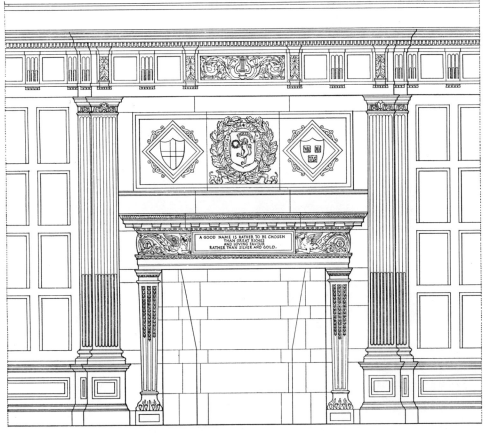

·ELEVATION OF MANTEL ON WEST WALL·

A GOOD NAME IS RATHER TO BE CHOSEN
THAN GREAT RICHES
AND LOVING FAVOUR
RATHER THAN SILVER AND GOLD.

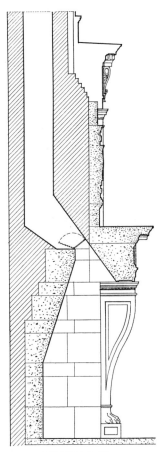

·SECTION·

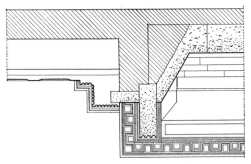

·PLAN OF ABOVE·

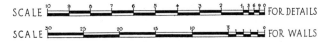

SCALE   FOR DETAILS

SCALE   FOR WALLS

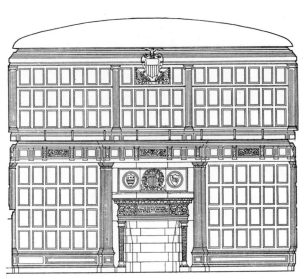

·EAST WALL·

DETAILS OF LIVING ROOM

THE HARVARD UNION, CAMBRIDGE, MASS.   Plate 161

NOTE: FOR "DINING HALL" READ "LIVING ROOM" ON PAGE NO. 160

1902

RESIDENCE OF THOMAS B. CLARKE, NEW YORK CITY.
1902

Plate 162

RESIDENCE OF PHILIP A. ROLLINS, NEW YORK CITY.
1902

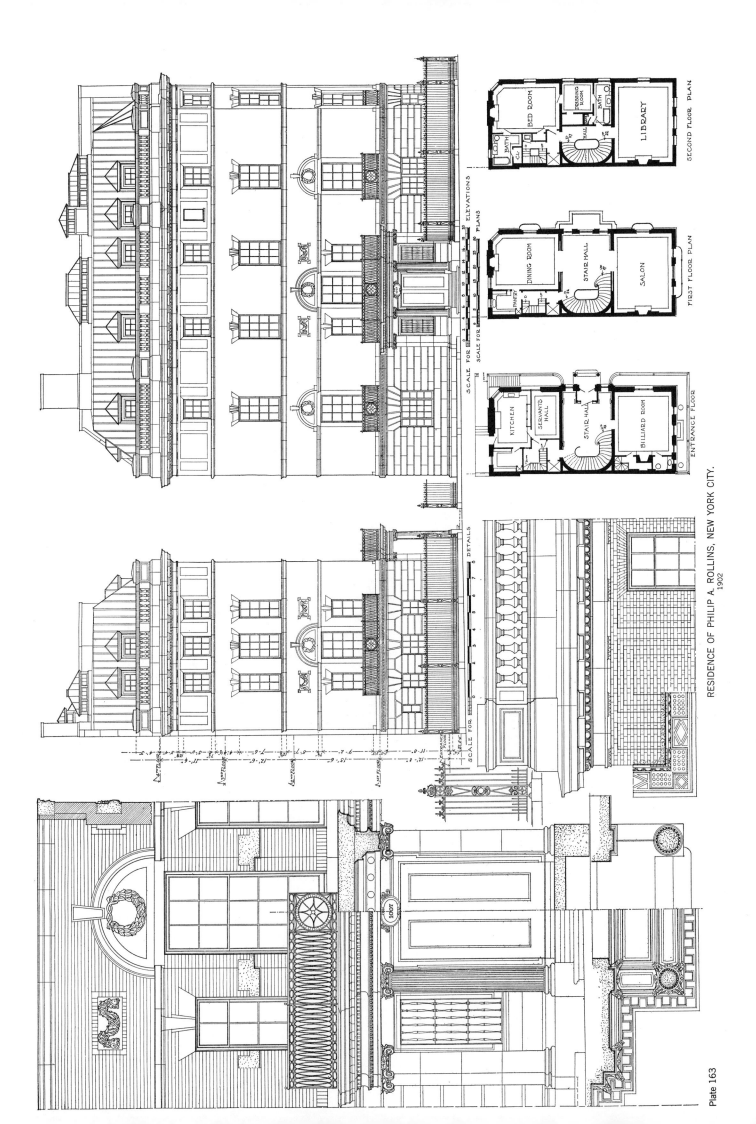

SECOND FLOOR PLAN

BED ROOM

DRESSING ROOM

BATH

LIBRARY

BATH

CL.

HALL

FIRST FLOOR PLAN

DINING ROOM

STAIR HALL

SALON

PANTRY

ENTRANCE FLOOR

KITCHEN

SERVANTS HALL

STAIR HALL

BILLIARD ROOM

ELEVATIONS

PLANS

SCALE FOR

SCALE FOR

DETAILS

SCALE FOR

RESIDENCE OF PHILIP A. ROLLINS, NEW YORK CITY.
1902

Plate 163

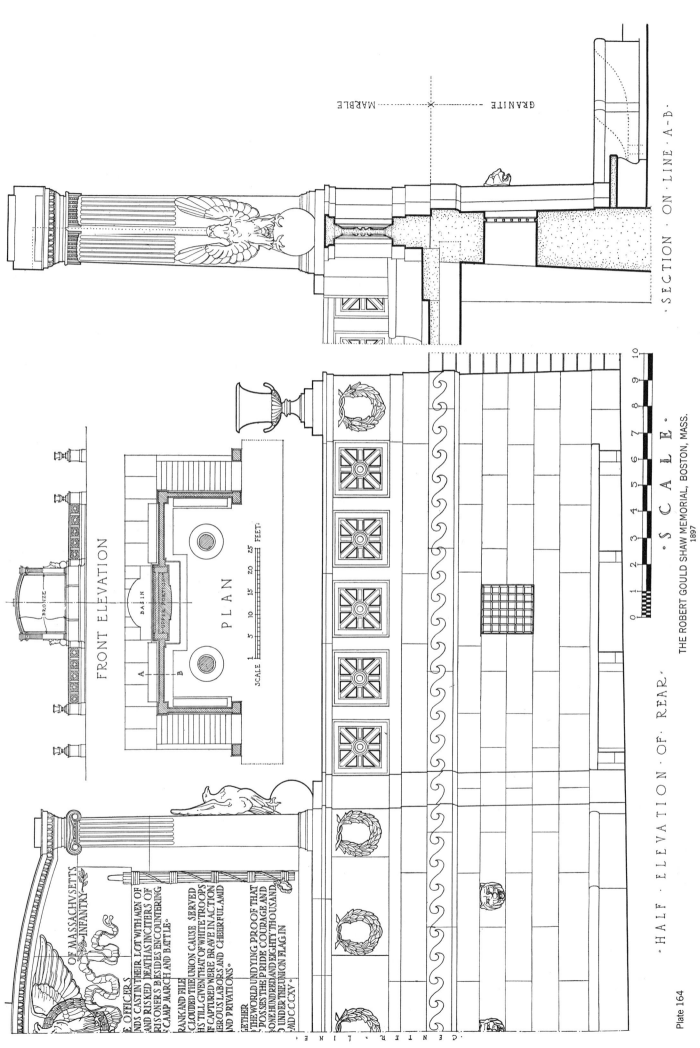

THE ROBERT GOULD SHAW MEMORIAL, BOSTON, MASS.
1897

Plate 164

FRONT TOWARD STATE HOUSE

REAR TOWARD COMMON

ROBERT GOULD SHAW MEMORIAL, BOSTON, MASS.

Plate 165

ENTRANCE FRONT

TERRACE AT ENTRANCE

DETAIL OF DOORWAY

Plate 166

"HARBOR HILL", C. H. MACKAY RESIDENCE, ROSLYN, L. I.

THE STONE ROOM

DINING ROOM

"HARBOR HILL", C. H. MACKAY RESIDENCE, ROSLYN, L. I.
1902

Plate 167

ENTRANCE HALL

STAIR HALL

"HARBOR HILL", C. H. MACKAY RESIDENCE, ROSLYN, L. I.
1902

Plate 168

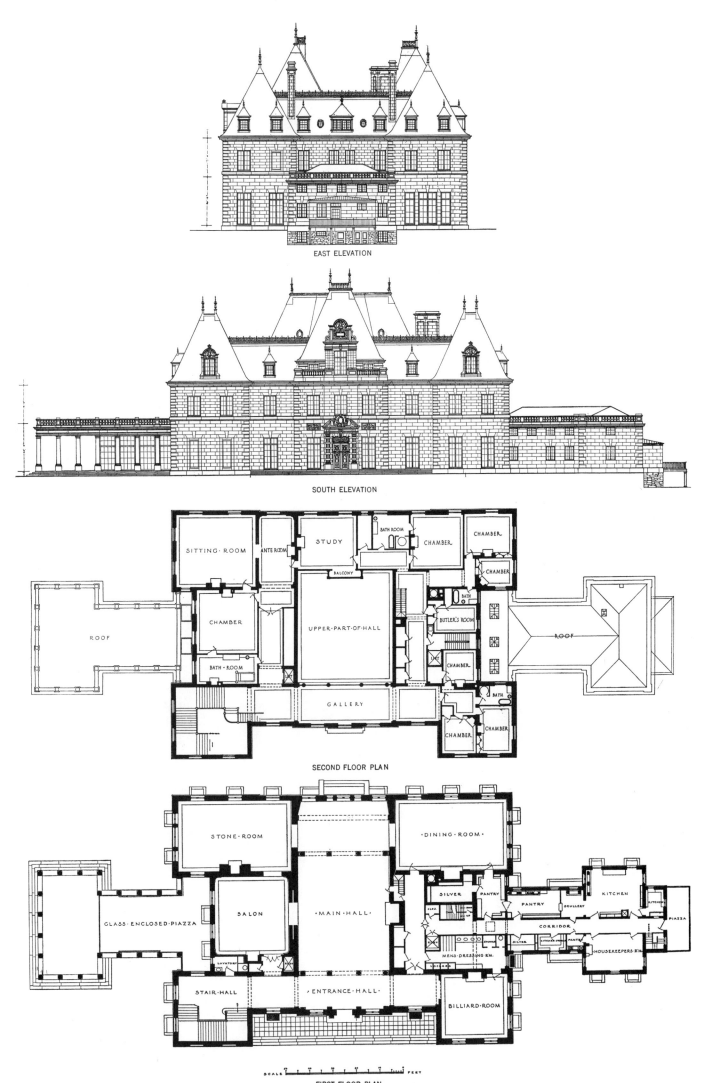

EAST ELEVATION

SOUTH ELEVATION

SECOND FLOOR PLAN

SITTING · ROOM

ANTE ROOM

STUDY

BATH ROOM

CHAMBER

CHAMBER

CHAMBER

ROOF

CHAMBER

BALCONY

UPPER · PART · OF · HALL

BATH

BUTLER'S · ROOM

ROOF

BATH · ROOM

LIFT

CHAMBER

GALLERY

BATH

CHAMBER

CHAMBER

FIRST FLOOR PLAN

STONE · ROOM

DINING · ROOM

GLASS · ENCLOSED · PIAZZA

SALON

MAIN · HALL

SILVER

PANTRY

PANTRY

SCULLERY

KITCHEN

KITCHEN

CORRIDOR

PIAZZA

LAVATORY

MENS · DRESSING · RM.

KITCHEN

PANTRY

HOUSEKEEPERS · RM.

STAIR · HALL

ENTRANCE · HALL

BILLIARD · ROOM

SCALE ┣━┿━┿━┿━┿━┿━┿━┿━┫━━━━┫ FEET

FIRST FLOOR PLAN

C. H. MACKAY RESIDENCE, ROSLYN, L. I.

1902

Plate 169

ELEVATION
AND SECTION
OF SMALLER
DORMERS

COPPER GUTTER

SLATE ROOF   COPPER GUTTER

SECTION THRO. WINDOW
AT SIDE OF CENTRAL DORMER

STONE WORK OF
INDIANA BLUE LIMESTONE

▾ELEVATION OF CENTRAL FEATURE OF FACADE▾

SCALE ▬▬▬▬▬▬▬▬▬▬ FEET

SECTION THRO.
CENTRAL DOOR
ON CENTERLINE

EXTERIOR DETAILS
C. H. MACKAY RESIDENCE, ROSLYN, L. I.
1902

Plate 170

RESIDENCE OF MRS. OELRICHS, NEWPORT, R. I.
1902

Plate 171

LIVING ROOM

STAIR HALL

Plate 172

RESIDENCE OF MRS. OELRICHS, NEWPORT, R. I.
1902

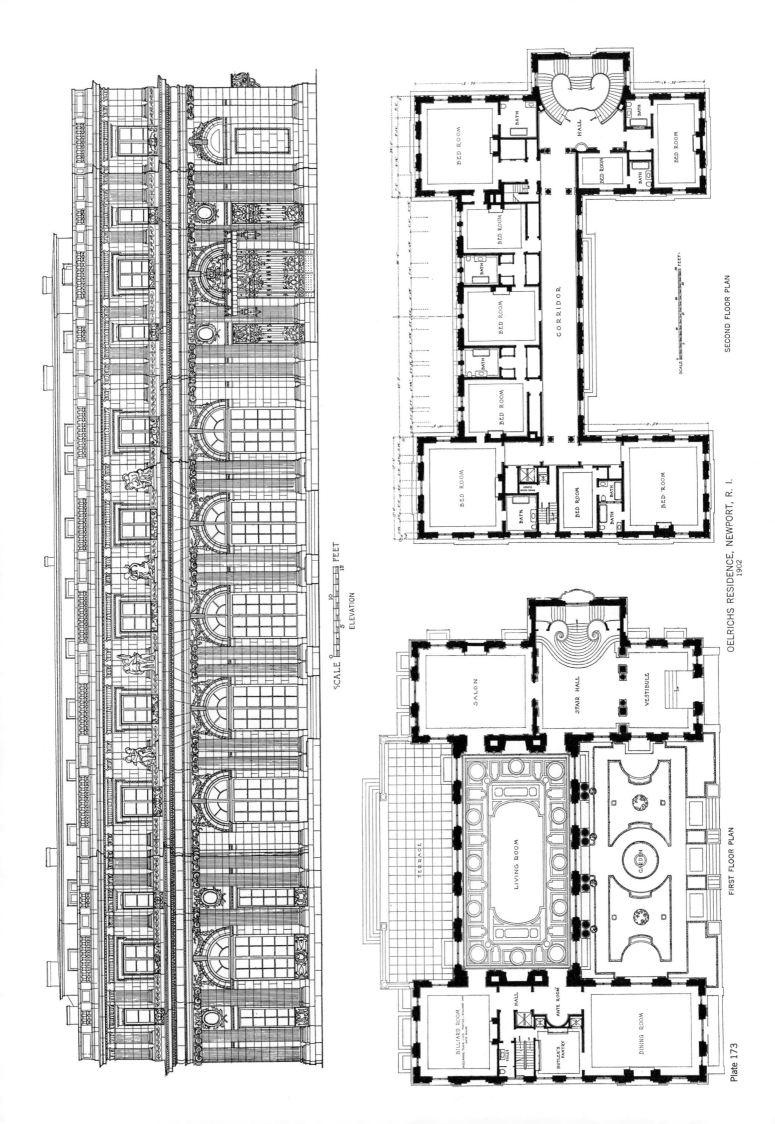

SCALE 0 5 10 15 FEET

ELEVATION

BED ROOM

BATH

BED ROOM

HALL

BATH

BED ROOM

BATH

BED ROOM

BED ROOM

BATH

BED ROOM

BATH

CORRIDOR

BED ROOM

BED ROOM

BATH

BED ROOM

BATH

BED ROOM

BED ROOM

BATH

BED ROOM

BED-ROOM

SCALE 0 8 FEET

SECOND FLOOR PLAN

OELRICHS RESIDENCE, NEWPORT, R. I.
1902

SALON

STAIR HALL

VESTIBULE

TERRACE

LIVING ROOM

GARDEN

BILLIARD ROOM

HALL

ANTE ROOM

BUTLER'S PANTRY

TOILET

DINING ROOM

FIRST FLOOR PLAN

Plate 173

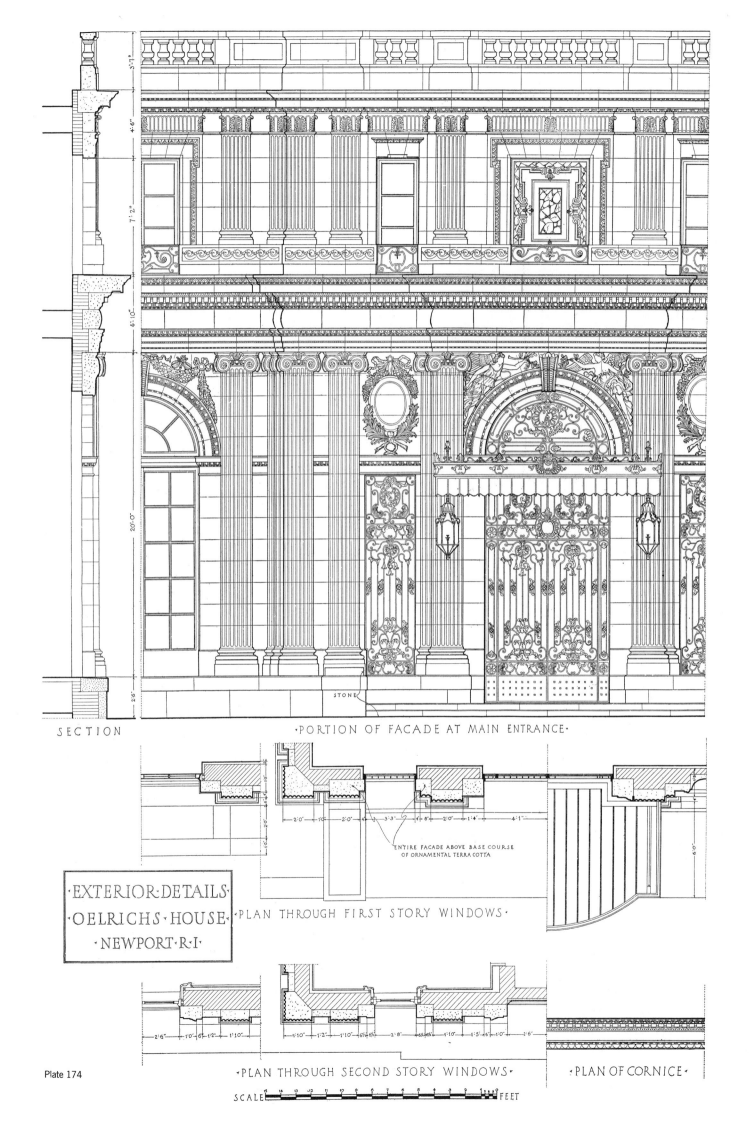

SECTION   ·PORTION·OF·FACADE·AT·MAIN·ENTRANCE·

STONE

ENTIRE FACADE ABOVE BASE COURSE
OF ORNAMENTAL TERRA COTTA

·PLAN·THROUGH·FIRST·STORY·WINDOWS·

·EXTERIOR·DETAILS·
·OELRICHS·HOUSE·
·NEWPORT·R·I·

·PLAN·THROUGH·SECOND·STORY·WINDOWS·   ·PLAN·OF·CORNICE·

Plate 174

SCALE   FEET

ENTRANCE UNDER EAST TERRACE

EAST TERRACE WITH PLAN OF BUILDINGS

THE WHITE HOUSE, WASHINGTON, D. C.
ADDITIONS AND RESTORATIONS
1903

Plate 175

ENTRANCE HALL

Plate 176

THE WHITE HOUSE, WASHINGTON, D. C.
RENOVATION OF INTERIOR
1903

DETAILS OF EAST ROOM

DETAILS OF DINING ROOM

0 1 2 3 4 5 6 7 8 9 10
· S C A L E ·

ALTERATIONS TO THE WHITE HOUSE, WASHINGTON, D. C.
1903

Plate 177

DETAIL OF EAST ROOM

THE WHITE HOUSE, WASHINGTON, D. C.
RENOVATION OF INTERIOR
1903

MANTEL IN STATE DINING ROOM

Plate 178

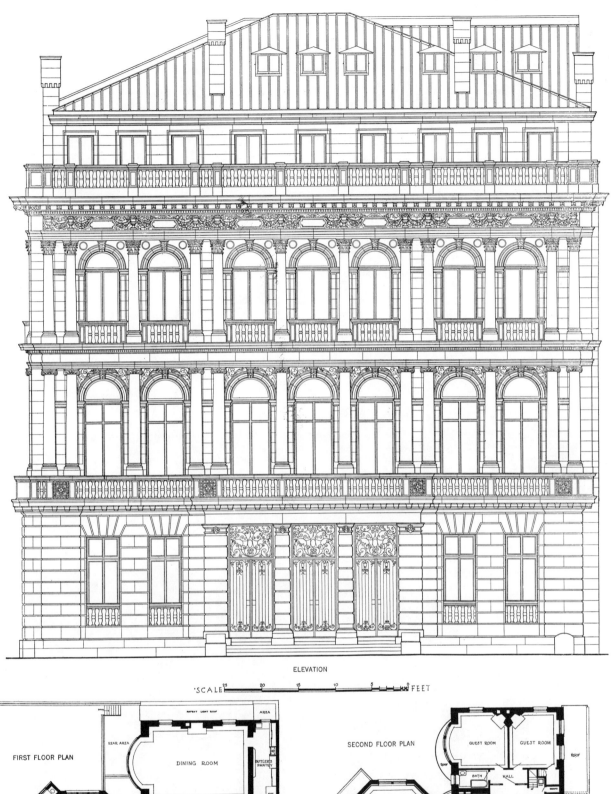

ELEVATION

SCALE 25 20 15 10 5 0 FEET

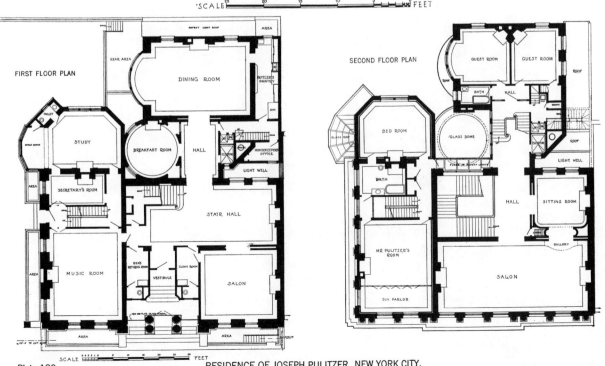

FIRST FLOOR PLAN

REAR AREA

PATENT LIGHT ROOF

AREA

DINING ROOM

BUTLER'S PANTRY

SAFE

STUDY

TOILET

BREAKFAST ROOM

HALL

HOUSEKEEPER'S OFFICE

LIGHT WELL

SECRETARY'S ROOM

AREA

STAIR HALL

MUSIC ROOM

AREA

MEN'S RETIRING ROOM

CLOAK ROOM

VESTIBULE

SALON

AREA

AREA

SCALE FEET

SECOND FLOOR PLAN

GUEST ROOM

GUEST ROOM

ROOF

BATH

HALL

GLASS DOME

BED ROOM

GLASS DOME

ROOF

BATH

ELEVATOR

LIGHT WELL

HALL

SITTING ROOM

MR PULITZER'S ROOM

GALLERY

SUN PARLOR

SALON

Plate 180

RESIDENCE OF JOSEPH PULITZER, NEW YORK CITY.
1903

BREAKFAST ROOM

EXTERIOR

RESIDENCE OF JOSEPH PULITZER, NEW YORK CITY
1903

Plate 181

DINING ROOM

RESIDENCE OF JOSEPH PULITZER, NEW YORK CITY.
1903

Plate 182

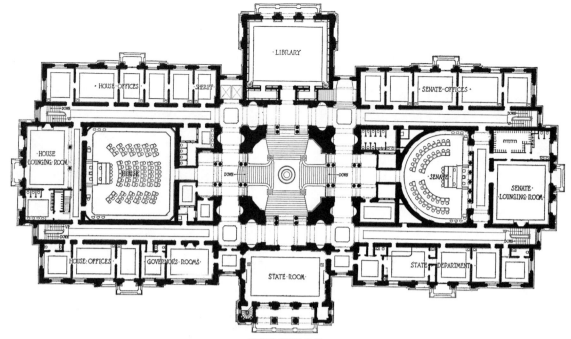

SECOND FLOOR PLAN

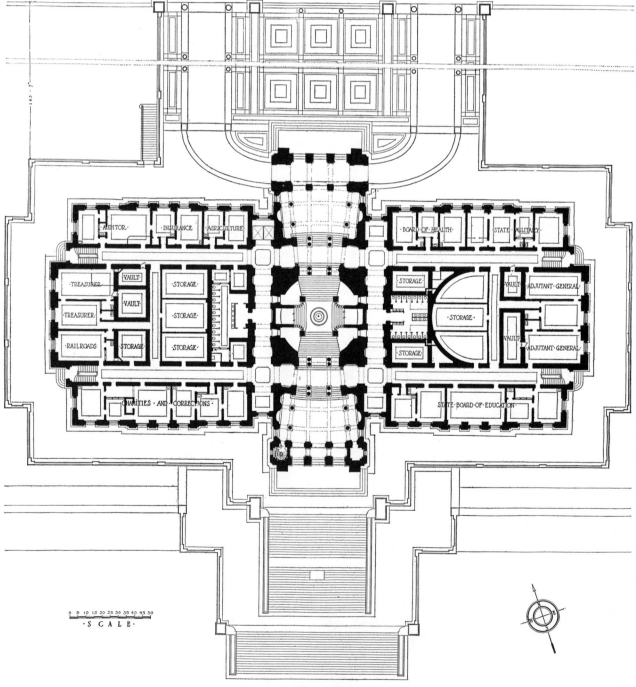

FIRST FLOOR PLAN

Plate 183

RHODE ISLAND STATE CAPITOL, PROVIDENCE, R. I.
BEGUN 1895. COMPLETED 1903.

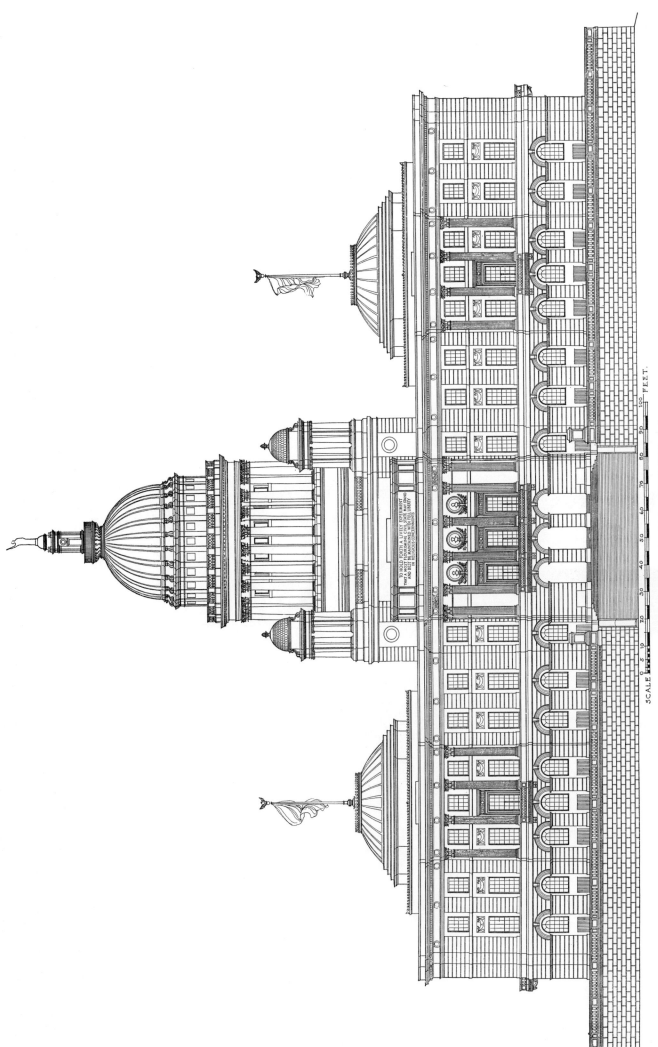

Plate 184

THE RHODE ISLAND STATE CAPITOL, PROVIDENCE, R. I.

FRONT ELEVATION

BEGUN 1895 · COMPLETED 1903

SCALE

0 5 10 20 30 40 50 60 70 80 90 100 FEET.

TO HOLD FORTH A LIVELY EXPERIMENT
THAT A MOST FLOURISHING CIVILL STATE MAY STAND
AND BEST BE MAINTAINED WITH FULL LIBERTY
IN RELIGIOUS CONCERNMENTS

GLASS

GRILLE

SAME AS BELOW

PAVONAZZA

SAME AS ABOVE

BRONZE

BRICK-ARCH

0 5' 10' 15' 20' 25' 30' 35' 40' 45' 50'
· S C A L E ·

Plate 185

THE RHODE ISLAND STATE CAPITOL, PROVIDENCE, R. I.
SECTION THROUGH ROTUNDA
1895 - 1903

THE RHODE ISLAND STATE CAPITOL, PROVIDENCE, R. I.
COMPLETED 1903

Plate 186

DETAIL OF MAIN ENTRANCE

THE RHODE ISLAND STATE CAPITOL, PROVIDENCE, R. I.
1903

STAIR IN ROTUNDA

Plate 187

PLAN OF CORNER

GRANITE

·SECTION·THRO·PORTICO·
·ON·CENTER·LINE·

·DETAIL·OF·CENTRAL·PORTION·OF·SOUTH·ELEVATION·
SCALE FEET

THE RHODE ISLAND STATE CAPITOL, PROVIDENCE, R. I.

Plate 188

HOUSE OF REPRESENTATIVES

GOVERNOR'S RECEPTION ROOM

Plate 189   THE RHODE ISLAND STATE CAPITOL, PROVIDENCE, R. I.

UPPER PART OF ROTUNDA

THE SENATE CHAMBER

THE RHODE ISLAND STATE CAPITOL, PROVIDENCE, R. I.

Plate 190

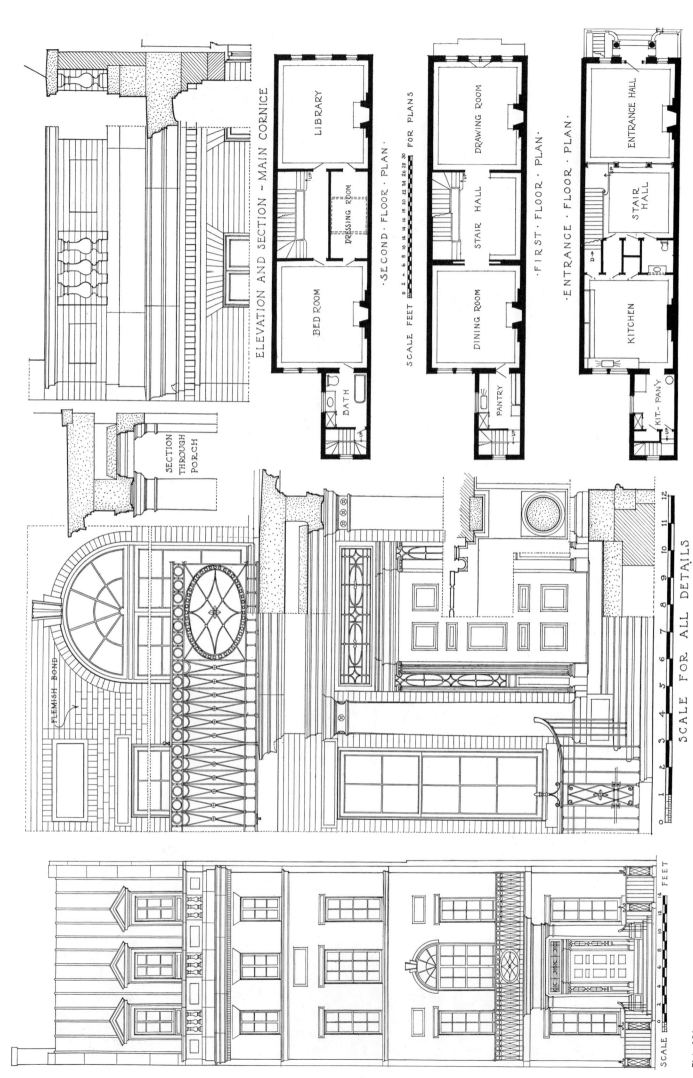

ELEVATION AND SECTION ~ MAIN CORNICE

SECTION THROUGH PORCH

·SECOND·FLOOR·PLAN·

BED ROOM

LIBRARY

DRESSING ROOM

BATH

·FIRST·FLOOR·PLAN·

DINING ROOM

DRAWING ROOM

STAIR HALL

PANTRY

·ENTRANCE·FLOOR·PLAN·

KITCHEN

STAIR HALL

ENTRANCE HALL

KIT.- PANY

SCALE FEET 0 2 4 6 8 10 12 14 16 18 20 22 24 26 28 30 FOR PLANS

FLEMISH BOND

SCALE FOR ALL DETAILS 0 1 2 3 4 5 6 7 8 9 10 11 12

RESIDENCE OF CHARLES DANA GIBSON, NEW YORK CITY.
1903

SCALE 0 2 4 6 8 10 12 14 FEET

Plate 191

LIVING ROOM

DINING ROOM

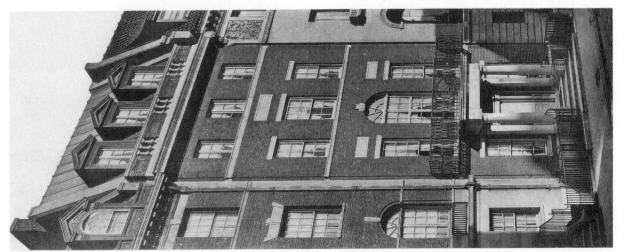

EXTERIOR

RESIDENCE OF C. D. GIBSON, NEW YORK CITY.
1903

Plate 192

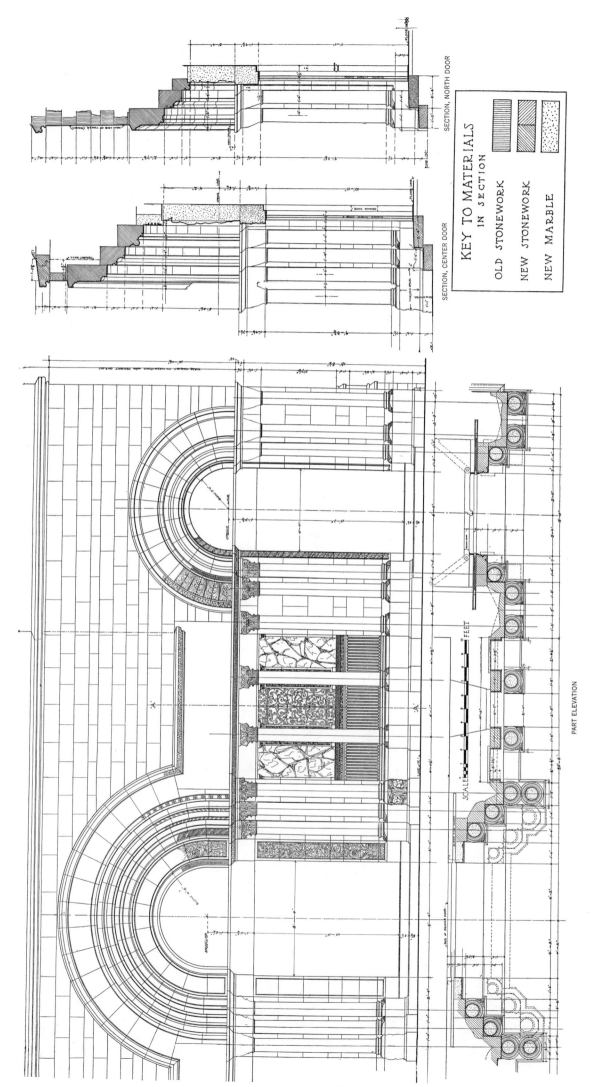

KEY TO MATERIALS
IN SECTION

OLD STONEWORK

NEW STONEWORK

NEW MARBLE

SECTION, NORTH DOOR

SECTION, CENTER DOOR

PART ELEVATION

DOORWAYS TO ST. BARTHOLOMEW'S CHURCH, NEW YORK CITY.
1903

Plate 193

EASTERLY DOORWAYS, ST. BARTHOLOMEW'S CHURCH, NEW YORK CITY.
1903

Plate 194

DETAILS OF EAST DOORWAYS
ST. BARTHOLOMEW'S CHURCH, NEW YORK CITY.
1903

Plate 195

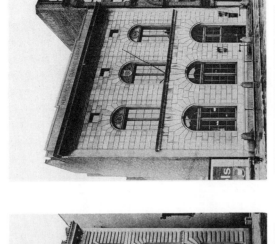

ONE HUNDRED AND TWENTY FIFTH ST. BRANCH
1904

ONE HUNDRED AND FIFTEENTH ST. BRANCH
1907

CHATHAM SQUARE BRANCH
1903

·ROOF READING ROOM PLAN·

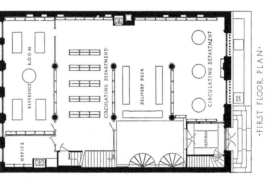

·SECOND FLOOR PLAN·

SCALE   FEET

PLANS OF ST. GABRIEL'S BRANCH

·FIRST FLOOR PLAN·

ST. GABRIEL'S BRANCH
1907

NEW YORK PUBLIC LIBRARY, BRANCH BUILDINGS

Plate 196

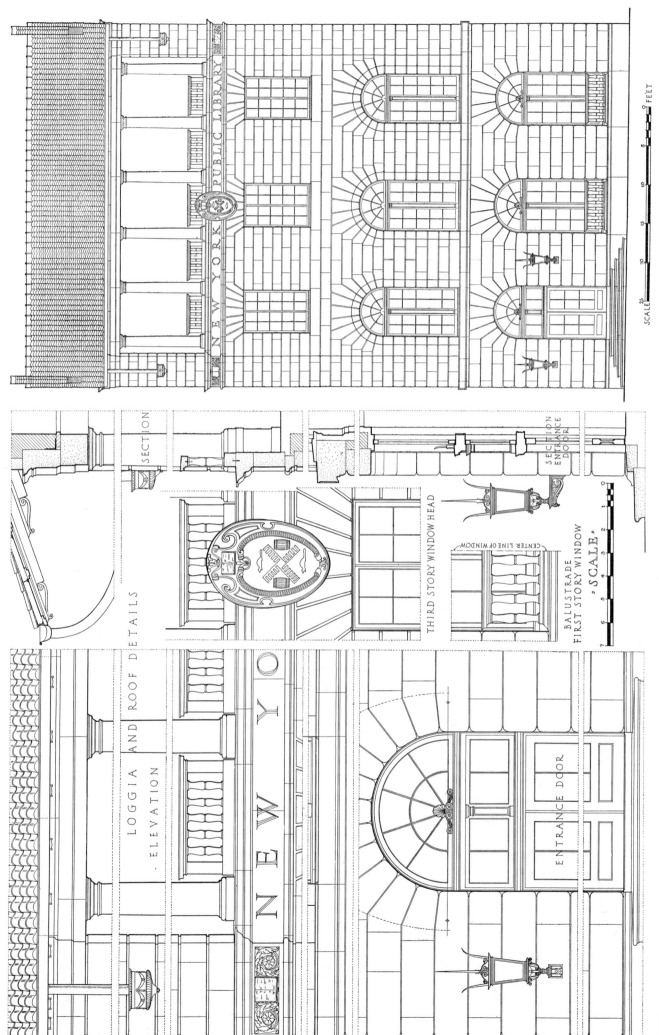

NEW YORK PUBLIC LIBRARY

NEW YORK

SECTION

LOGGIA AND ROOF DETAILS

· ELEVATION ·

N E W Y O R K

ENTRANCE DOOR

THIRD STORY WINDOW HEAD

SECTION ENTRANCE DOOR

CENTER LINE OF WINDOW

BALUSTRADE
FIRST STORY WINDOW

"SCALE"

SCALE   FEET

NEW YORK PUBLIC LIBRARY, ST. GABRIEL'S BRANCH
1906

Plate 197

TOMPKINS SQUARE, 1904

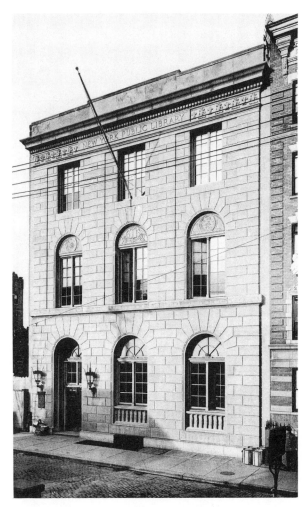

WOODSTOCK, 1913

MT. MORRIS, HARLEM, 1906

HAMILTON GRANGE, 1905

BRANCH BUILDINGS OF THE NEW YORK PUBLIC LIBRARY

Plate 198

NEW YORK PUBLIC LIBRARY

SECTION

ELEVATION

MT. MORRIS BRANCH

SECTION

NEW YORK PUBLIC LIBRARY, BRANCH BUILDINGS

NEW YORK PUBLIC LIBRARY

SCALE

ELEVATION

HAMILTON GRANGE BRANCH

Plate 199

SOUTH TERRACE WITH COLONNADE OF LIBRARY

EARL HALL · 1901

COLUMBIA UNIVERSITY, NEW YORK CITY.

Plate 200

FURNALD HALL, DORMITORY, 1912

FOUNTAIN IN SOUTH COURT, 1906

Plate 201   COLUMBIA UNIVERSITY, NEW YORK CITY.

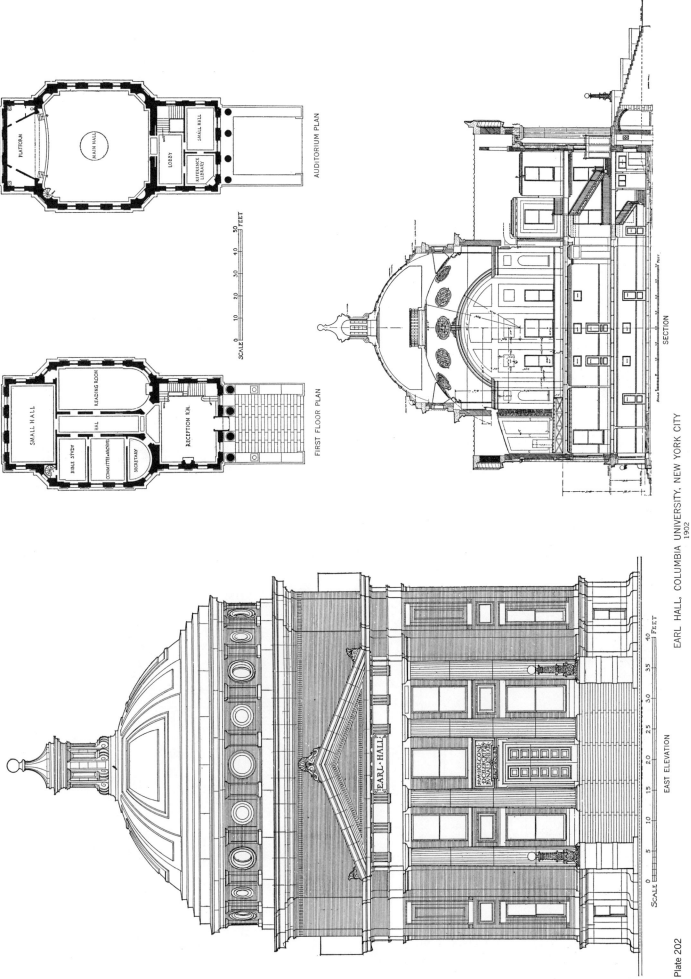

PLATFORM

MAIN HALL

SMALL HALL

LOBBY

REFERENCE LIBRARY

AUDITORIUM PLAN

SMALL HALL

READING ROOM

HALL

BIBLE STUDY

COMMITTEE MEETING

SECRETARY

RECEPTION R.M.

FIRST FLOOR PLAN

SCALE 0 10 20 30 40 50 FEET

SECTION

EARL · HALL

EAST ELEVATION

SCALE 0 5 10 15 20 25 30 35 40 FEET

EARL HALL, COLUMBIA UNIVERSITY, NEW YORK CITY
1902

Plate 202

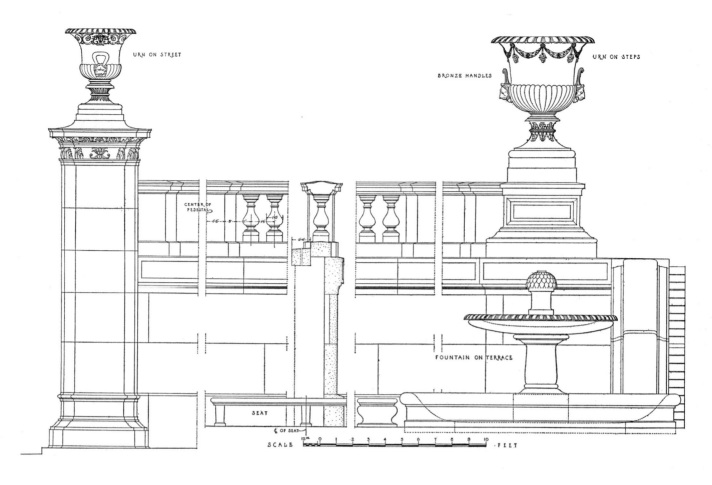

URN ON STREET

BRONZE HANDLES

URN ON STEPS

CENTER OF
PEDESTAL

FOUNTAIN ON TERRACE

SEAT

℄ OF SEAT

SCALE 12ᴵᴺ 0 1 2 3 4 5 6 7 8 9 10 FEET

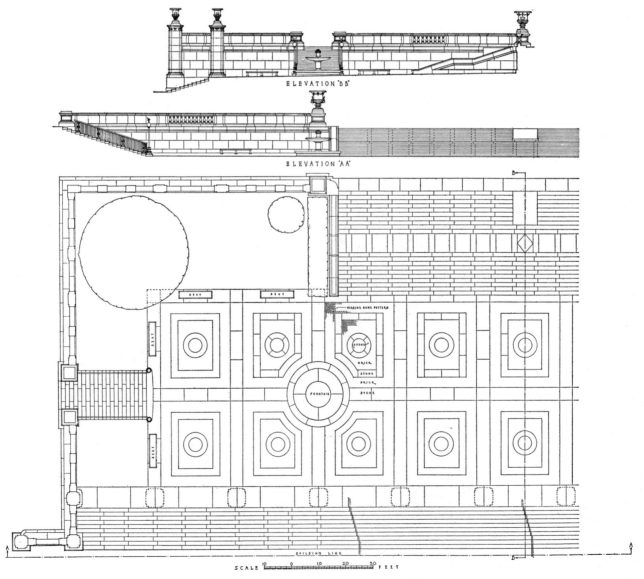

ELEVATION "BB"

ELEVATION "AA"

HERRING BONE PATTERN

STONE
BRICK
STONE
BRICK
STONE

SEAT   SEAT

SEAT

FOUNTAIN

SEAT

BUILDING LINE

SCALE 10 0 10 20 30 FEET

PLAN

Plate 203

DETAILS OF SOUTH COURT, COLUMBIA UNIVERSITY, NEW YORK CITY

ROBINSON HALL, ARCHITECTURAL SCHOOL
1904

MEMORIAL GATEWAY, CLASS 1885

HARVARD UNIVERSITY, CAMBRIDGE, MASS.

Plate 204

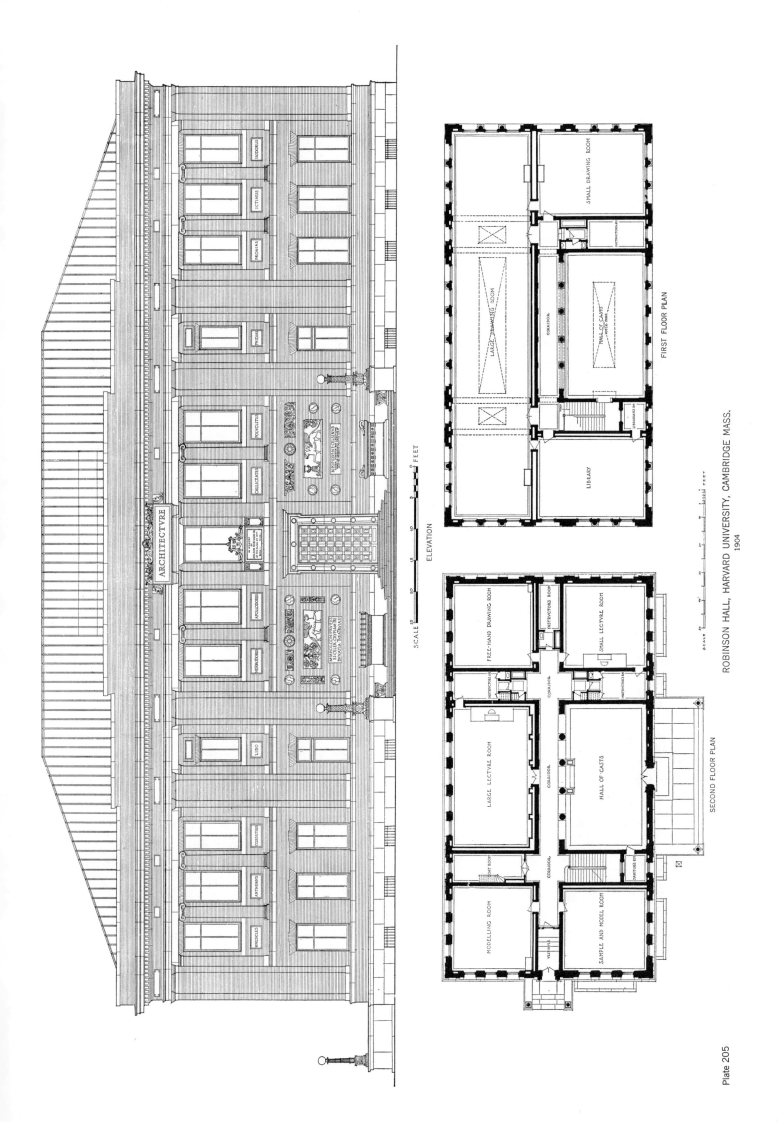

ARCHITECTVRE

ELEVATION

SCALE

FIRST FLOOR PLAN

SECOND FLOOR PLAN

ROBINSON HALL, HARVARD UNIVERSITY, CAMBRIDGE MASS.
1904

Plate 205

SCALE |‚‚‚‚| ‚‚‚‚‚|‚‚‚‚‚|‚‚‚‚‚|‚‚‚‚‚| FEET

BRONZE ENTRANCE DOORWAY

SCALE |12 11 10 9 8 7 6 5 4 3 2 1| INCHES

ROBINSON HALL SCHOOL OF ARCHITECTURE.
HARVARD UNIVERSITY, CAMBRIDGE, MASS.
1904

Plate 206

Plate 207

INTERBOROUGH RAPID TRANSIT COMPANY, NEW YORK CITY
POWER HOUSE
1903

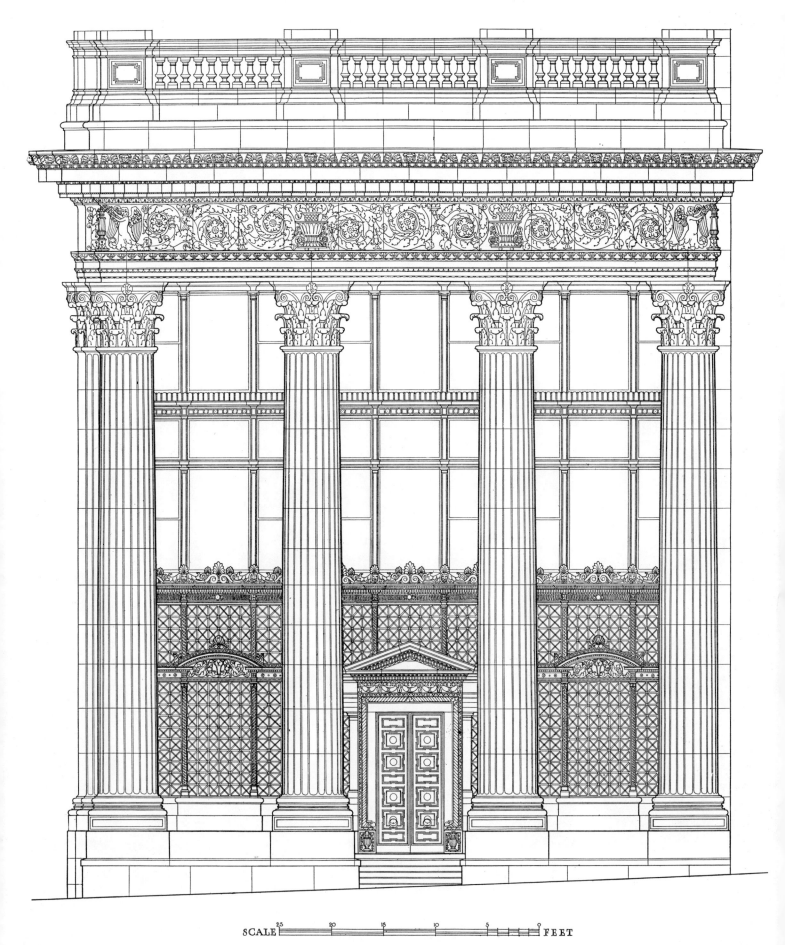

SCALE 25 20 15 10 5 0 FEET

FIFTH AVENUE ELEVATION

BUILDING FOR THE KNICKERBOCKER TRUST CO., NEW YORK CITY.
1904

Plate 208

Plate 209

THE KNICKERBOCKER TRUST COMPANY, NEW YORK CITY
(NOW COLUMBIA TRUST COMPANY)
1904

DETAIL OF ENTABLATURE

THE KNICKERBOCKER TRUST COMPANY, NEW YORK CITY
(NOW COLUMBIA TRUST COMPANY)
1904

DETAIL OF DOORWAY

Plate 210

VIEW OF BANKING ROOM

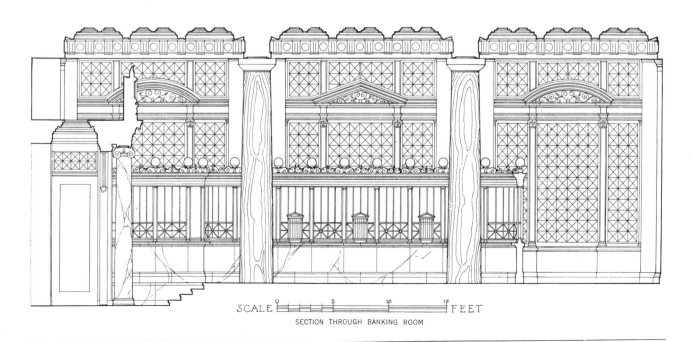

SCALE |0   5   10   15| FEET

SECTION THROUGH BANKING ROOM

Plate 211   BUILDING FOR THE KNICKERBOCKER TRUST CO., NEW YORK CITY.
1904

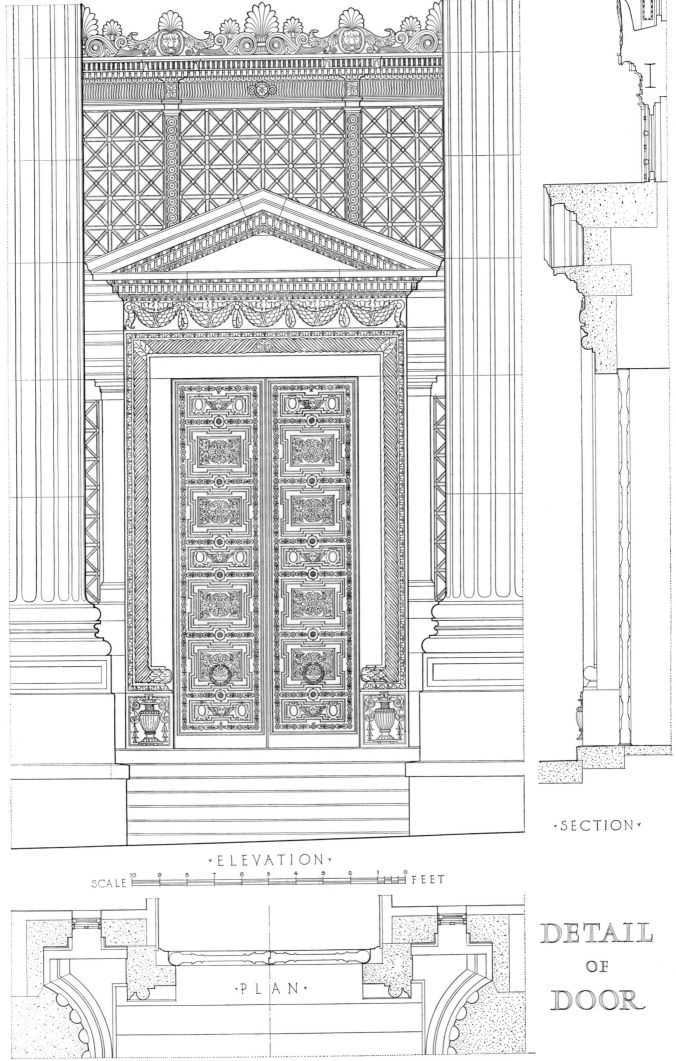

·ELEVATION·

SCALE 10 9 8 7 6 5 4 3 2 1 0 FEET

·PLAN·

·SECTION·

DETAIL
OF
DOOR

BUILDING FOR THE KNICKERBOCKER TRUST CO., NEW YORK CITY.
BRONZE ENTRANCE DOORS WITH MARBLE TRIM
1904

Plate 212

THE BANK OF MONTREAL, MONTREAL, CANADA.
1904

Plate 213

BANK OF MONTREAL, MONTREAL, CANADA.
1904

Plate 214

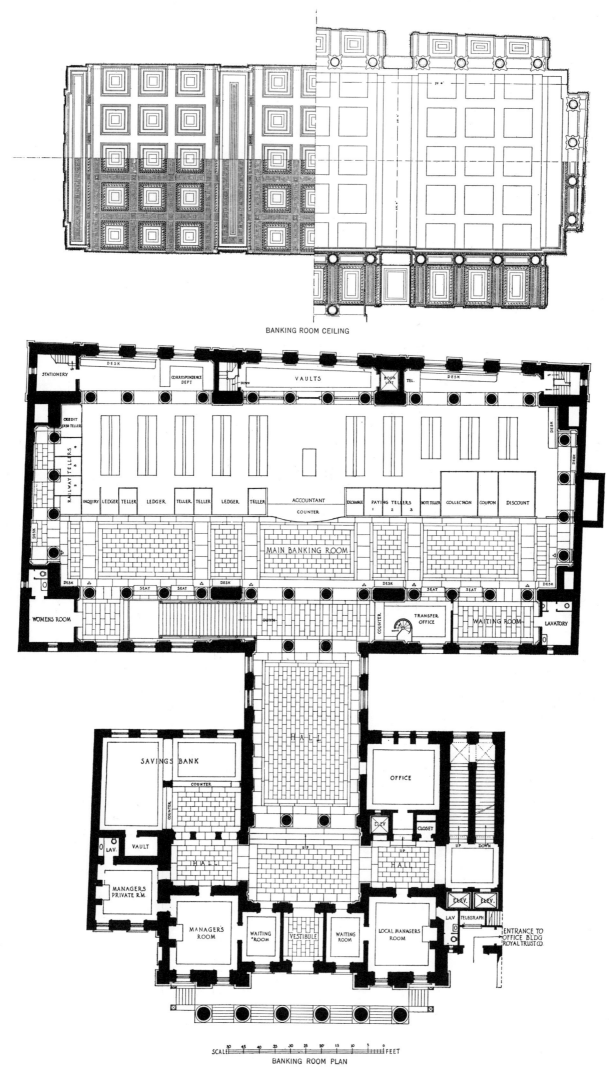

BANKING ROOM CEILING

BANKING ROOM PLAN

Plate 215 THE BANK OF MONTREAL, MONTREAL, CANADA.
1904

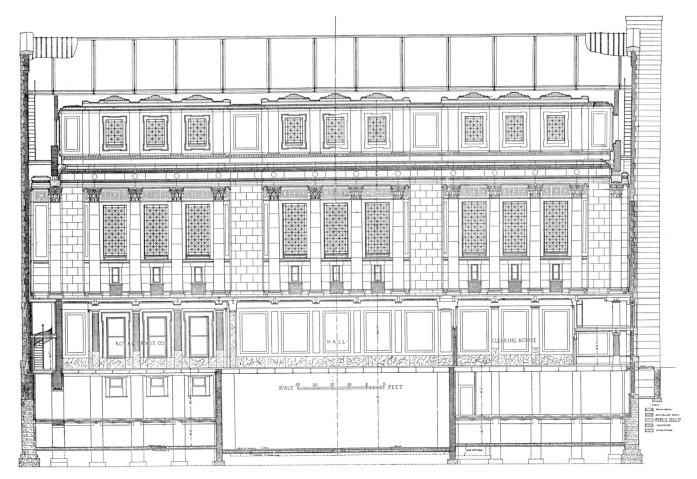

SECTION, MAIN BANKING ROOM

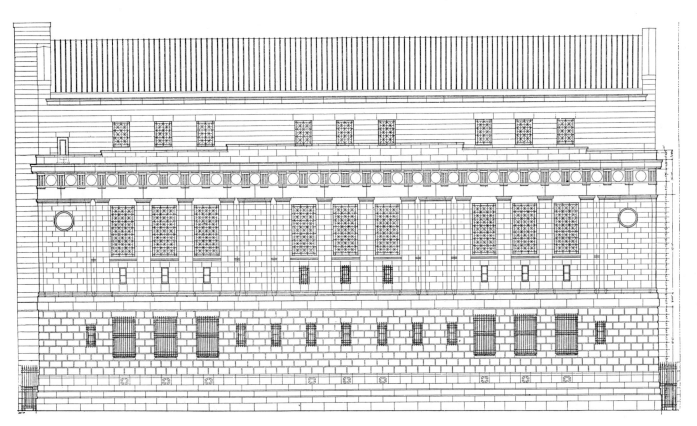

CRAIG STREET ELEVATION

THE BANK OF MONTREAL, MONTREAL, CANADA

Plate 216

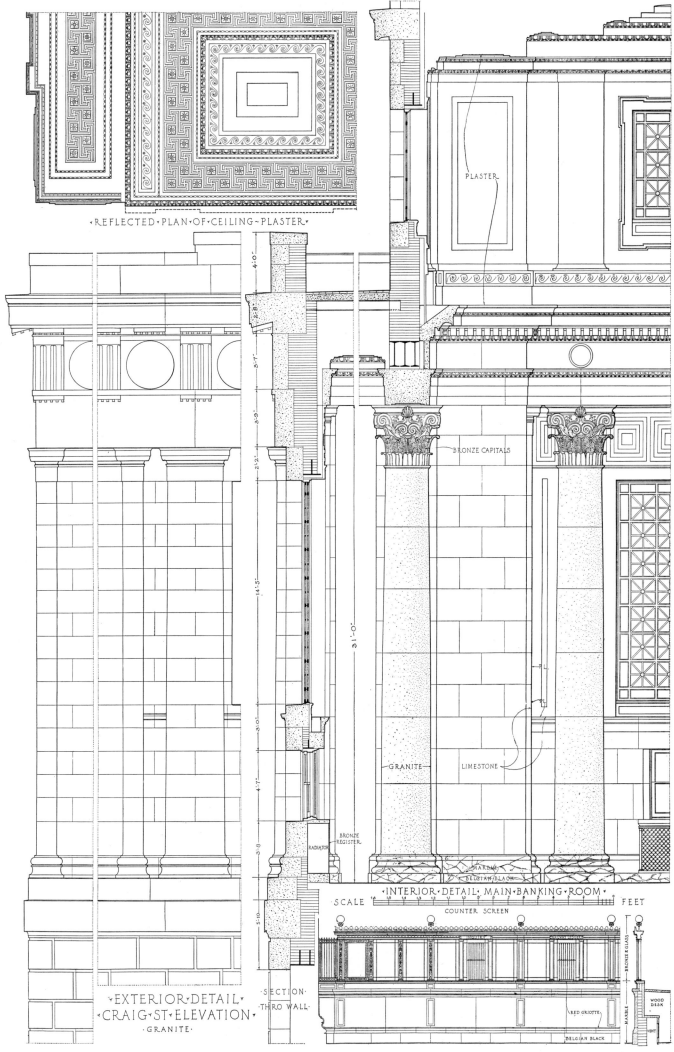

·REFLECTED·PLAN·OF·CEILING~PLASTER·

PLASTER

BRONZE CAPITALS

PLASTER

FL.

GRANITE   LIMESTONE

BRONZE
REGISTER

RADIATOR

MARBLE
BELGIAN·BLACK

·INTERIOR·DETAIL·MAIN·BANKING·ROOM·

SCALE ·························· FEET

COUNTER SCREEN

·EXTERIOR·DETAIL·
·CRAIG·ST·ELEVATION·
·GRANITE·

·SECTION·
THRO·WALL·

RED GRIOTTE

MARBLE   BRONZE & GLASS   WOOD
                                        DESK

BELGIAN BLACK   VENT

EXTERIOR AND INTERIOR DETAILS

Plate 216A   THE BANK OF MONTREAL, MONTREAL, CANADA
                                         1904

OSBORN

H. A. C. TAYLOR

GOELET

RUSSELL

WOODLAWN CEMETERY

Plate 217

SOUTH ELEVATION

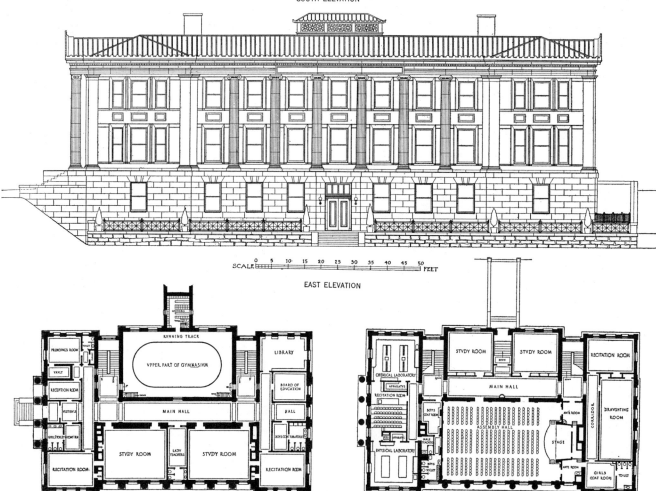

EAST ELEVATION

SCALE 0 5 10 15 20 25 30 35 40 45 50 FEET

MAIN FLOOR PLAN

SECOND FLOOR PLAN

SCALE 0 5 10 15 20 25 30 35 40 45 50 FEET

Plate 219

NAUGATUCK HIGH SCHOOL, NAUGATUCK, CONN.
1904

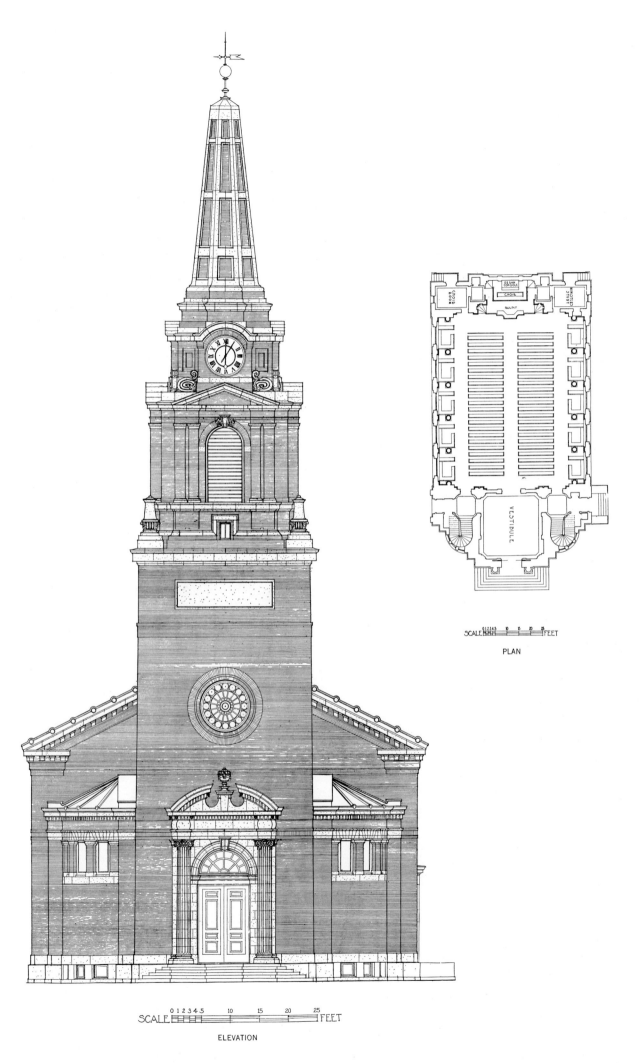

SCALE 0 1 2 3 4 5   10   15   20   25   FEET

PLAN

SCALE 0 1 2 3 4 5   10   15   20   25   FEET

ELEVATION

THE CONGREGATIONAL CHURCH, NAUGATUCK, CONN.
1905

Plate 220

NAUGATUCK, CONNECTICUT.
1903 - 1905

Plate 221

RESIDENCE OF T. JEFFERSON COOLIDGE, JR., MANCHESTER, MASS.
1904

Plate 222

REAR ELEVATION

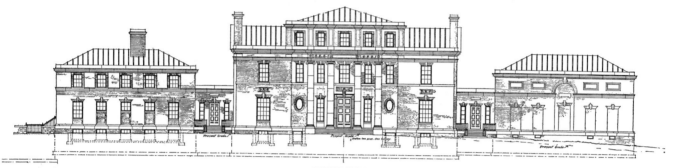

FRONT ELEVATION

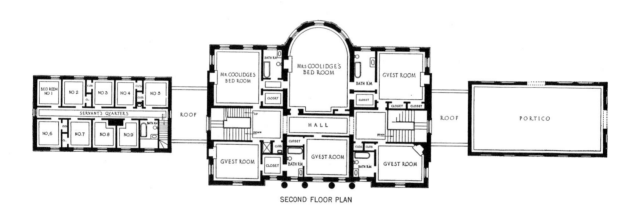

SECOND FLOOR PLAN

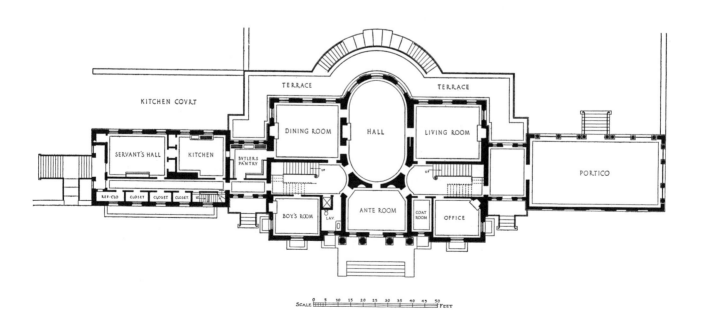

FIRST FLOOR PLAN

Plate 223

RESIDENCE OF T. JEFFERSON COOLIDGE, MANCHESTER, MASS.
1904

THE HALL

MANTEL IN HALL

INTERIOR OF LOGGIA

RESIDENCE OF T. JEFFERSON COOLIDGE, MANCHESTER, MASS.
1904

Plate 224

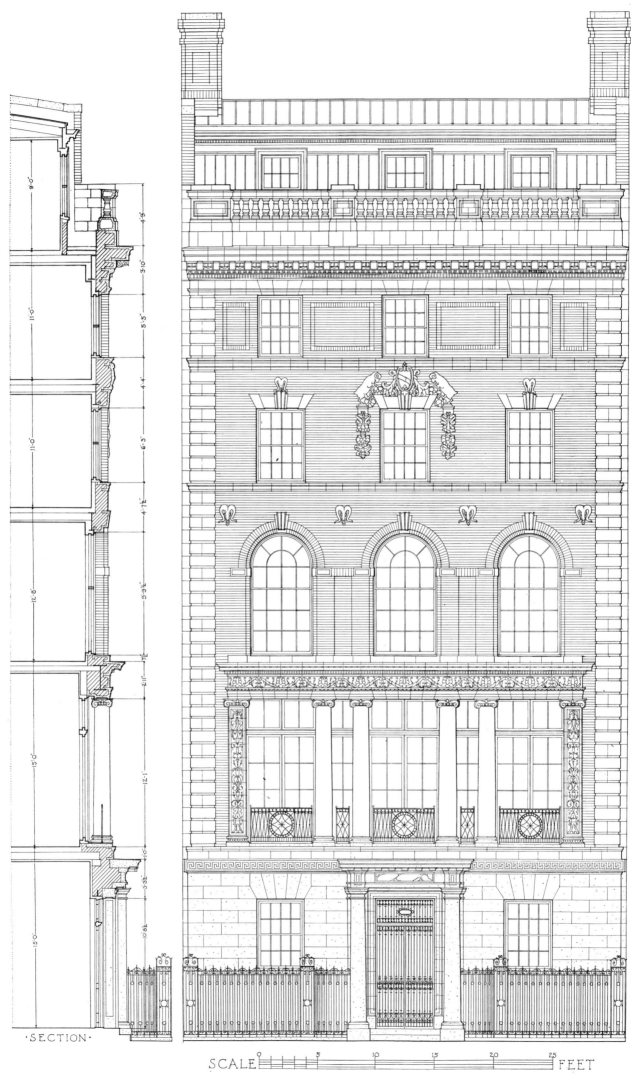

·SECTION·

9'-0"
4'-9"
3'-10"
11'-0"
5'-5"
4'-4"
6'-3"
11'-0"
4'-7½"
3'-9½"
12'-6"
7½"
2'-11"
3'-10"
12'-1"
3'-3½"
15'-0"
10½"

SCALE 0 5 10 15 20 25 FEET

THE LAMBS' CLUB, NEW YORK CITY.

Plate 225

THE LAMBS' CLUB, NEW YORK CITY.
1906

Plate 226

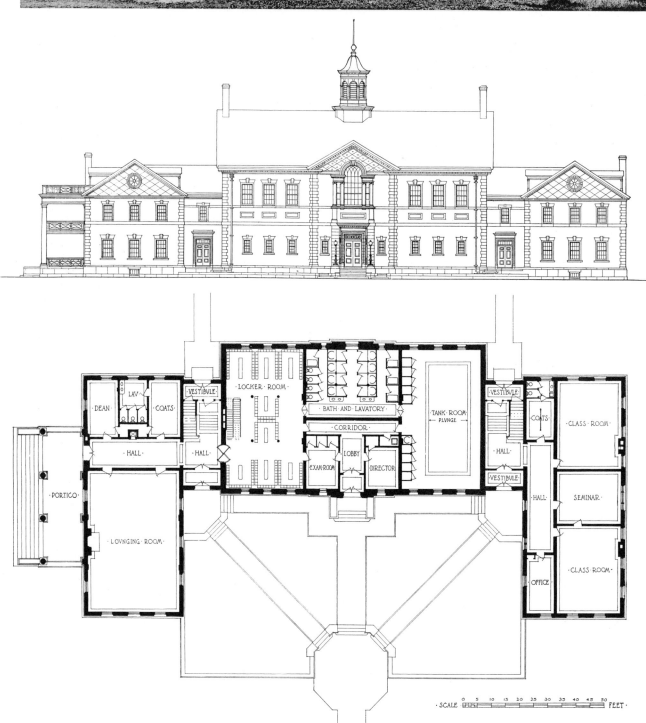

Plate 227

UNIVERSITY OF ILLINOIS, URBANA, ILL.
WOMENS' BUILDING
1905

THE HARMONIE CLUB, NEW YORK CITY.
1906

Plate 228

TERRA COTTA

MARBLE

GRANITE

6'-0"

10'-5"

38'-5¼"

3'-1½" 2'-9¾"

11'-1½"

5'-11½"

23'-5"

1'-11"

SCALE 25 20 15 10 5 0 FEET

PLANS·OF·GROVND·AND·THIRD·FLOOR·FRONTS

Plate 229

THE HARMONIE CLUB, NEW YORK CITY.
FRONT ELEVATION
1906

BUILDING FOR THE NEW ENGLAND TRUST CO., BOSTON, MASS.
1906

Plate 230

SCALE 25 20 15 10 5 0 FEET

ELEVATION

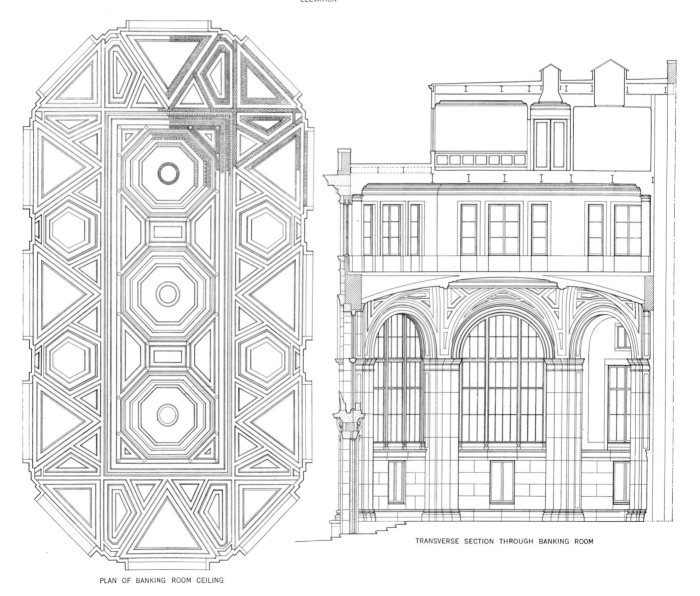

PLAN OF BANKING ROOM CEILING

TRANSVERSE SECTION THROUGH BANKING ROOM

Plate 231

BUILDING FOR THE NEW ENGLAND TRUST CO., BOSTON, MASS.
1906

SCALE 5 10 15 20 25 30 35 40 FEET

SCALE 0 1 2 3 4 8 12 FEET

TERRA COTTA

TERRA COTTA

SCRAFFITO

BUCKINGHAM BUILDING, WATERBURY, CONN.
ELEVATION AND DETAILS
1906

Plate 232

Plate 234

BUILDING FOR THE GORHAM COMPANY, NEW YORK CITY.
1906

EXTERIOR DETAILS
BUILDING FOR THE GORHAM COMPANY, NEW YORK CITY.
1906

Plate 235

BUILDING FOR THE GORHAM COMPANY, NEW YORK CITY.
1906

Plate 236

SCALE 0 5 10 15 20 25 30 FEET

SIDE ELEVATION

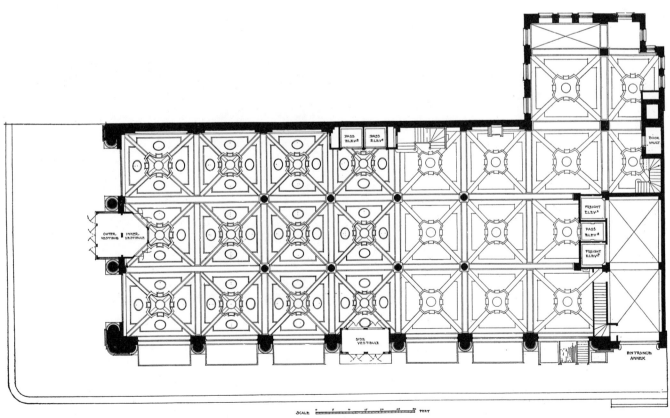

SCALE 0 5 10 15 20 25 30 FEET

FIRST FLOOR PLAN

THE GORHAM BUILDING, NEW YORK CITY
1906

Plate 237

Plate 238

SCALE   0   5   10   15   20   FEET

THE GORHAM BUILDING, NEW YORK CITY
FIFTH AVENUE ELEVATION
1906

APPLIED
BRONZE
ORNAMENT

ENTANCE VESTIBULE SHOWN IN PLAN AND ELEVATION

SECTION THROUGH WALL

FLOOR PLAN   CEILING PLAN

BRONZE BALCONY RAIL

SCALE · OF · FEET ·

GRANITE   LIMESTONE

THE GORHAM BUILDING, NEW YORK CITY
DETAILS OF LOWER STORIES
1906

Plate 239

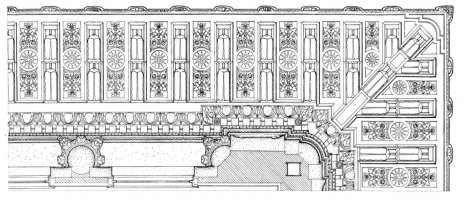

DETAILS
OF
VPPER
STORIES

SCALE |0 1 2 3 4 5 6 7 8 9 10 11 12 13 14 15| FEET

DETAILS OF UPPER STORIES

Plate 240

BUILDING FOR THE GORHAM CO., NEW YORK CITY.
1906

LIBRARY OF J. PIERPONT MORGAN, NEW YORK CITY
1906

Plate 241

LIBRARY OF J. PIERPONT MORGAN, NEW YORK CITY.

1906

Plate 242

LIBRARY OF J. PIERPONT MORGAN, NEW YORK CITY
1906

Plate 242A

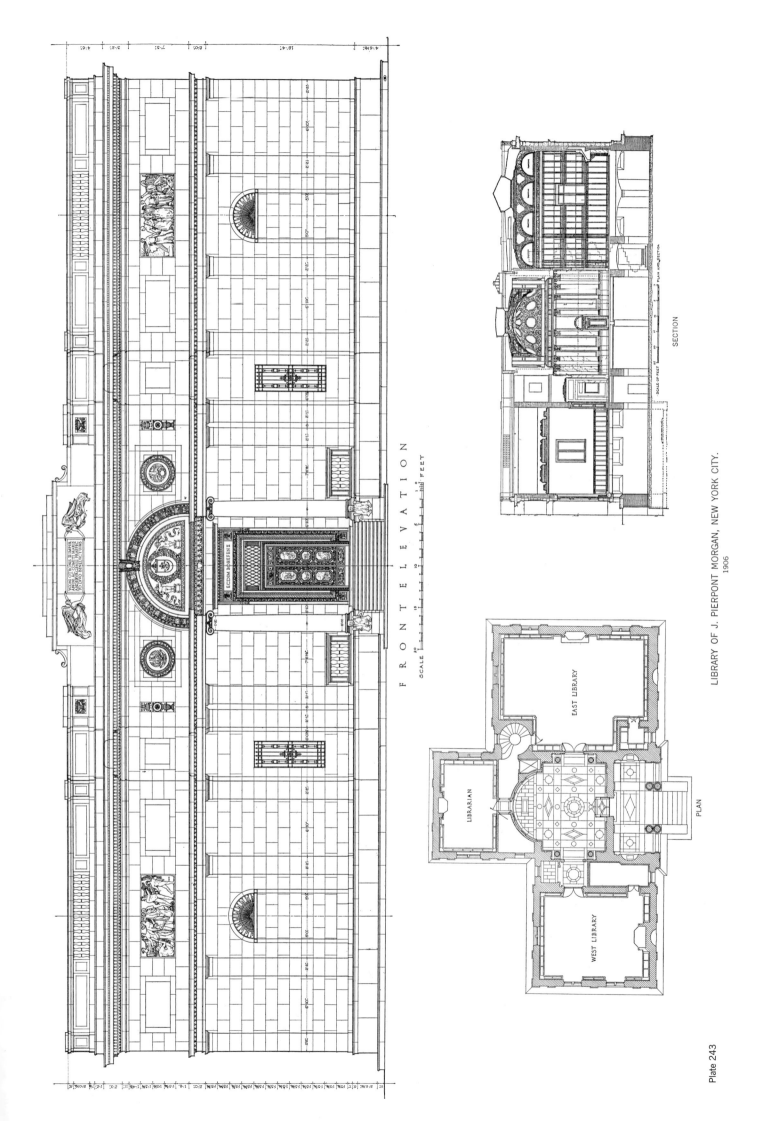

FRONT ELEVATION

SCALE [ ] FEET

SECTION

SCALE OF FEET

EAST LIBRARY

LIBRARIAN

WEST LIBRARY

PLAN

LIBRARY OF J. PIERPONT MORGAN, NEW YORK CITY.

1906

Plate 243

·EXTERIOR·DETAILS·
·OF·THE·
·MORGAN·LIBRARY·
·SCALE·

PLAN OF
LOGGIA

BENCH

VERDE·ANTICO

LEVANTO

VERDE·ANTICO

LEVANTO

KNOXVILLE MARBLE

·WINDOW·GRILLE·
·FRONT·ELEVATION·

·WINDOW·SIDE·ELEVATION·
·CARVED·PANEL·OVER·

·NICHE·FRONT·ELEVATION·

·BRONZE·FENCE·WITH·MARBLE·POSTS·FRONT·ELEVATION·

LIBRARY OF J. PIERPONT MORGAN, NEW YORK CITY
1906

Plate 244

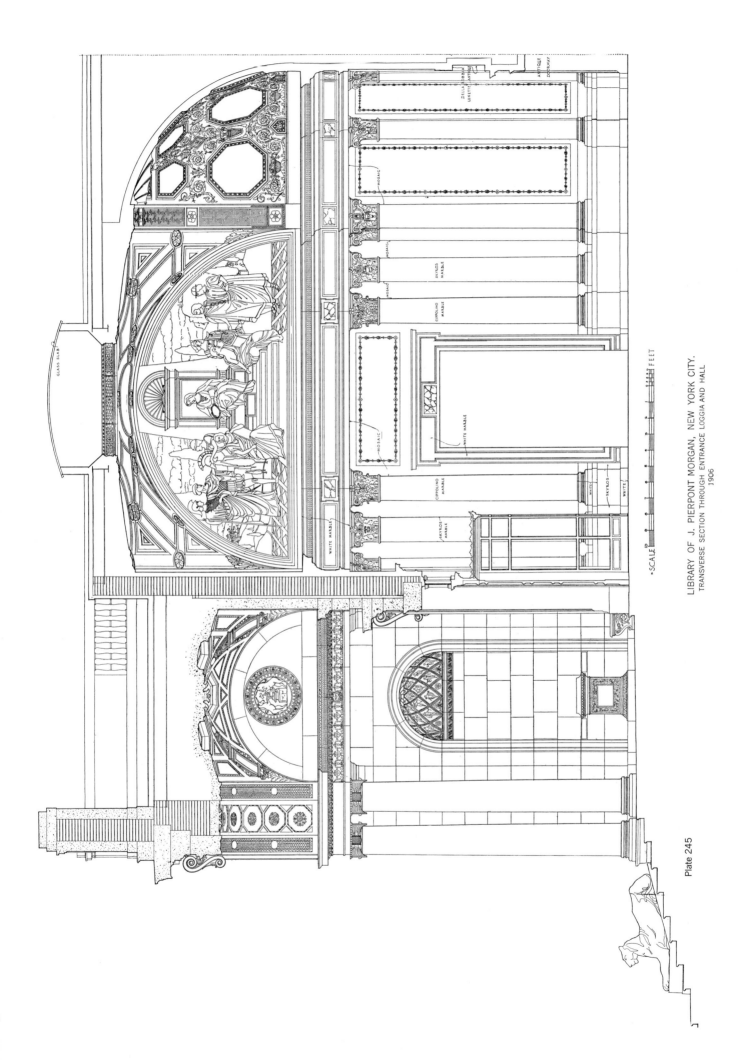

LIBRARY OF J. PIERPONT MORGAN, NEW YORK CITY.

TRANSVERSE SECTION THROUGH ENTRANCE LOGGIA AND HALL

1906

Plate 245

LIBRARY OF J. PIERPONT MORGAN, NEW YORK CITY.
1906

Plate 246

Plate 247

LIBRARY OF J. PIERPONT MORGAN, NEW YORK CITY.
VIEWS OF EAST ROOM
1906

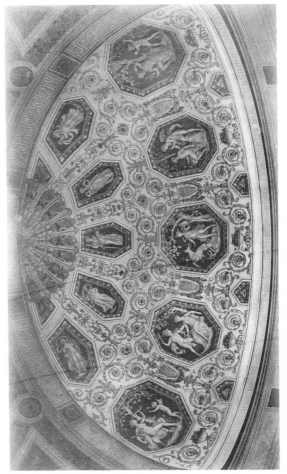

LIBRARY OF J. PIERPONT MORGAN, NEW YORK CITY.
1906

Plate 248

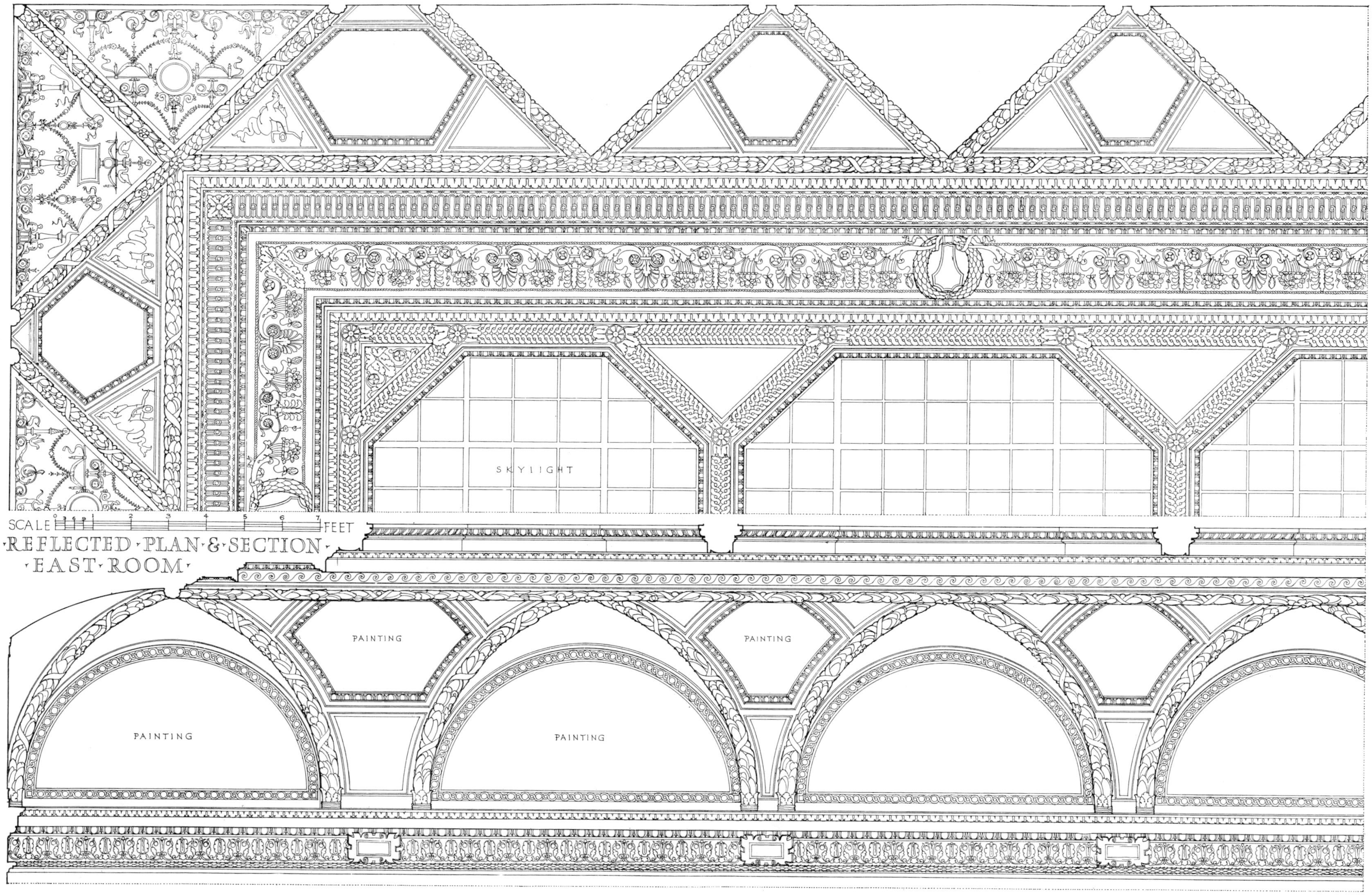

SCALE   1   2   3   4   5   6   7   FEET

·REFLECTED·PLAN·&·SECTION·
·EAST·ROOM·

SKYLIGHT

PAINTING   PAINTING   PAINTING   PAINTING   PAINTING

LIBRARY OF J. P. MORGAN, NEW YORK CITY.
DETAIL OF CEILING IN EAST ROOM
1906

Plate 249

MADISON SQUARE PRESBYTERIAN CHURCH
NEW YORK CITY
1906

Plate 251

MADISON SQUARE PRESBYTERIAN CHURCH, NEW YORK CITY.
1906

Plate 252

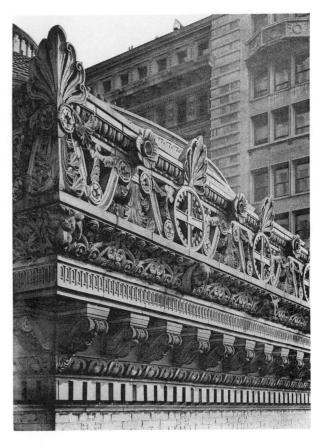

MADISON SQUARE PRESBYTERIAN CHURCH, NEW YORK CITY.
1906

Plate 253

· FRONT · ELEVATION ·
· MADISON SQVARE PRESBYTERIAN CHVRCH ·
· SCALE ¼ INCH EQVALS ONE FOOT ·

Plate 254

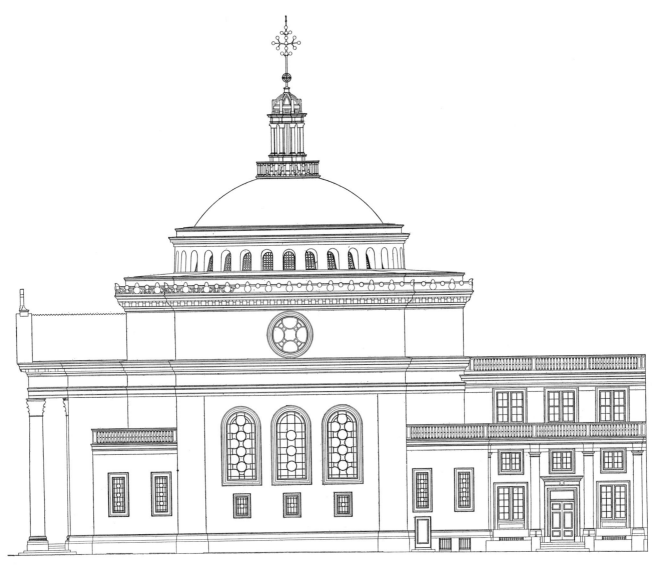

STREET ELEVATION

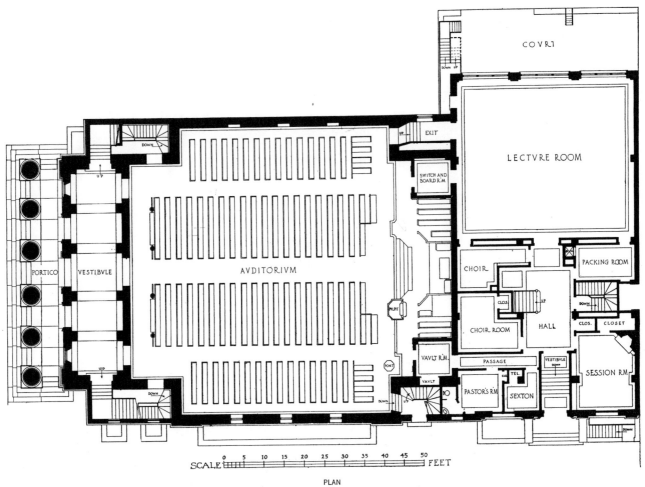

PLAN

MADISON SQUARE PRESBYTERIAN CHURCH, NEW YORK CITY
1906

Plate 255

SCALE 0 1 2 3 4 5 FEET

· DETAIL · OF ·
· PORTICO ·

· BALVSTRADE ·

CAPITALS, ENTABLATURE, BALUSTRADE, WINDOW TRIM OF ORNAMENTAL TERRA COTTA, SHAFT OF COLUMN, POLISHED GREEN GRANITE. BASE, WHITE MARBLE. WALLS, LIGHT BRICK.

Plate 256
MADISON SQUARE PRESBYTERIAN CHURCH, NEW YORK CITY.
1906

·VPPER·
·CORNICE·

·MAIN·DOORWAY·

SCALE 0 1 2 3 4 5 FEET

MARBLE JAMB

SECTION

WALLS, LIGHT BRICK. CORNICES AND DOOR TRIM, ORNAMENTAL TERRA COTTA MARBLE INSERTS, PAVONAZZO. OAK DOORS WITH IRON STUDS.
MADISON SQUARE PRESBYTERIAN CHURCH, NEW YORK CITY.

Plate 257

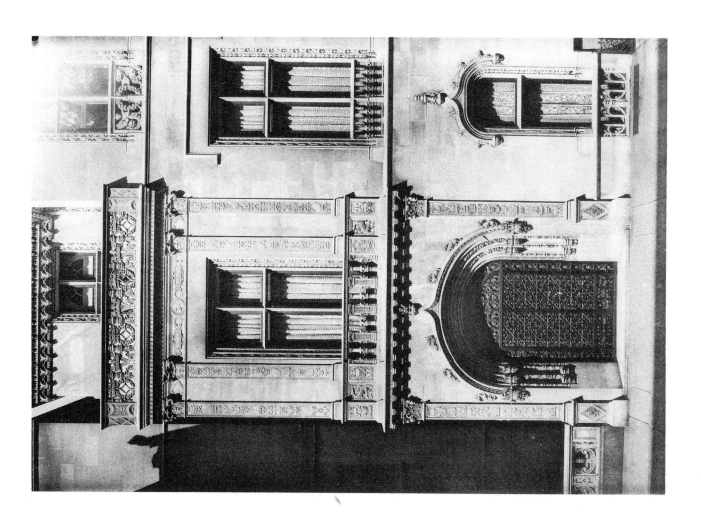

RESIDENCE OF MRS. W. K. VANDERBILT, JR., NEW YORK CITY
1906

Plate 259

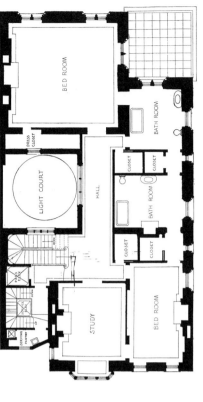

THIRD FLOOR PLAN

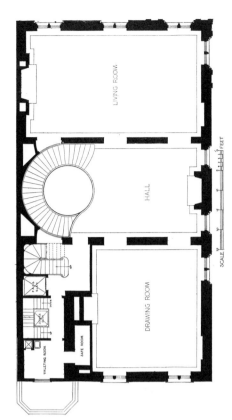

SECOND FLOOR PLAN

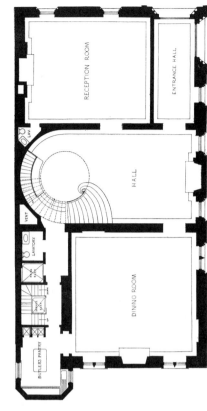

FIRST FLOOR PLAN
1906

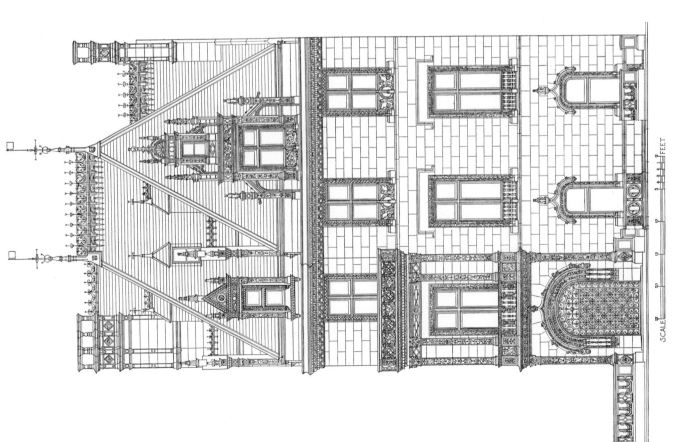

FRONT ELEVATION

RESIDENCE OF MRS. W. K. VANDERBILT, JR., NEW YORK CITY.

Plate 259

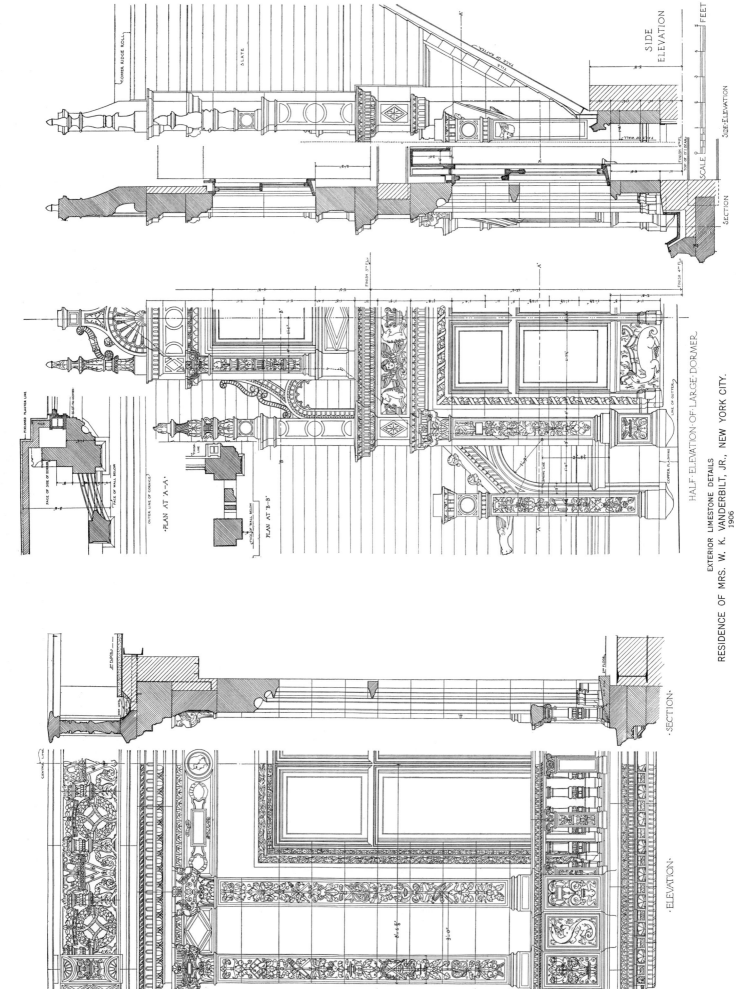

SIDE ELEVATION

SIDE-ELEVATION

SECTION

SCALE

FEET

PLAN AT 'A-A'

PLAN AT 'B-B'

HALF·ELEVATION·OF·LARGE·DORMER.

SECTION·

·ELEVATION·

EXTERIOR LIMESTONE DETAILS
RESIDENCE OF MRS. W. K. VANDERBILT, JR., NEW YORK CITY.
1906

Plate 260

BUILDING FOR TIFFANY & CO., NEW YORK CITY.
1906
ADJOINING BUILDING, 391 FIFTH AVENUE
1910

Plate 261

GENERAL VIEW OF STORE

STAIR AND ELEVATOR ENCLOSURE

BUILDING FOR TIFFANY & CO., NEW YORK CITY.
1906

Plate 262

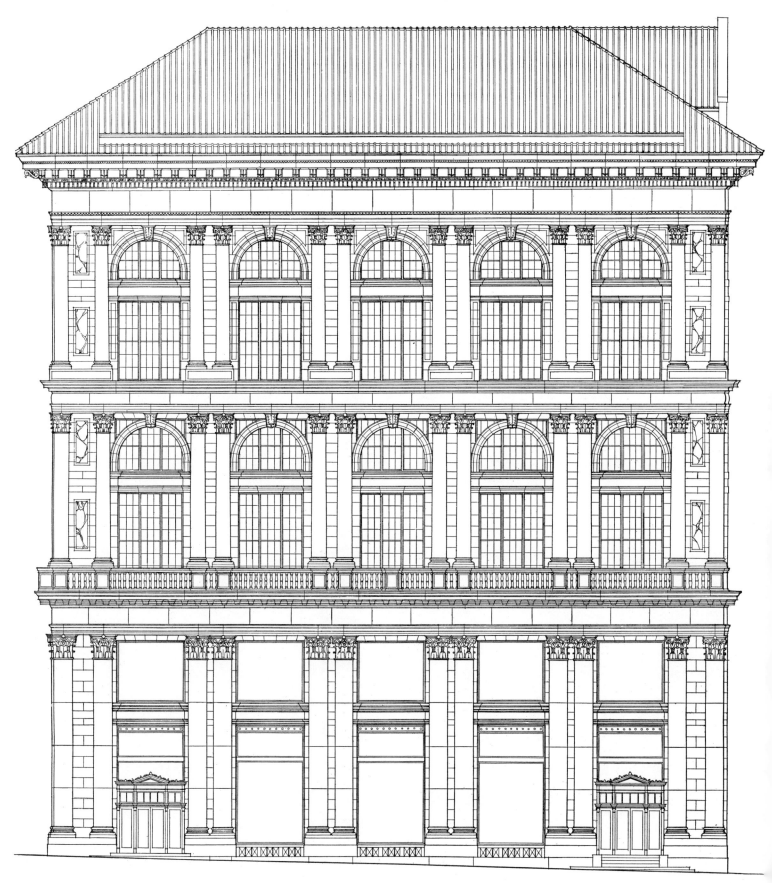

SCALE 25 20 15 10 5 0 FEET

FIFTH AVENUE ELEVATION

BUILDING FOR TIFFANY & CO., NEW YORK CITY.
1906

Plate 263

MAIN
CORNICE

FIFTH
STORY
ORDER

THIRD STORY ORDER

ROLLING
SHUTTER

PLASTER
CEILING

TERRAZZO

TERRAZZO

FAMOSA
MARBLE COLUMNS

METAL
SHUTTER

BRONZE

BRONZE

FAMOSA MARBLE

SCALE 0 1 2 3 4 5 6 7 8 9 10 11 12 13 14 15 FEET

EXTERIOR AND INTERIOR DETAILS

BUILDING FOR TIFFANY & CO., NEW YORK CITY.

Plate 264

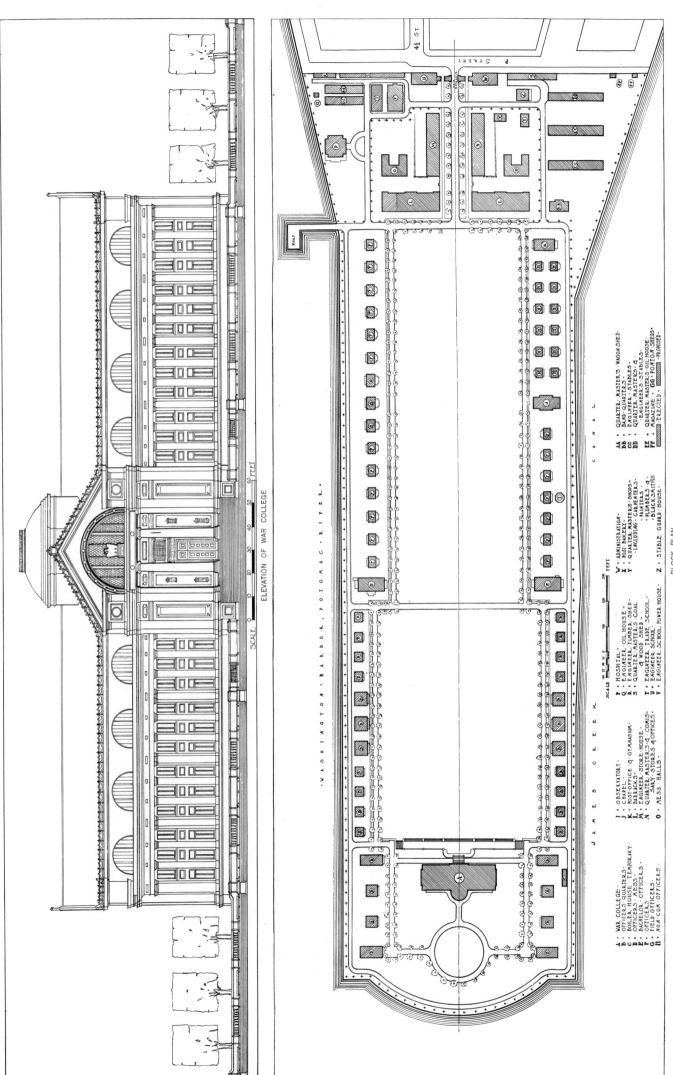

ELEVATION OF WAR COLLEGE

SCALE · 0 · 10 · 20 · 30 · 40 · 50 · 60 FEET

· WASHINGTON · HARBOR · POTOMAC · RIVER ·

JAMES CREEK

CANAL

4½ ST.

P STREET

SCALE 100 50 0 100 200 300 FEET

A · WAR COLLEGE ·
B · OFFICERS QUARTERS ·
C · BOILER HOUSE TEMPORARY ·
D · OFFICERS MESS ·
E · BACHELOR OFFICERS ·
F · OFFICERS ·
G · FIELD OFFICERS ·
H · NON-COM OFFICERS ·

I · OBSERVATORY ·
J · CHAPEL ·
K · POST OFFICE & GYMNASIUM ·
L · BARRACKS ·
M · ENGINEER STORE HOUSE ·
N · QUARTER MASTERS COMMISSARY STORES & OFFICES ·
O · MESS HALLS ·

P · HOSPITAL ·
Q · ENGINEER OIL HOUSE ·
R · ENGINEER TIMBER SHED ·
S · QUARTER MASTERS COAL & WOOD SHED ·
T · ENGINEER TRADE SCHOOL ·
U · ENGINEER SCHOOL ·
V · ENGINEER SCHOOL POWER HOUSE ·

W · ADMINISTRATION ·
X · POST BAKERY ·
Y · QUARTER MASTERS SHOPS INCLUDING CARPENTERS PAINTERS PLUMBERS & BLACKSMITHS ·
Z · STABLE GUARD HOUSE ·

AA · QUARTER MASTERS WAGON SHED ·
BB · BAND QUARTERS ·
CC · ENGINEER STABLES ·
DD · QUARTER MASTERS Q. ·
EE · ENGINEERS STABLES ·
FF · QUARTER MASTERS OIL HOUSE ·
GG · PONTOON SHEDS ·
HH · MAGAZINE ·

ERECTED · PROJECTED ·

BLOCK PLAN

ARMY WAR COLLEGE AND ENGINEERS' POST, WASHINGTON, D. C.

1908

Plate 265

THE ARMY WAR COLLEGE, WASHINGTON, D. C.
1908

Plate 266

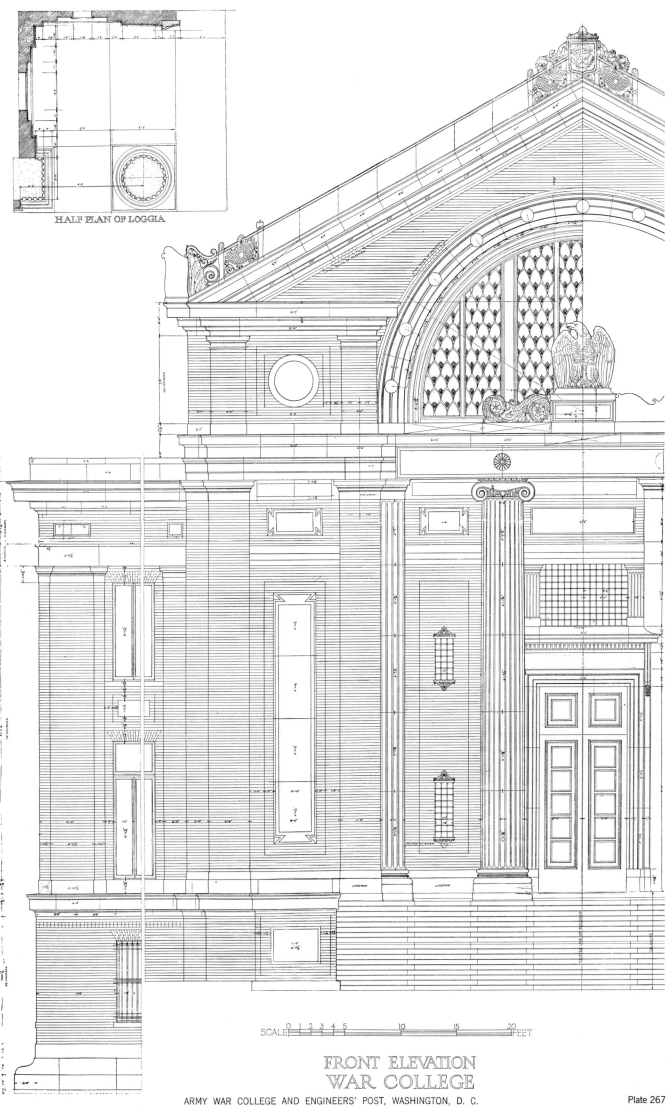

HALF PLAN OF LOGGIA

SCALE 0 1 2 3 4 5   10   15   20 FEET

FRONT ELEVATION
WAR COLLEGE

ARMY WAR COLLEGE AND ENGINEERS' POST, WASHINGTON, D. C.   Plate 267

Plate 268 RESIDENCE OF JAMES L. BREESE, SOUTHAMPTON, L. I.
1906

RESIDENCE OF JAMES L. BREESE, SOUTHAMPTON, L. I.
1906

Plate 269

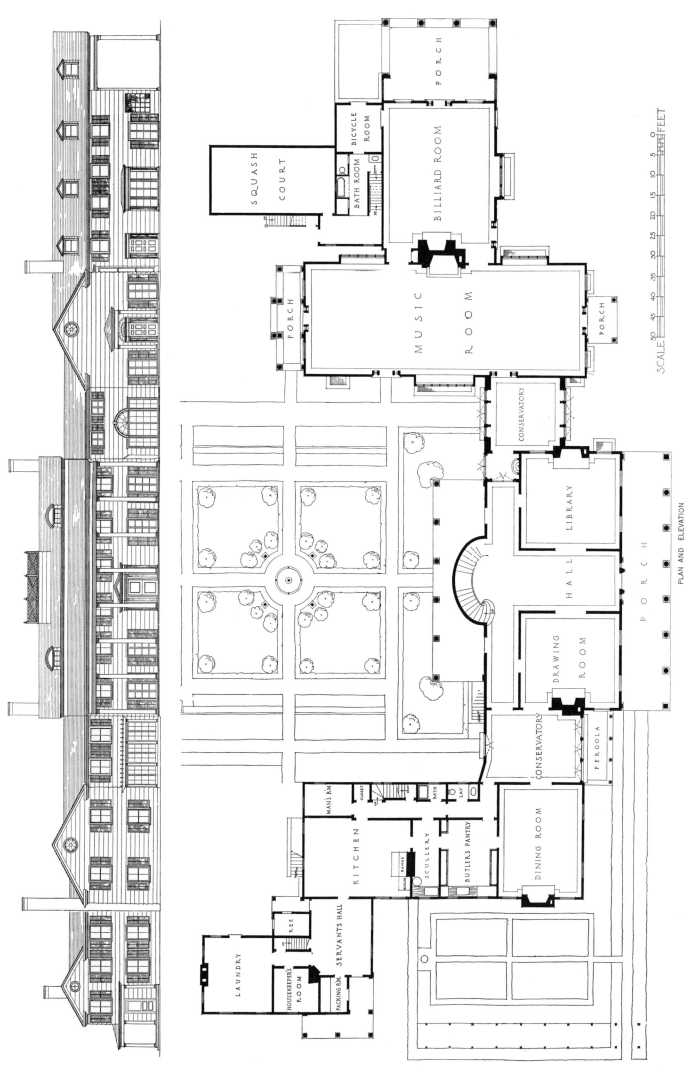

SQUASH COURT

BICYCLE ROOM

BATH ROOM

BILLIARD ROOM

PORCH

PORCH

MUSIC ROOM

PORCH

CONSERVATORY

LIBRARY

HALL

PORCH

DRAWING ROOM

CONSERVATORY

PERGOLA

MAN'S RM.

CLOSET

BATH

LAV.

KITCHEN

RANGE

BOILER

SCULLERY

BUTLER'S PANTRY

DINING ROOM

SERVANTS HALL

REF.

LAUNDRY

HOUSEKEEPER'S ROOM

PACKING RM.

SCALE

50 45 40 35 30 25 20 15 10 5 0   FEET

PLAN AND ELEVATION
RESIDENCE OF JAMES L. BREESE, SOUTHAMPTON, L. I.
1906

Plate 270

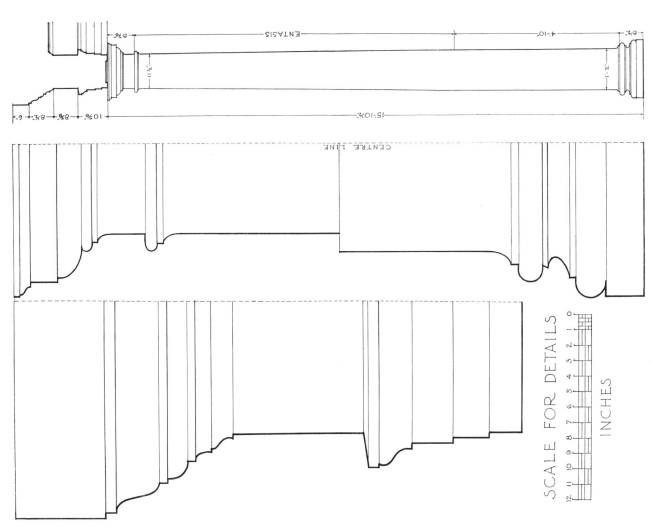

SCALE FOR DETAILS

INCHES

RESIDENCE OF JAMES L. BREESE, SOUTHAMPTON L. I.
DETAILS OF PORCH, ENTRANCE FRONT
1906

Plate 271

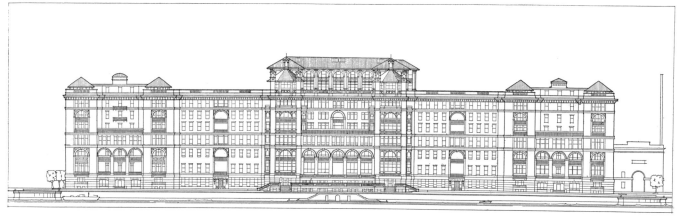

ELEVATION ON EAST RIVER

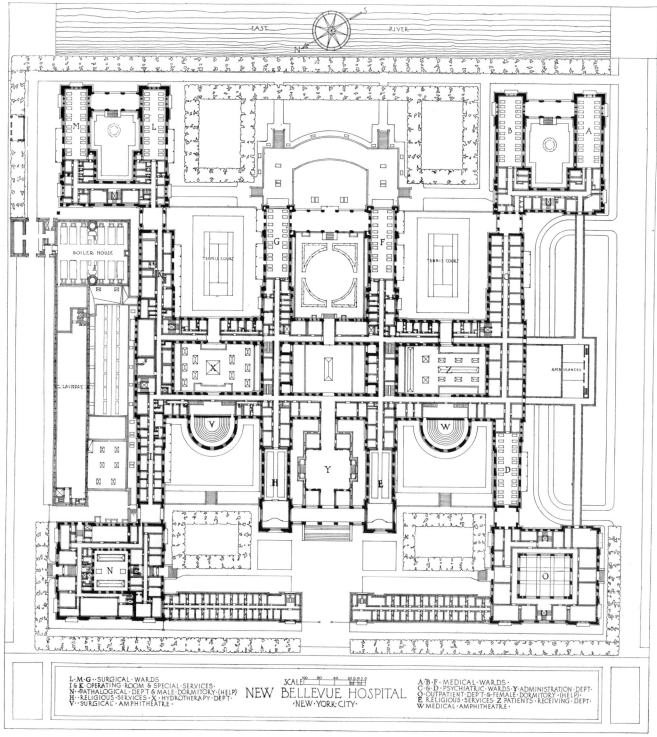

L·M·G·SURGICAL·WARDS
I & K·OPERATING·ROOM & SPECIAL·SERVICES·
N·PATHALOGICAL·DEPT & MALE·DORMITORY·(HELP)
H·RELIGIOUS·SERVICES·X·HYDROTHERAPY·DEPT·
V·SURGICAL·AMPHITHEATRE·

SCALE
NEW BELLEVUE HOSPITAL
·NEW·YORK·CITY·

A·B·F·MEDICAL·WARDS·
C & D·PSYCHIATRIC·WARDS·Y·ADMINISTRATION·DEPT·
O·OUTPATIENT·DEPT·& FEMALE·DORMITORY·(HELP)
E·RELIGIOUS·SERVICES·Z·PATIENTS·RECEIVING·DEPT·
W·MEDICAL·AMPHITHEATRE·

BLOCK PLAN

Plate 274

BELLEVUE HOSPITAL, NEW YORK CITY.
1906 - 1916

BELLEVUE HOSPITAL, NEW YORK CITY.
1906 - 1916

Plate 275

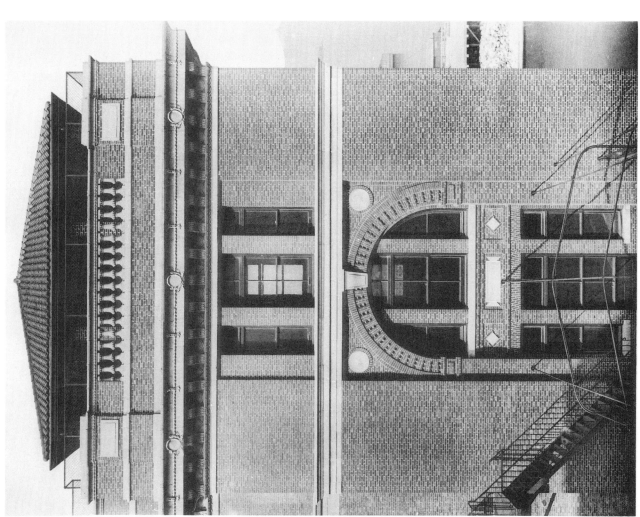

BELLEVUE HOSPITAL, NEW YORK CITY.
1906 · 1916

Plate 276

ADDITION E

ADDITION H

ADDITIONS TO THE METROPOLITAN MUSEUM OF ART, NEW YORK CITY.
1908   1912

Plate 275X

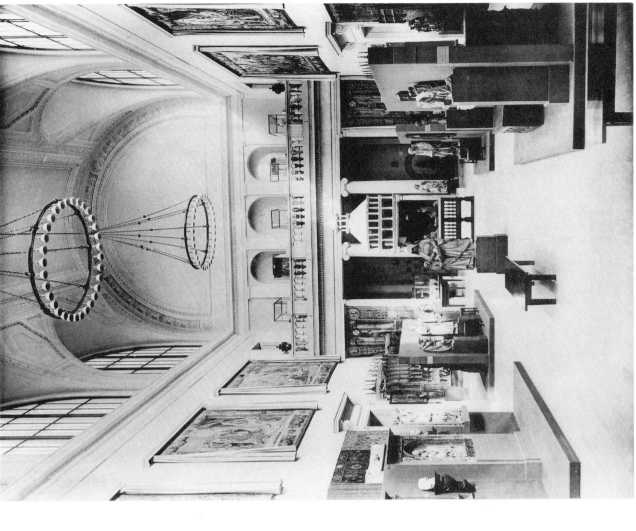

HALL OF DECORATIVE ARTS - ADDITION F - 1908

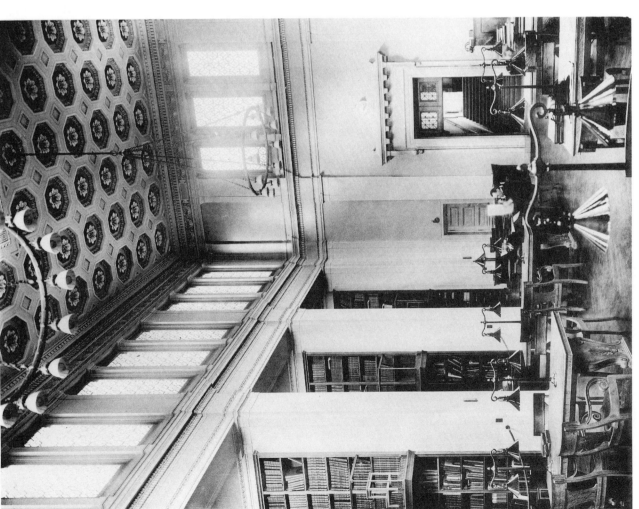

LIBRARY - 1910

ADDITIONS TO THE METROPOLITAN MUSEUM OF ART, NEW YORK CITY.

Plate 277

ADDITIONS TO THE METROPOLITAN MUSEUM OF ART, NEW YORK CITY.
COURT AND ROOM FOR ARMOR COLLECTION, ADDITION H.
1912

Plate 278

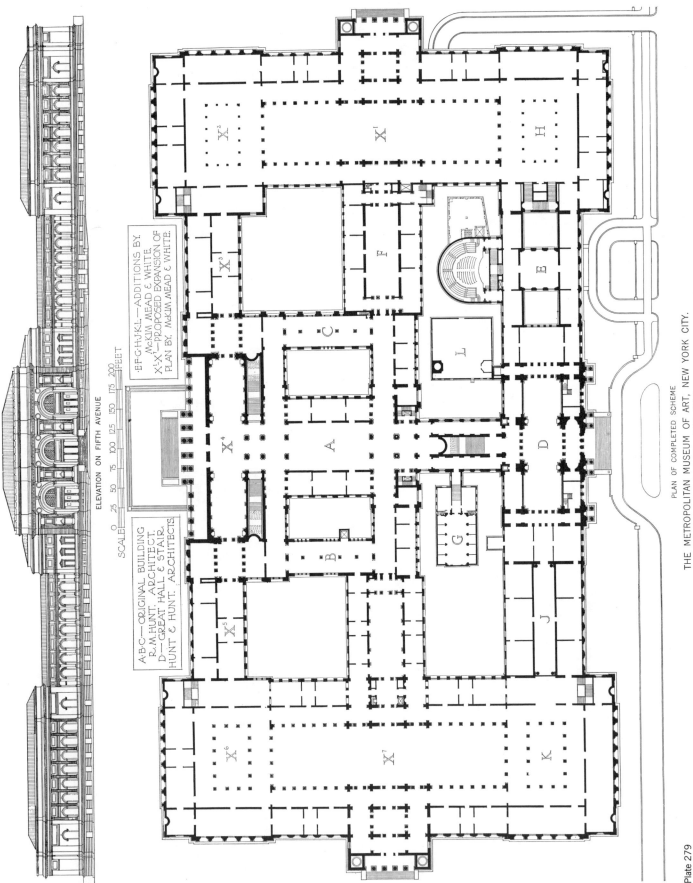

ELEVATION ON FIFTH AVENUE

SCALE 0 25 50 75 100 125 150 175 200 FEET

A·B·C—ORIGINAL BUILDING
R·M·HUNT. ARCHITECT.
D—GREAT HALL & STAIR.
HUNT & HUNT. ARCHITECTS.

·E·F·G·H·J·K·L—ADDITIONS BY
McKIM MEAD & WHITE.
X¹-X⁷—PROPOSED EXPANSION OF
PLAN BY. McKIM MEAD & WHITE.

X²   X¹   H

X³   F   E

C   L

X⁴   A   D

B   G   J

X⁵   X⁶   X⁷   K

PLAN OF COMPLETED SCHEME
THE METROPOLITAN MUSEUM OF ART, NEW YORK CITY.
ADDITIONS, 1908 - 1916

Plate 279

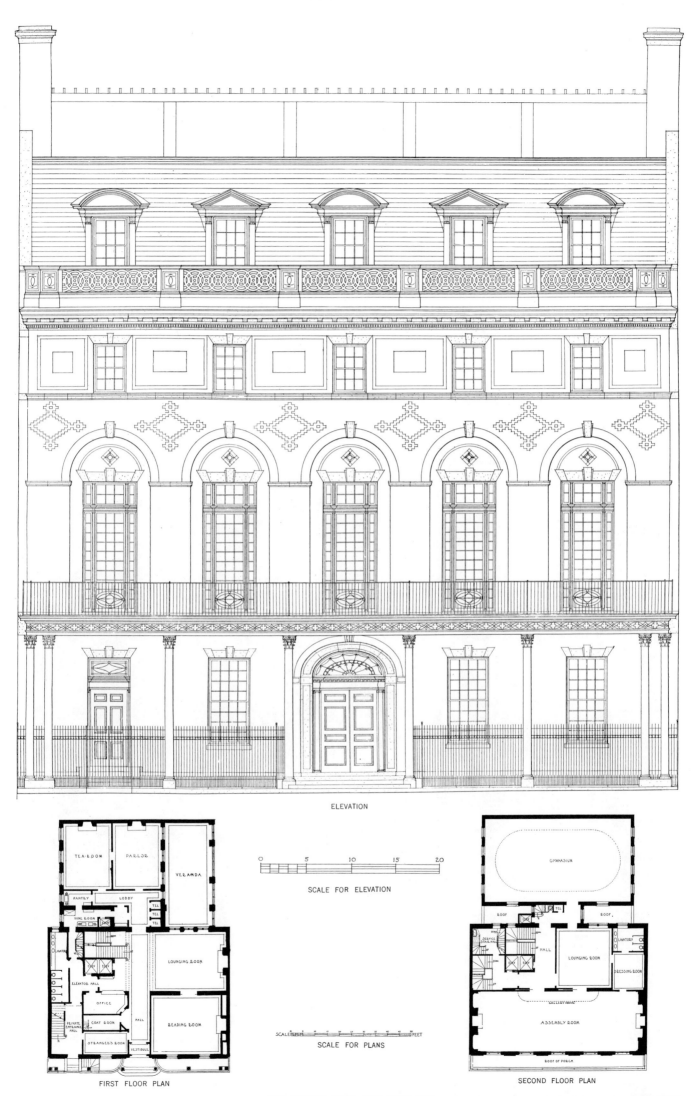

ELEVATION

TEA ROOM · PARLOR · VERANDA · PANTRY · LOBBY · GIRL ROOM · ELEVATOR HALL · OFFICE · COAT ROOM · PRIVATE ENTRANCE HALL · STRANGER'S ROOM · VESTIBULE · HALL · LOUNGING ROOM · READING ROOM · TEL

FIRST FLOOR PLAN

SCALE FOR ELEVATION

0   5   10   15   20

SCALE   FEET

SCALE FOR PLANS

GYMNASIUM · ROOF · SERVICE STAIR HALL · TEL · HALL · LAVATORY · LOUNGING ROOM · DRESSING ROOM · GALLERY ABOVE · ASSEMBLY ROOM · ROOF OF PORCH

SECOND FLOOR PLAN

THE COLONY CLUB, NEW YORK CITY.

Plate 280

Plate 281

THE COLONY CLUB, NEW YORK CITY.
1906

CAST IRON

MARBLE WOOD →

· SECTION ·

SECTION · THRO
MAIN · DOORWAY

· PLAN ·

SCALE ⊢⊢⊢⊢ 0 1 2 3 4 5 6 7 8 9 10 FEET

EXTERIOR DETAILS
THE COLONY CLUB, NEW YORK CITY

Plate 282

ATHLETIC FIELD GATES · 1913

MAIN ENTRANCE GATES, NASSAU STREET · 1905

Plate 283   MEMORIAL GATEWAYS, PRINCETON UNIVERSITY.

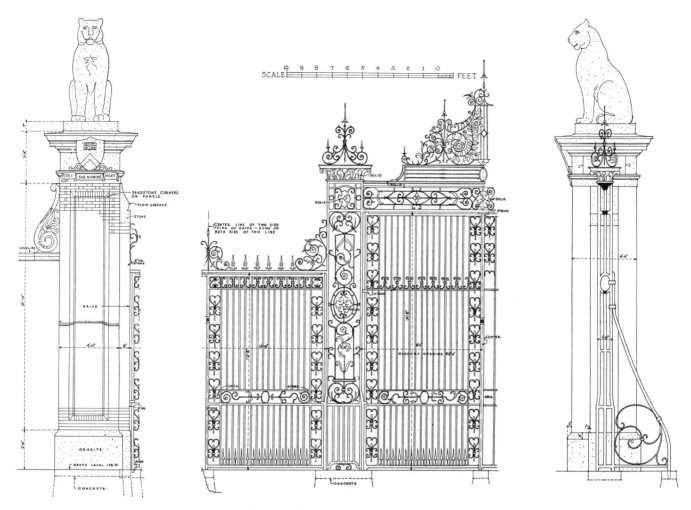

SCALE 10 9 8 7 6 5 4 3 2 1 0 FEET

ATHLETIC FIELD GATES, PROSPECT STREET.
1913

ELEVATION

PLAN

SECTION

SCALE 10 9 8 7 6 5 4 3 2 1 0 FEET

MAIN ENTRANCE GATEWAY, NASSAU STREET.
1905

MEMORIAL GATEWAYS, PRINCETON UNIVERSITY

Plate 284

RESIDENCE OF JOHN INNES KANE NEW YORK CITY.
1907

Plate 285

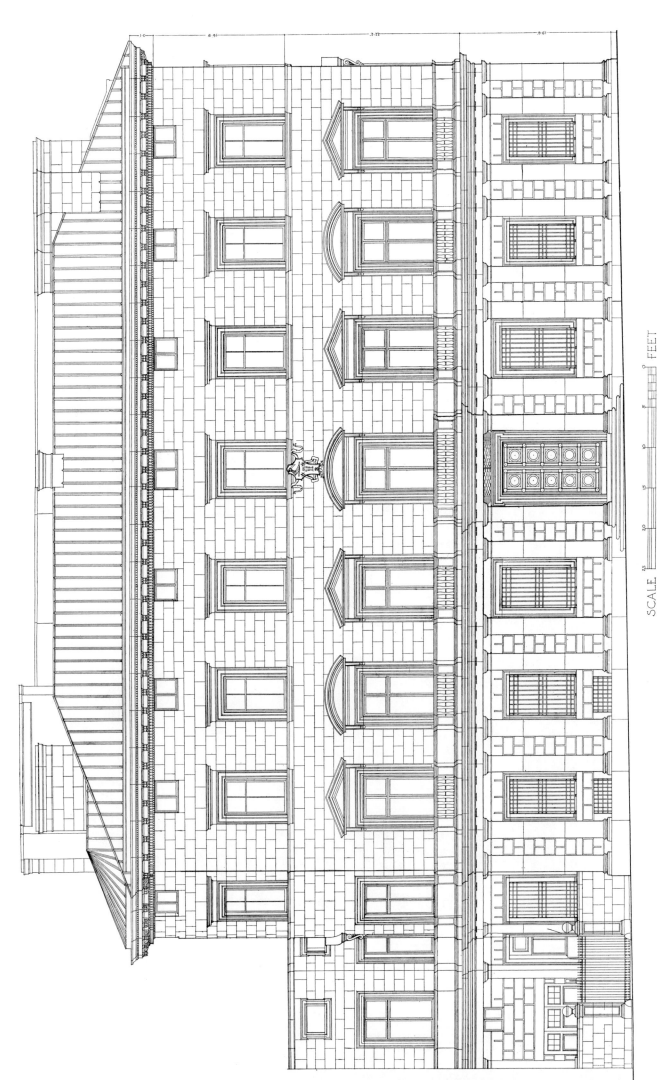

SCALE |———————|———|——|—| FEET

RESIDENCE OF JOHN INNES KANE, NEW YORK CITY.

SOUTH ELEVATION
1906

Plate 286

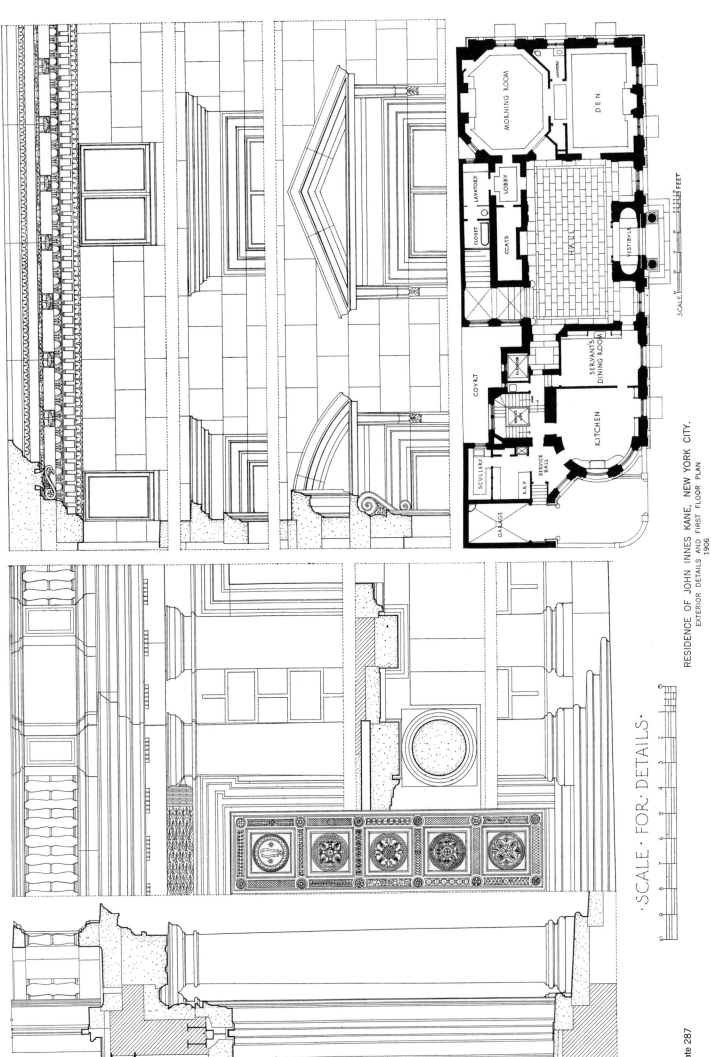

· SCALE · FOR · DETAILS ·

MORNING ROOM

DEN

CLOSET LAVATORY

LOBBY

COATS

HALL

VESTIBULE

COURT

ELEVATOR

SERVICE ELEV.

SERVANT'S DINING ROOM

KITCHEN

SCULLERY

R.E.F

SERVICE HALL

GARAGE

SCALE FEET

RESIDENCE OF JOHN INNES KANE, NEW YORK CITY.
EXTERIOR DETAILS AND FIRST FLOOR PLAN
1906

Plate 287

VIEWS OF ENTRANCE HALL

RESIDENCE OF JOHN INNES KANE, NEW YORK CITY.

Plate 288

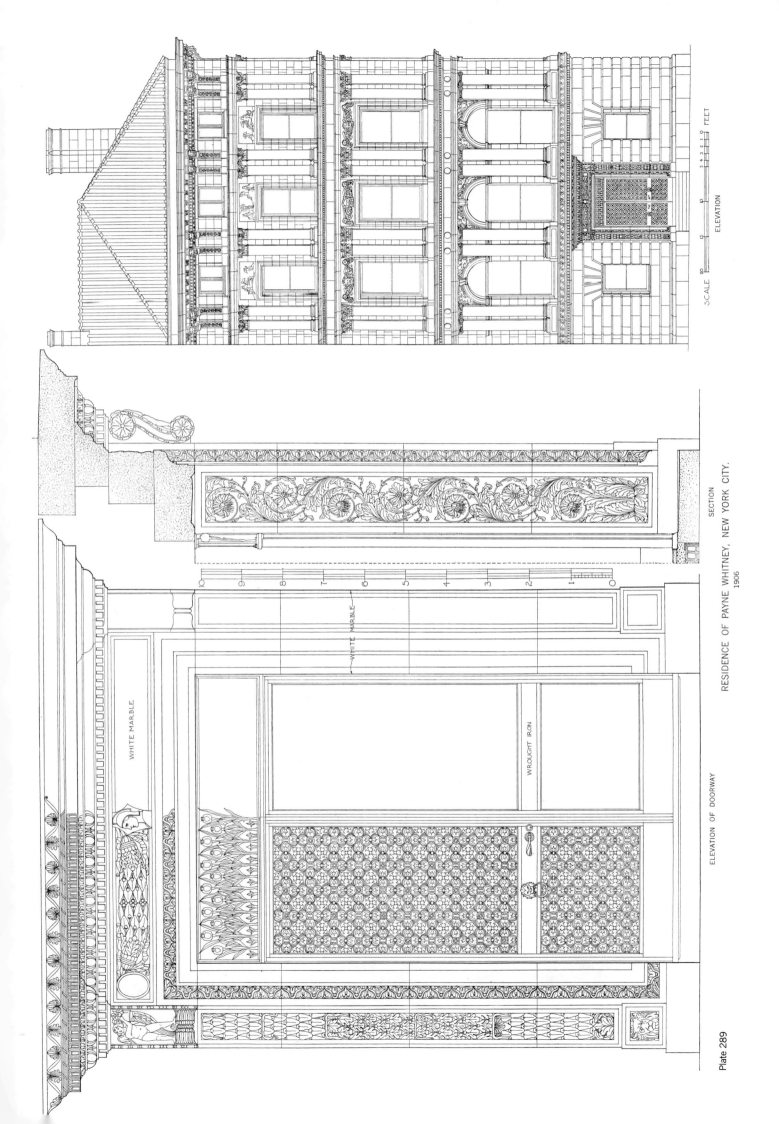

SCALE

ELEVATION

SECTION

RESIDENCE OF PAYNE WHITNEY, NEW YORK CITY.
1906

WHITE MARBLE

WHITE MARBLE

WROUGHT IRON

ELEVATION OF DOORWAY

Plate 289

VIEW OF EXTERIOR

ENTRANCE HALL

PAYNE WHITNEY RESIDENCE, NEW YORK CITY.

1906

Plate 290

DINING ROOM

LIVING ROOM

Plate 291   PAYNE WHITNEY RESIDENCE, NEW YORK CITY.

STAIR HALL

OFFICE

PAYNE WHITNEY RESIDENCE, NEW YORK CITY.
1906

Plate 292

ENTRANCE FRONT

THE HALL

Plate 293

THE UNIVERSITY COTTAGE CLUB, PRINCETON, N. J.
1906

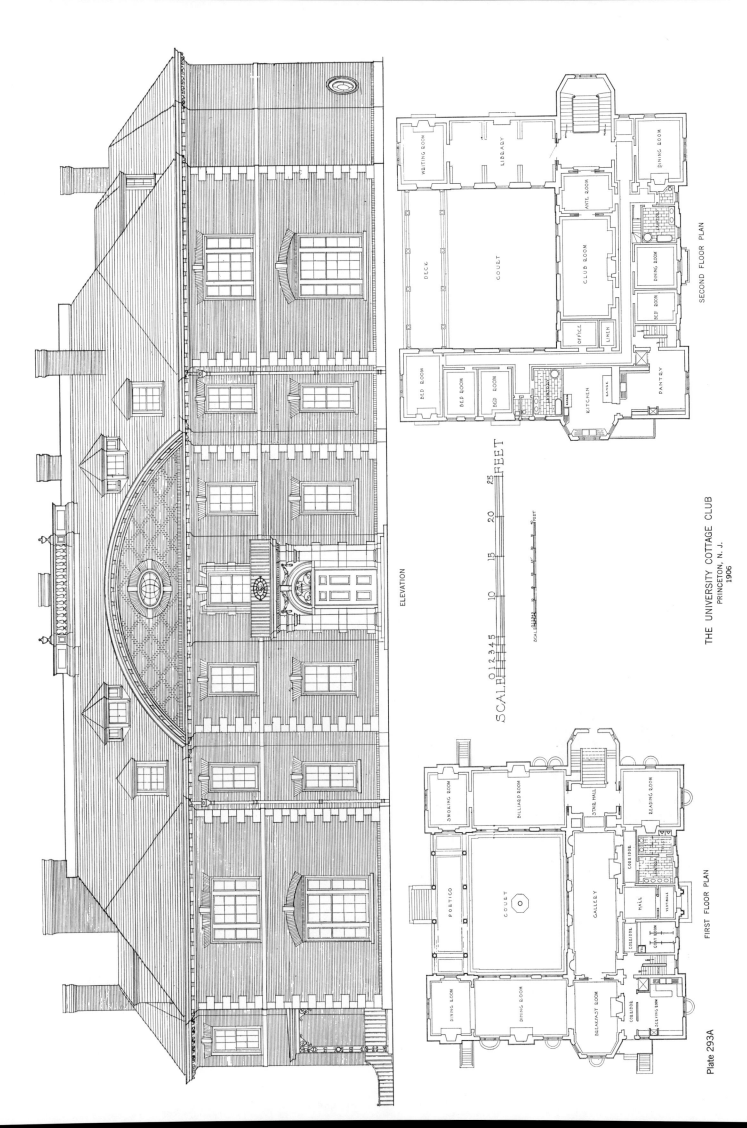

ELEVATION

SECOND FLOOR PLAN

FIRST FLOOR PLAN

SCALE 0 1 2 3 4 5   10   15   20   25   FEET

SCALE

THE UNIVERSITY COTTAGE CLUB
PRINCETON, N. J.
1906

Plate 293A

EXTERIOR

INTERIOR

Plate 294

TRINITY CHURCH, ROSLYN, L. I.
1906

THE NATIONAL CITY BANK, NEW YORK CITY.
BANKING ROOM
1909

Plate 295

THE NATIONAL CITY BANK, NEW YORK CITY.
VIEWS IN BANKING ROOM
1909

Plate 296

PRESIDENT'S OFFICE - 1914

DETAIL OF COUNTER SCREEN

CHECK DESK IN PUBLIC SPACE

THE NATIONAL CITY BANK, NEW YORK CITY.
1909

Plate 297

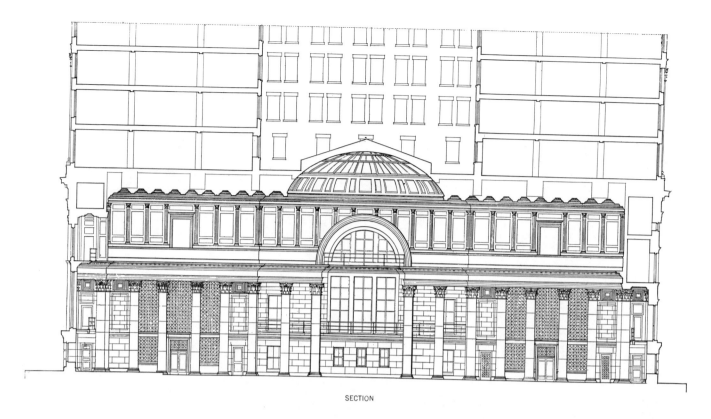

SECTION

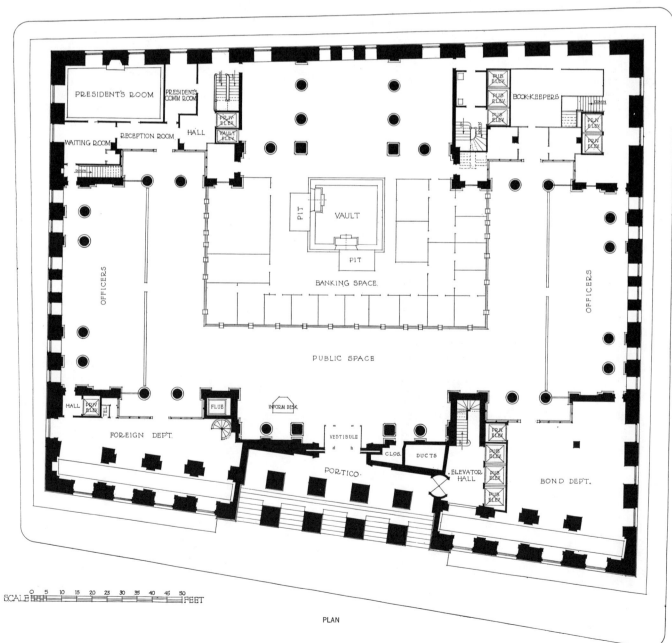

PRESIDENT'S ROOM   PRESIDENT'S COMM. ROOM

PUB. ELEV.   PUB. ELEV.   PUB. ELEV.   BOOK-KEEPERS

RECEPTION ROOM   HALL

PRIV. ELEV.

VAULT ELEV.

PRIV. ELEV.   PRIV. ELEV.

WAITING ROOM

DOWN

PIT   VAULT   PIT

OFFICERS

OFFICERS

BANKING SPACE.

PUBLIC SPACE

HALL   PRIV. ELEV.   TEL.

FLUE   INFORM DESK

FOREIGN DEPT.

VESTIBULE

PRIV. ELEV.

PUB. ELEV.

CLOS.   DUCTS

PORTICO.   ELEVATOR HALL   PUB. ELEV.

BOND DEPT.

PUB. ELEV.

SCALE   0 5 10 15 20 25 30 35 40 45 50   FEET

PLAN

Plate 298

THE NATIONAL CITY BANK, NEW YORK CITY.
1909

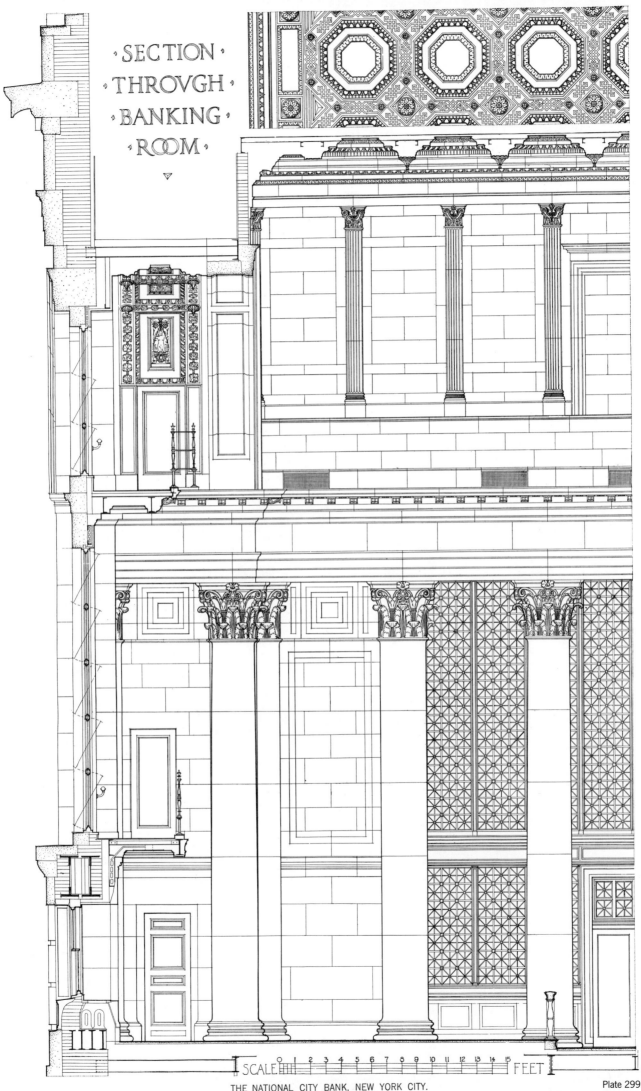

· SECTION ·
· THROVGH ·
· BANKING ·
· ROOM ·

SCALE 0 1 2 3 4 5 6 7 8 9 10 11 12 13 14 15 FEET

THE NATIONAL CITY BANK, NEW YORK CITY.
DETAILS OF BANKING ROOM
1909

Plate 299

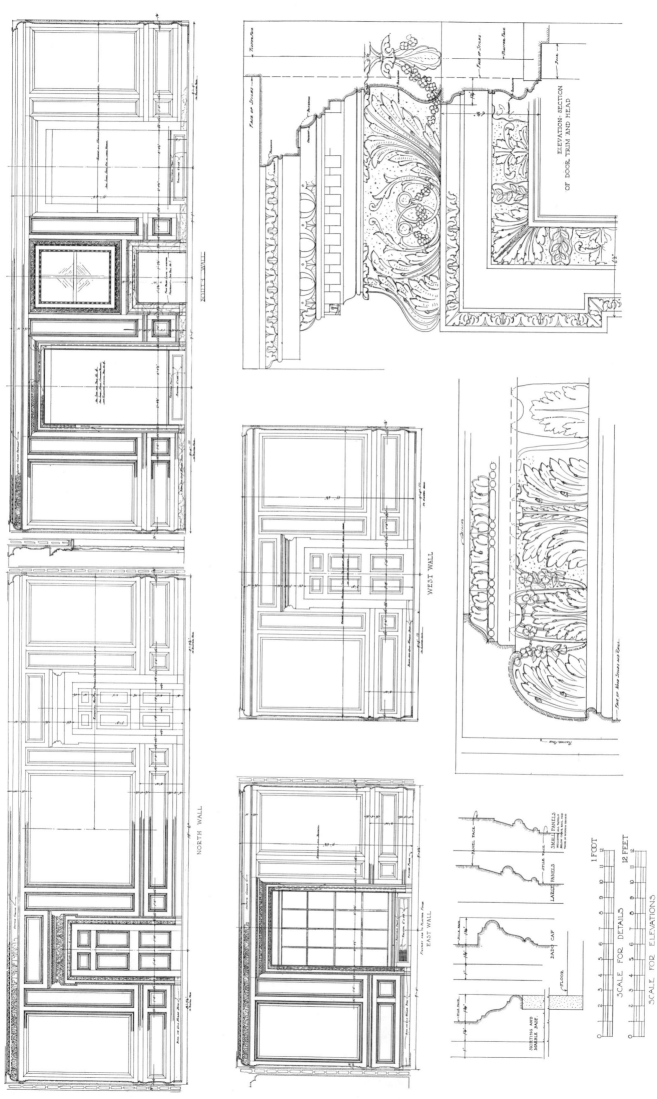

NORTH WALL

WEST WALL

EAST WALL

ELEVATION-SECTION
OF DOOR TRIM AND HEAD

DETAILS OF PRESIDENT'S ROOM
THE NATIONAL CITY BANK, NEW YORK CITY.
1913

SCALE FOR DETAILS

SCALE FOR ELEVATIONS

Plate 299A

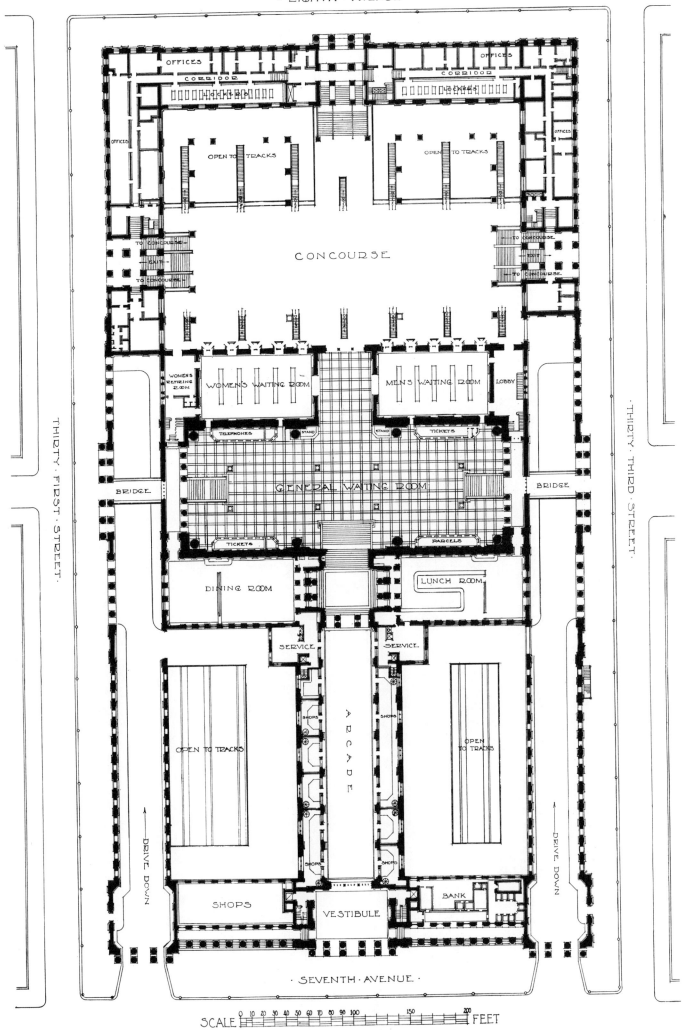

· EIGHTH · AVENUE ·

OFFICES   OFFICES

CORRIDOR   CORRIDOR

LOCKERS

OFFICES

OPEN TO TRACKS   OPEN TO TRACKS

OFFICES

TO CONCOURSE   TO CONCOURSE

CONCOURSE

TO CONCOURSE   TO CONCOURSE

WOMENS RETIRING ROOM

WOMEN'S WAITING ROOM   MEN'S WAITING ROOM

LOBBY

TELEPHONES   STAND   STAND   TICKETS

BRIDGE   GENERAL WAITING ROOM   BRIDGE

TICKETS   PARCELS

DINING ROOM   LUNCH ROOM

SERVICE   SERVICE

SHOPS   SHOPS

OPEN TO TRACKS   ARCADE   OPEN TO TRACKS

DRIVE DOWN   DRIVE DOWN

SHOPS   SHOPS

SHOPS   BANK

SHOPS   VESTIBULE

THIRTY · FIRST · STREET.

THIRTY · THIRD · STREET.

· SEVENTH · AVENUE ·

SCALE   0 10 20 30 40 50 60 70 80 90 100   150   200   FEET

BLOCK PLAN
THE PENNSYLVANIA RAILROAD STATION, NEW YORK CITY.
1906 - 1910

Plate 300

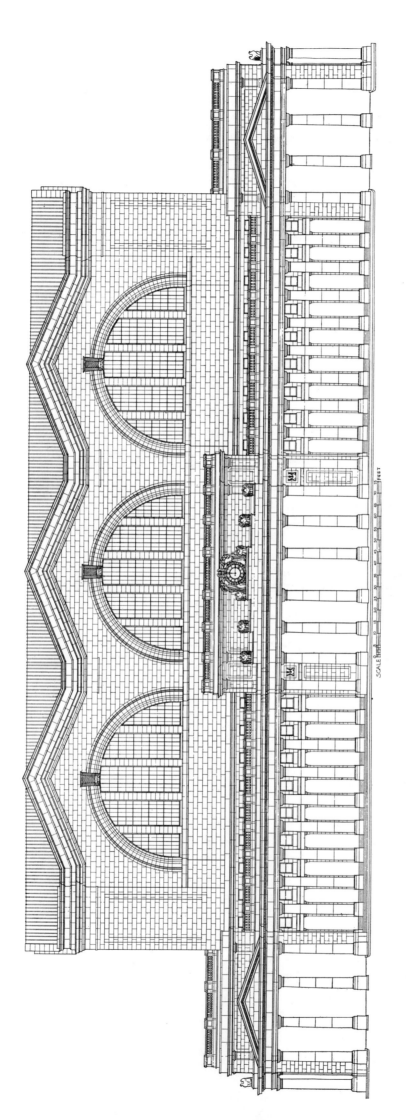

THE PENNSYLVANIA RAILROAD STATION, NEW YORK CITY.
SEVENTH AVENUE ELEVATION
1906 - 1910

SCALE

Plate 301

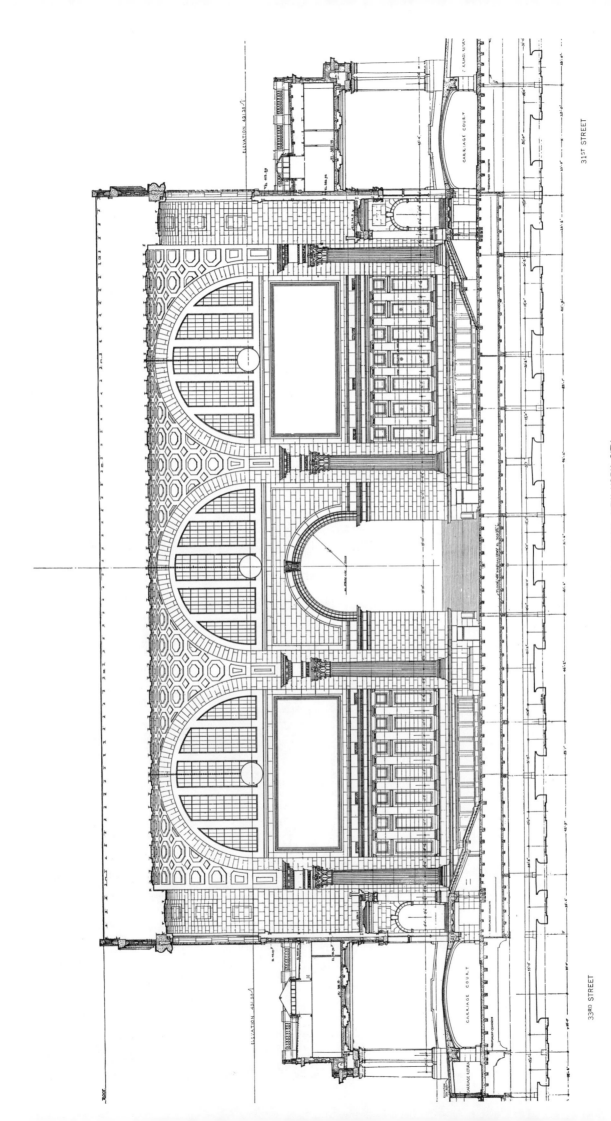

31ST STREET

33RD STREET

THE PENNSYLVANIA RAILROAD STATION, NEW YORK CITY
SECTION THROUGH MAIN WAITING ROOM
1906 - 1910

Plate 302

THE PENNSYLVANIA RAILROAD STATION, NEW YORK CITY.
1906 - 1910

Plate 303

THE PENNSYLVANIA RAILROAD STATION, NEW YORK CITY.

SEVENTH AVENUE FACADE
1906 - 1910

Plate 304

ARCADE FROM MAIN ENTRANCE TO WAITING ROOM

CARRIAGE DRIVEWAY

Plate 305

THE PENNSYLVANIA RAILROAD STATION, NEW YORK CITY.
1906 - 1910

MAIN WAITING ROOM
THE PENNSYLVANIA RAILROAD STATION, NEW YORK CITY.
1906 - 1910

Plate 306

RESTAURANT

CONCOURSE

Plate 307 THE PENNSYLVANIA RAILROAD STATION, NEW YORK CITY
1906 - 1910

DETAILS OF MAIN WAITING ROOM
THE PENNSYLVANIA RAILROAD STATION, NEW YORK CITY.
1906 - 1910

Plate 308

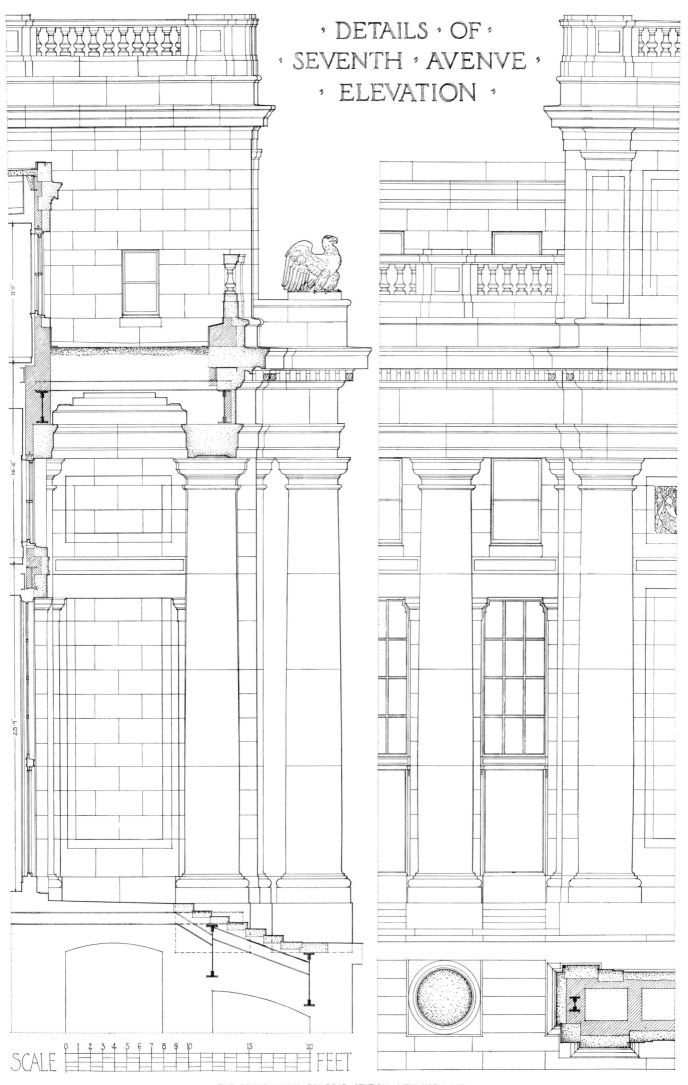

' DETAILS · OF ·
· SEVENTH · AVENVE ·
· ELEVATION ·

SCALE 0 1 2 3 4 5 6 7 8 9 10   15   20 FEET

Plate 309

THE PENNSYLVANIA RAILROAD STATION, NEW YORK CITY.
1906 - 1910

SCALE 0 1 2 3 4 5 10 15 20 25 30 FEET

SPRING LINE

DETAILS
MAIN
WAITING ROOM

THE PENNSYLVANIA RAILROAD STATION, NEW YORK CITY

INTERIOR DETAILS

1906 - 1910

Plate 310

INTERIOR OF WAITING ROOM

GENERAL VIEW OF EXTERIOR

STATION AT WATERBURY, CONNECTICUT, FOR THE NEW HAVEN RAILWAY
1909

Plate 311

HAMILTON HALL, 1907

SCHOOL OF JOURNALISM, 1913

COLUMBIA UNIVERSITY, NEW YORK CITY.

Plate 313

AVERY BUILDING, SCHOOL OF ARCHITECTURE, 1912

KENT HALL, SCHOOL OF LAW, 1910

Plate 314   COLUMBIA UNIVERSITY, NEW YORK CITY.

AVERY LIBRARY 1912

KENT HALL, LAW LIBRARY 1911

COLUMBIA UNIVERSITY, NEW YORK CITY.

Plate 315

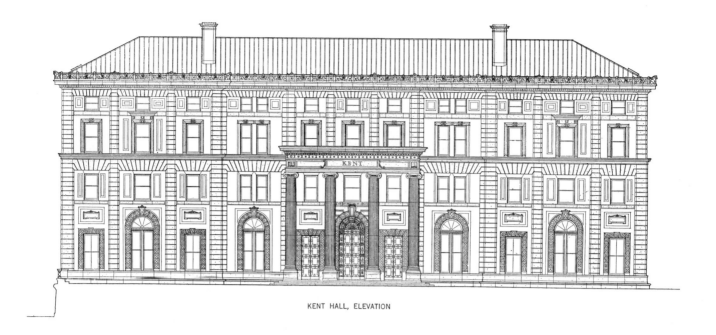

KENT HALL, ELEVATION

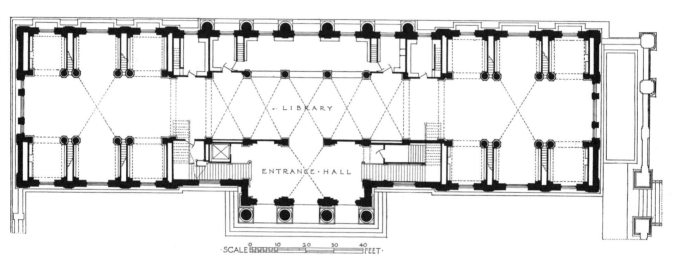

·SCALE· 0 10 20 30 40 ·FEET·

KENT HALL, PLAN OF FIRST FLOOR
1910

SCHOOL OF JOURNALISM, ELEVATION, 1913

Plate 316

COLUMBIA UNIVERSITY, NEW YORK CITY

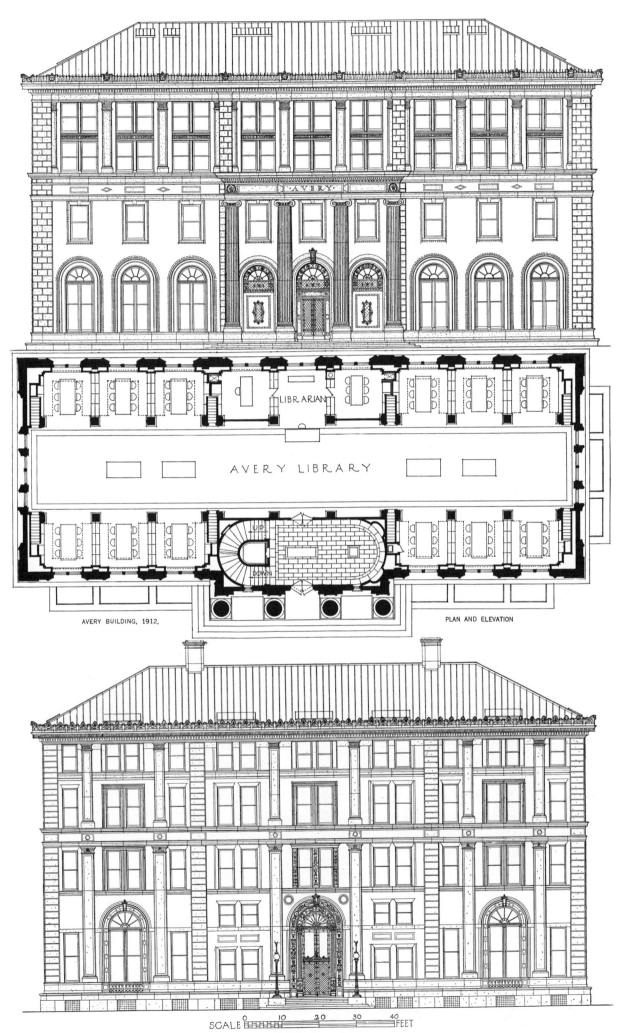

AVERY BUILDING, 1912,

LIBRARIAN

AVERY LIBRARY

UP

DOWN

PLAN AND ELEVATION

SCALE 0 10 20 30 40 FEET

PHILOSOPHY BUILDING, ELEVATION, 1910
COLUMBIA UNIVERSITY, NEW YORK CITY

Plate 317

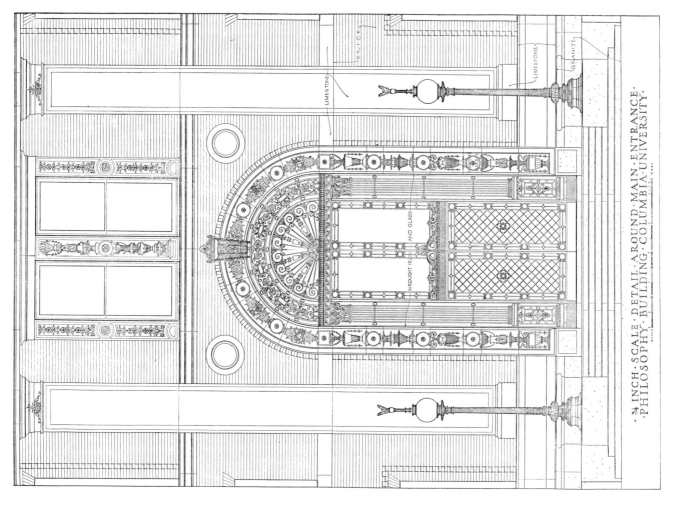

·¾·INCH·SCALE·DETAIL·AROUND·MAIN·ENTRANCE·
·PHILOSOPHY·BUILDING·COLUMBIA·UNIVERSITY·

ENTRANCE TO PHILOSOPHY BUILDING
COLUMBIA UNIVERSITY, NEW YORK CITY.
1911

Plate 318

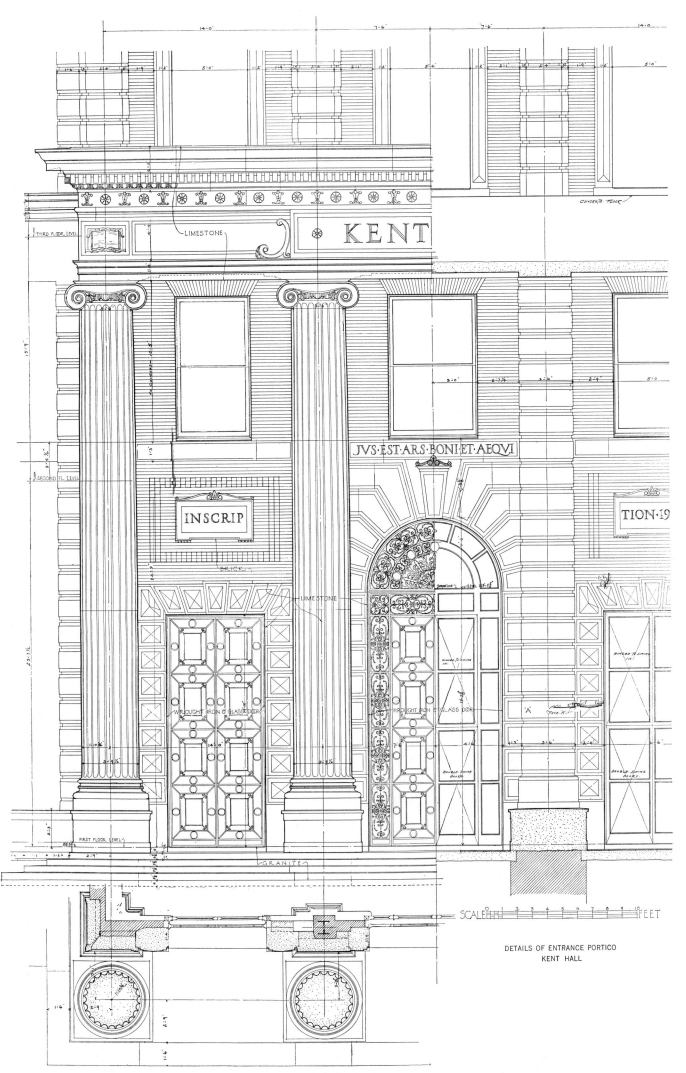

KENT

JVS·EST·ARS·BONI·ET·AEQVI

INSCRIP

TION·19

DETAILS OF ENTRANCE PORTICO
KENT HALL

SCALE _____ FEET

COLUMBIA UNIVERSITY, NEW YORK CITY

Plate 319

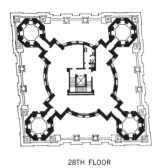

28TH FLOOR

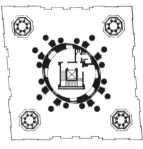

32ND FLOOR

36TH FLOOR

PLANS OF TOWER

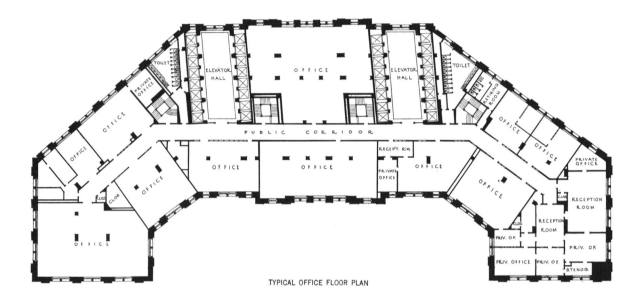

TYPICAL OFFICE FLOOR PLAN

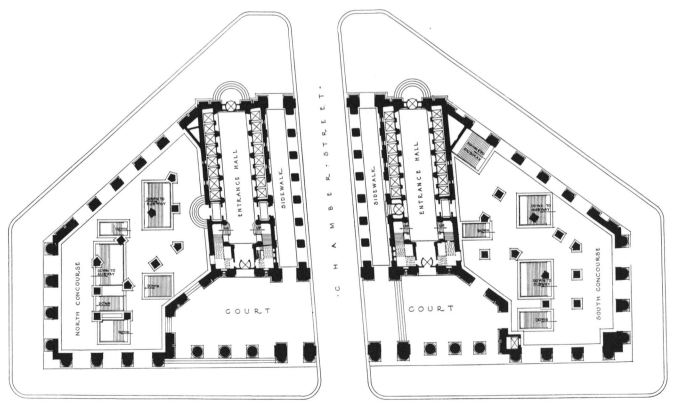

GROUND FLOOR PLAN

SCALE FEET

Plate 320

THE MUNICIPAL BUILDING, NEW YORK CITY
1908

NEW·AMSTERDAM·MDCXXV   MANHATTAN   NEW·YORK·MDCLXIV

SCALE |0 10 20 30 40 50 60 70 80 90 100| FEET

THE MUNICIPAL BUILDING, NEW YORK CITY
WEST ELEVATION
· 1908

Plate 321

Plate 322

THE MUNICIPAL BUILDING, NEW YORK CITY
1908 - 1910

THE MUNICIPAL BUILDING, NEW YORK CITY.
DETAILS OF COLONNADE AND ARCHWAY AT BASE
1908

Plate 323

DETAIL OF TOWER AND UPPER STORIES

DETAIL OF COLONNADE AT BASE

Plate 324   THE MUNICIPAL BUILDING, NEW YORK CITY.
1908

START OF STAIRWAY FIRST FLOOR

ELEVATOR HALL, FIRST FLOOR

THE MUNICIPAL BUILDING, NEW YORK CITY
1908 - 1910

Plate 325

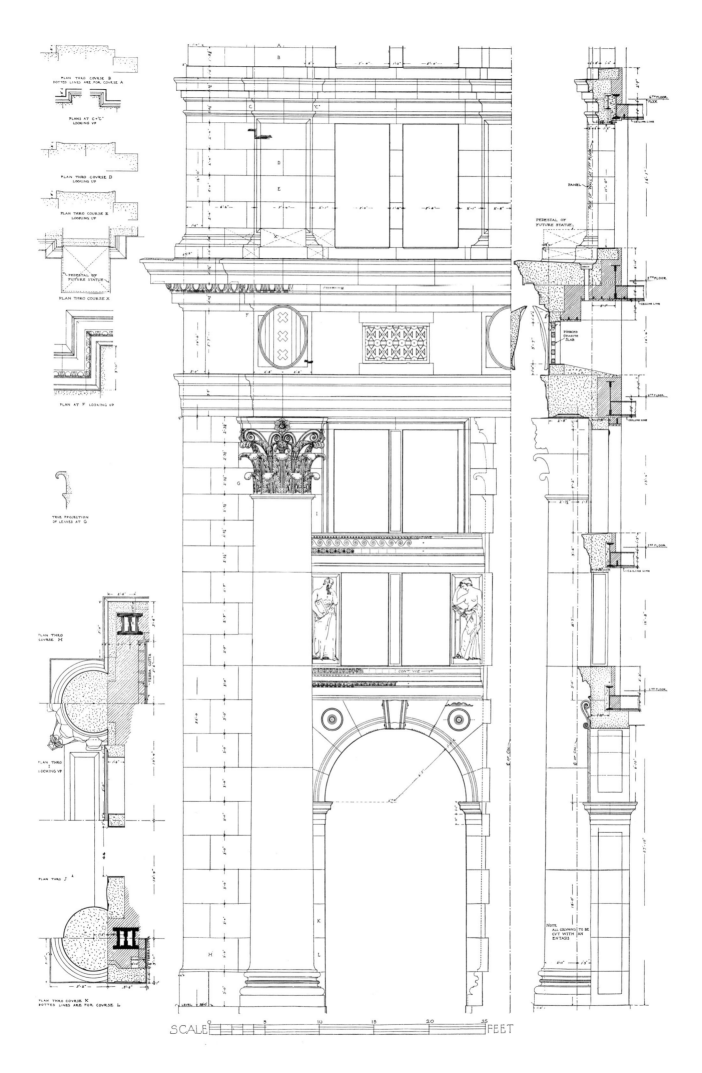

SCALE |—|—|—|—|—| FEET
0   5   10   15   20   25

Plate 326

THE MUNICIPAL BUILDING, NEW YORK CITY.
DETAIL OF LOWER STORIES
1908

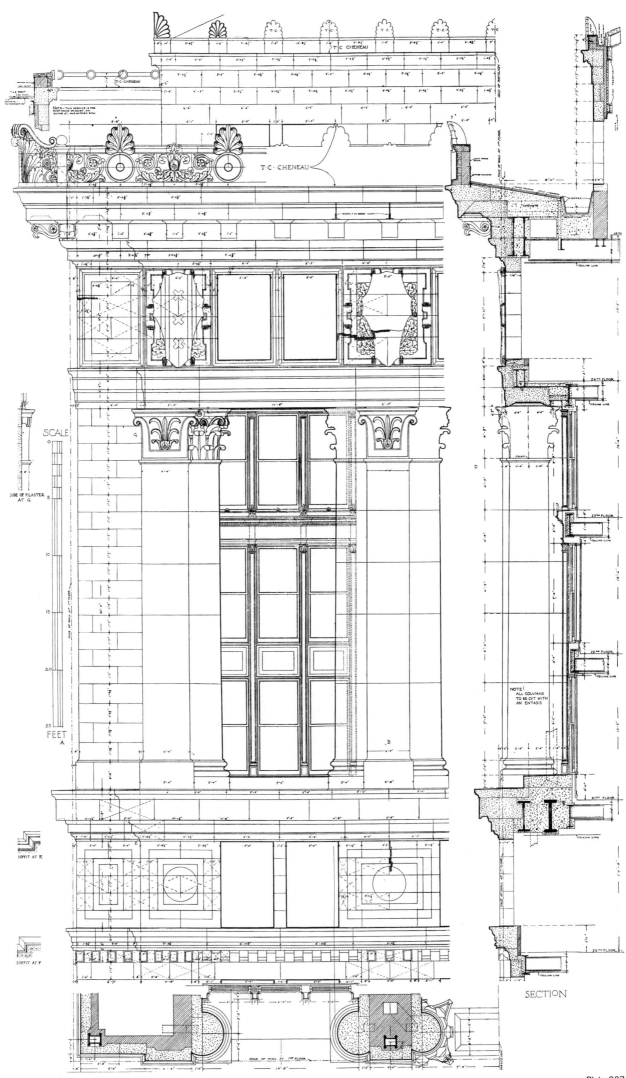

THE MUNICIPAL BUILDING, NEW YORK CITY.
DETAIL OF UPPER STORIES

Plate 327

EXTERIOR

MAIN BANKING ROOM

Plate 329   BUILDING FOR THE GIRARD TRUST CO., PHILADELPHIA, PA.

1908

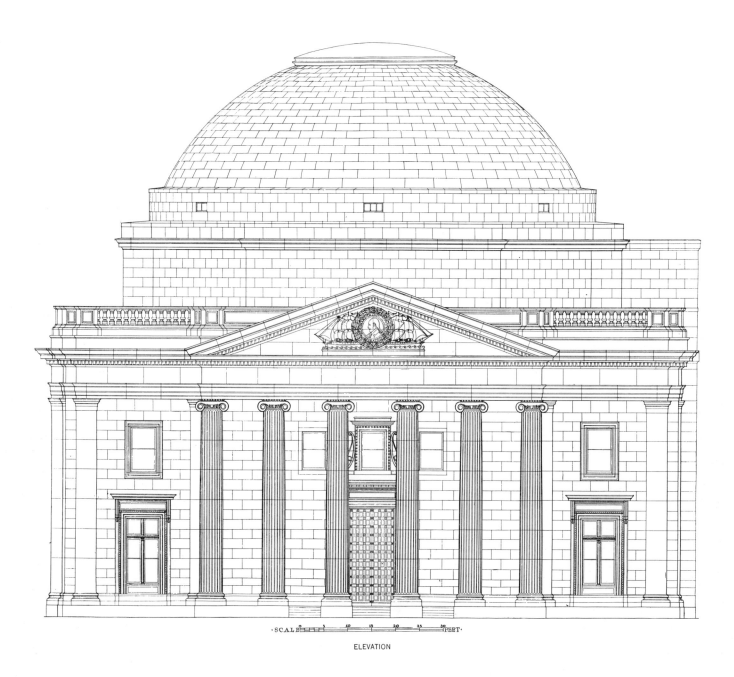

·SCALE· 0 5 10 15 20 25 30 ·FEET·

ELEVATION

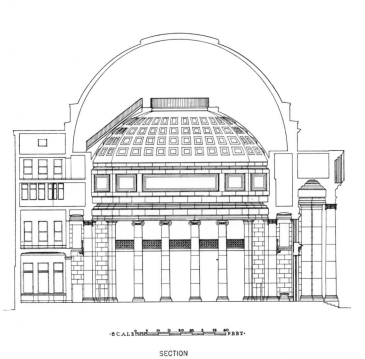

·SCALE· 0 5 10 20 30 40 50 60 ·FEET·

SECTION

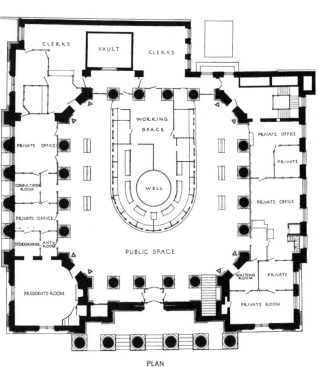

PLAN

THE GIRARD TRUST CO., PHILADELPHIA, PA.
1908

Plate 330

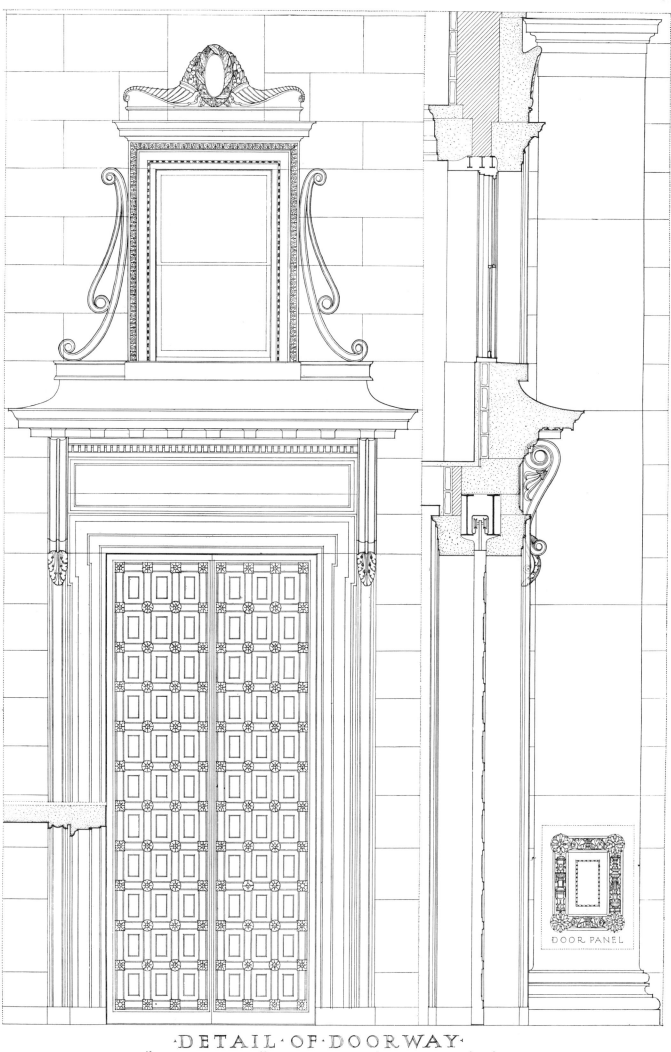

·DETAIL·OF·DOORWAY·

·SCALE· 1⁵ _____ 1⁰ _____ 5 _____ 0 |||| ·FEET·

MATERIALS, WHITE GEORGIA MARBLE AND CAST BRONZE.

DOOR PANEL

Plate 331   BUILDING FOR THE GIRARD TRUST COMPANY, PHILADELPHIA, PA.

DETAIL OF LOWER STORIES

GENERAL VIEW

BANK AND OFFICE BUILDING FOR THE COLUMBIA TRUST CO., NEW YORK CITY.
1910

Plate 333

Plate 334   DOWNTOWN BUILDING, COLUMBIA TRUST CO., NEW YORK CITY
SIDE ELEVATION
1910

DOWNTOWN BUILDING, COLUMBIA TRUST CO., NEW YORK CITY
EXTERIOR DETAILS,   FRONT ELEVATION
1910

Plate 335

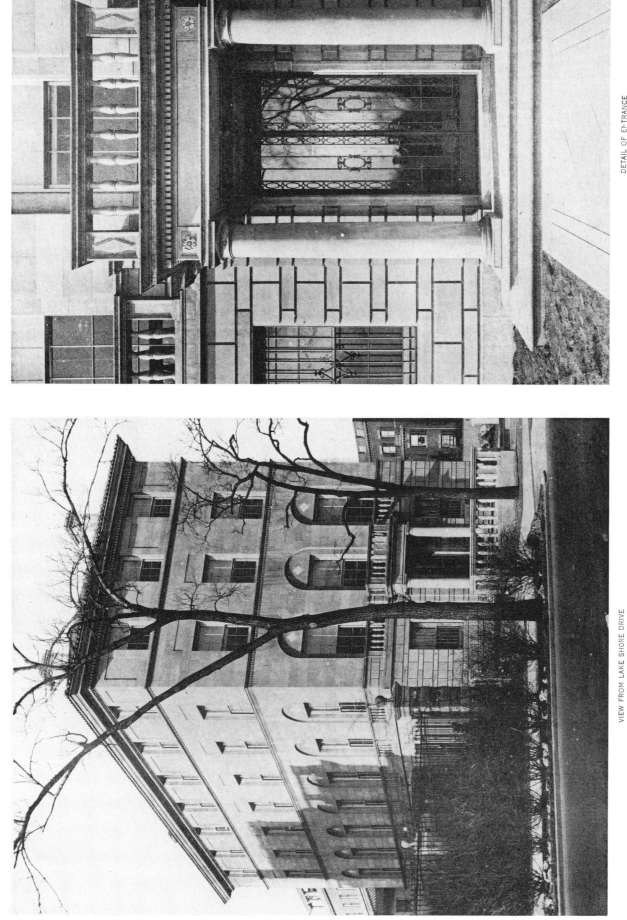

DETAIL OF ENTRANCE

VIEW FROM LAKE SHORE DRIVE

RESIDENCE OF EDWARD T. BLAIR, CHICAGO ILL.
1912

Plate 336

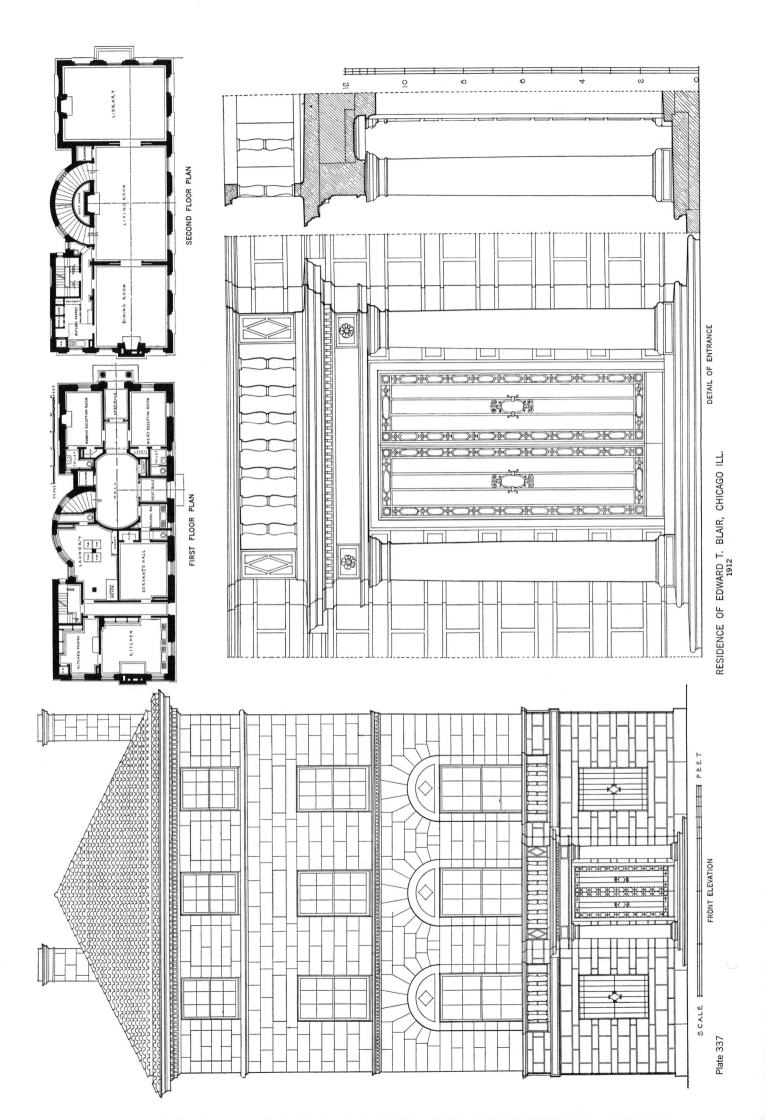

LIBRARY

LIVING ROOM

DINING ROOM

SECOND FLOOR PLAN

WOMAN'S RECEPTION ROOM

VESTIBULE

MEN'S RECEPTION ROOM

TOILET

TOILET

HALL

LAUNDRY

SERVANT'S HALL

KITCHEN PANTRY

KITCHEN

FIRST FLOOR PLAN

DETAIL OF ENTRANCE

RESIDENCE OF EDWARD T. BLAIR, CHICAGO ILL.
1912

FRONT ELEVATION

SCALE

FEET

Plate 337

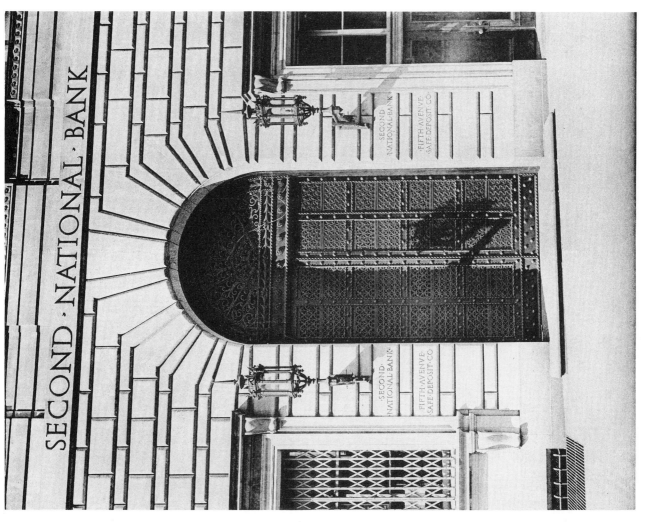

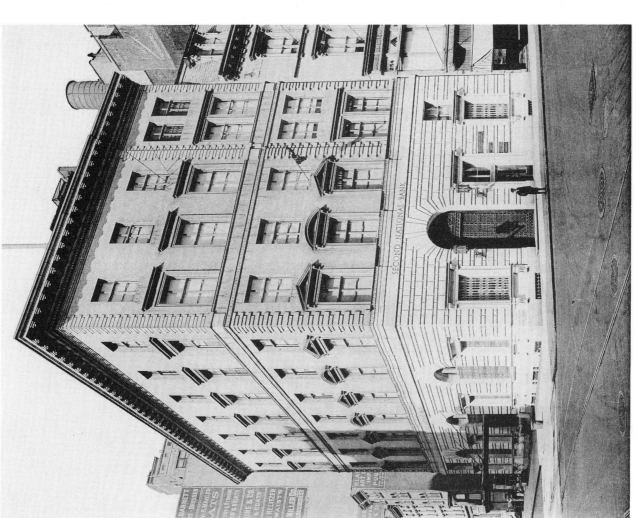

THE SECOND NATIONAL BANK, NEW YORK CITY
1908

Plate 338

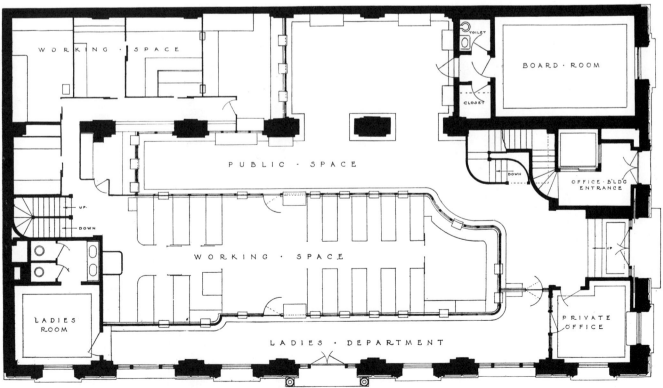

THE SECOND NATIONAL BANK, NEW YORK CITY.
1907

Plate 339

FORTY-FIFTH STREET FACADE

FORTY-FOURTH STREET FACADE

THE HARVARD CLUB OF NEW YORK CITY
1902 - 1915

FORTY-FIFTH STREET FACADE

Plate 340

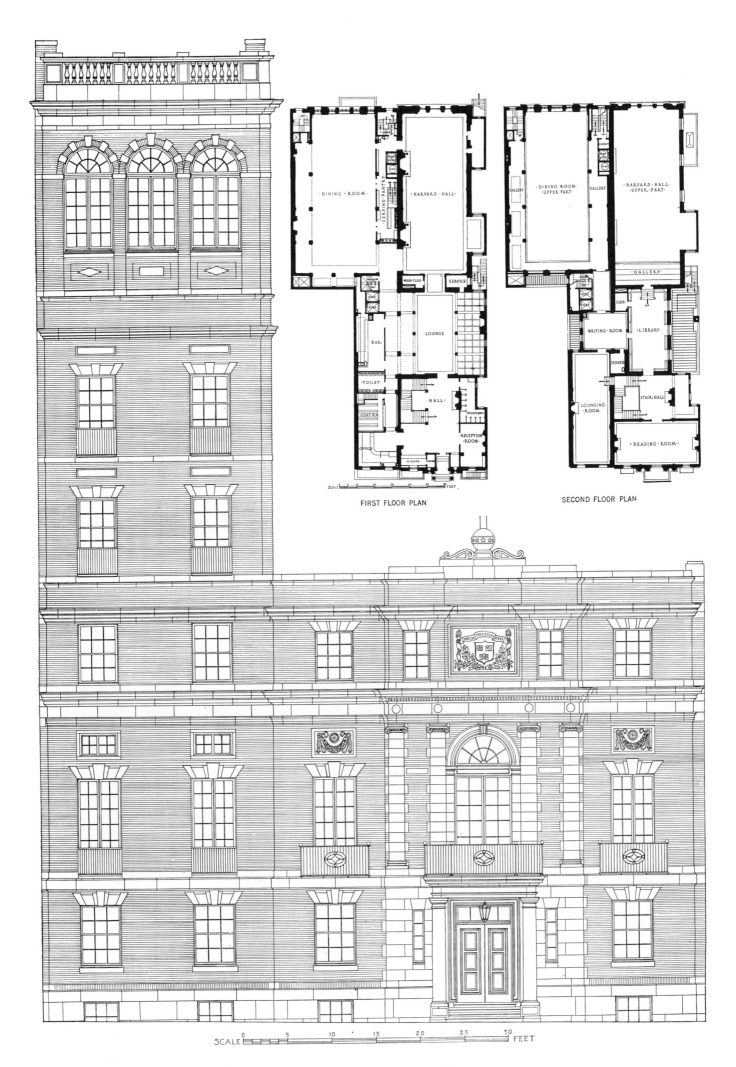

DINING·ROOM·

HARVARD·HALL·

SERVING·PANTRY·

WOOD·CLOS·   SERVICE·

·BAR·   ·LOUNGE·

·TOILET·

COAT·RM·   ·HALL·

OFFICE·   TELEPHONES·

·CIGARS·   ·RECEPTION·
ROOM·

SCALE   10   20   30   40   50   60   FEET·

FIRST FLOOR PLAN

GALLERY·

·DINING·ROOM·
UPPER·PART·   GALLERY·

HARVARD·HALL·
UPPER·PART·

·GALLERY·

CLOS·

WRITING·ROOM·   ·LIBRARY·

SERVICE·

LOUNGING·
·ROOM·   STAIR·HALL·

·READING·ROOM·

SECOND FLOOR PLAN

SCALE   0   5   10   15   20   25   30   FEET

THE HARVARD CLUB, NEW YORK CITY.
ORIGINAL BUILDING ON RIGHT 1902, ADDITION ON LEFT, 1915.

Plate 341

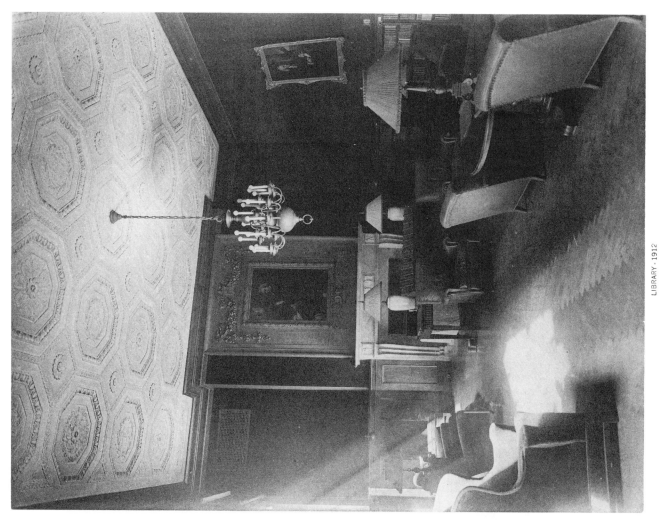

LIBRARY · 1912

HARVARD HALL, LOUNGING ROOM · 1905

THE HARVARD CLUB OF NEW YORK CITY.

Plate 343

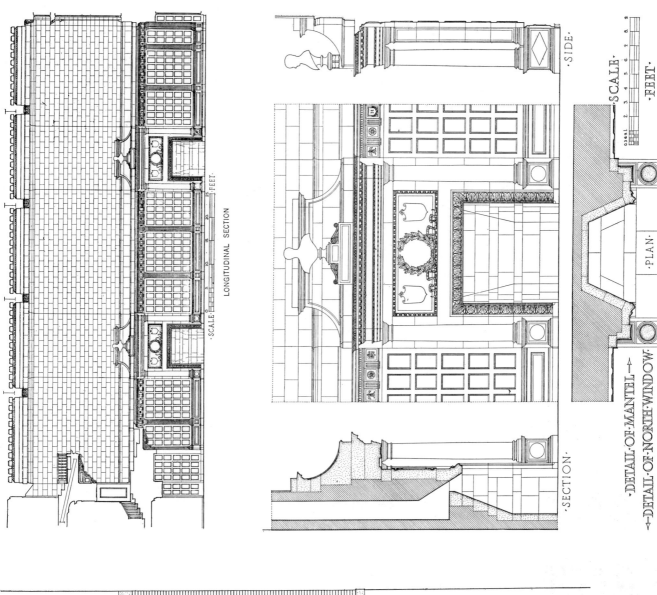

·LONGITUDINAL SECTION·

·SCALE· |0 5 10 15 20 25 |FEET·

·SECTION·

·DETAIL·OF·MANTEL·

·DETAIL·OF·NORTH·WINDOW·

·SIDE·

·PLAN·

·SCALE· 0 1 2 3 4 5 6 7 8 9 |FEET·

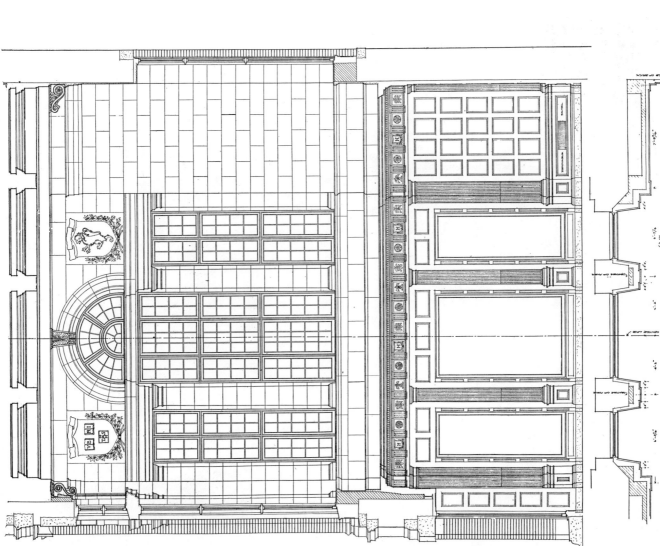

HARVARD HALL, LOUNGING ROOM OF HARVARD CLUB, NEW YORK CITY
1905

Plate 344

DINING ROOM 1914

HARVARD HALL · 1905

THE HARVARD CLUB OF NEW YORK

Plate 345

APARTMENT HOUSE, 998 FIFTH AVE., FOR THE CENTURY HOLDING CO.
1911

Plate 346

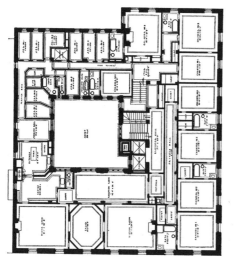

UPPER FLOOR.

TYPICAL DUPLEX APARTMENT

TYPICAL UPPER FLOOR PLAN SHOWING SINGLE APARTMENT
ON LEFT AND PART OF DUPLEX ON RIGHT

LOWER FLOOR.

FIRST FLOOR PLAN

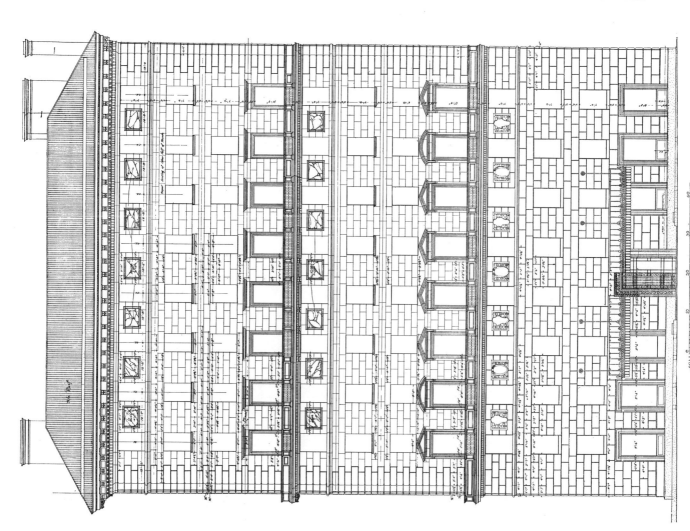

ELEVATION

Plate 347   APARTMENT HOUSE, 998 FIFTH AVENUE, FOR THE CENTURY HOLDING CO.
1911

ELEVATION

FIRST FLOOR PLAN

SECOND FLOOR PLAN

RESIDENCE OF P. H. B. FRELINGHUYSEN, MORRISTOWN, N. J.
1912

Plate 348

SCALE 0 5 10 15 20 25 30 FEET

SCALE 0 5 10 FEET

VALET ROOM

KITCHEN

PANTRY

STORE

CL

STORE

CLOS

ENTRY

CL

CLOS

SERVANT'S DINING RM.

HALL

TOILET

SERVT'S RM.

DR. SO. RM.

BILLIARD RM.

RECP'TN ROOM

VESTIB.

SCALE 0 10 20 30 40 FEET

DINING ROOM

PANTRY

CL.

SALON

HALL

LIBRARY

DEN

TOIL.

Plate 349

RESIDENCE OF PERCY PYNE, ESQ., NEW YORK CITY
ABOVE, SIDE ELEVATION,   BELOW, DETAIL OF ENTRANCE, FIRST AND SECOND FLOOR PLANS
1911

DETAIL OF ENTRANCE

GENERAL VIEW

RESIDENCE OF PERCY PYNE, ESQ., NEW YORK CITY
1911

Plate 350

SALON

LIBRARY

RESIDENCE OF PERCY PYNE, ESQ., NEW YORK CITY
1911

Plate 351

DINING ROOM

SALON

STAIR HALL

RECEPTION ROOM

RESIDENCE OF PERCY PYNE, ESQ., NEW YORK CITY
1911

Plate 351A

FACADE

DETAIL OF ENTRANCE

Plate 352

PRESIDENT'S HOUSE, COLUMBIA UNIVERSITY, NEW YORK CITY.

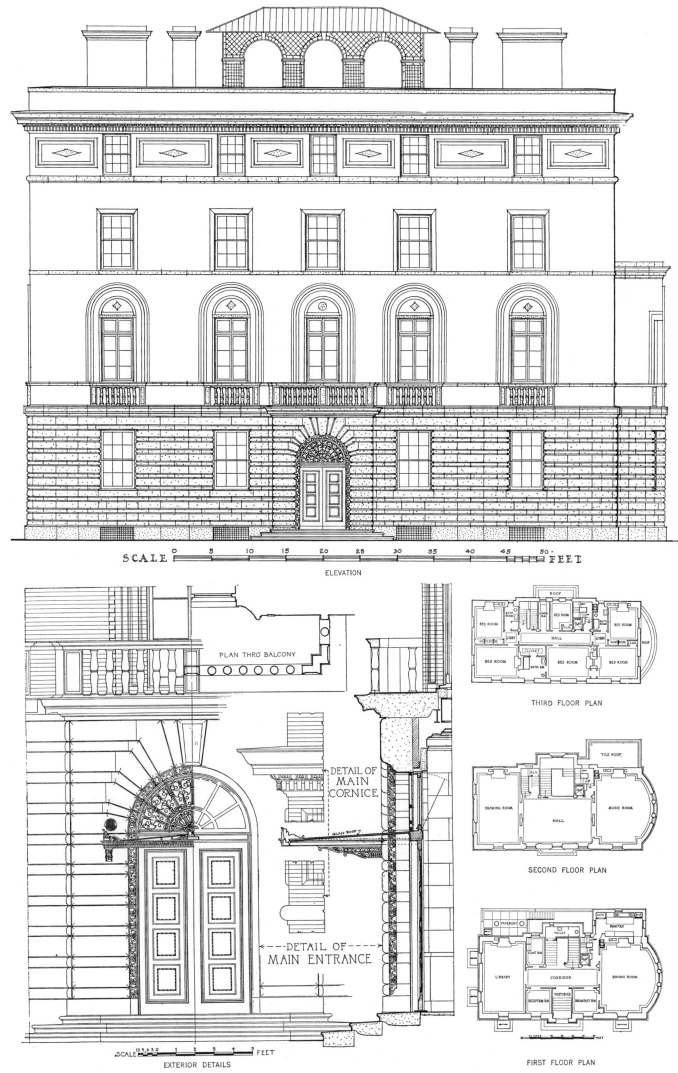

SCALE $\overline{0\quad\quad 5\quad\quad 10\quad\quad 15\quad\quad 20\quad\quad 25\quad\quad 30\quad\quad 35\quad\quad 40\quad\quad 45\quad\quad 50}$ FEET

ELEVATION

PLAN THRO' BALCONY

DETAIL OF
MAIN
CORNICE

GLASS ROOF

---DETAIL OF---
MAIN ENTRANCE

SCALE 1 2 9 6 3 0   1   2   3   4   5 FEET

EXTERIOR DETAILS

ROOF

THIRD FLOOR PLAN

BED ROOM · BATH ROOM · BED ROOM · BED ROOM
WARDROBE · LOBBY · HALL · LOBBY · WARDROBE · CLO. · ROOF
BED ROOM · CLOSET · BED ROOM · BED ROOM · BATH RM.

TILE ROOF

DRAWING ROOM · HALL · MUSIC ROOM

SECOND FLOOR PLAN

PAVEMENT · TOILET · SAFE · PANTRY
COAT RM.
LIBRARY · CORRIDOR · DINING ROOM
RECEPTION RM. · VESTIBULE · BREAKFAST RM.

SCALE FEET

FIRST FLOOR PLAN

PRESIDENT'S HOUSE, COLUMBIA UNIVERSITY, NEW YORK CITY
1912

Plate 353

ENTRANCE PORCH

GARDEN FRONT

ALTERATIONS TO HOUSE OF ELON H. HOOKER, GREENWICH, CONN.
1911

Plate 354

EXTERIOR

VIEW OF BANKING ROOM

THE BANK OF MONTREAL, WINNIPEG BRANCH, WINNIPEG, MANITOBA.
1911

Plate 355

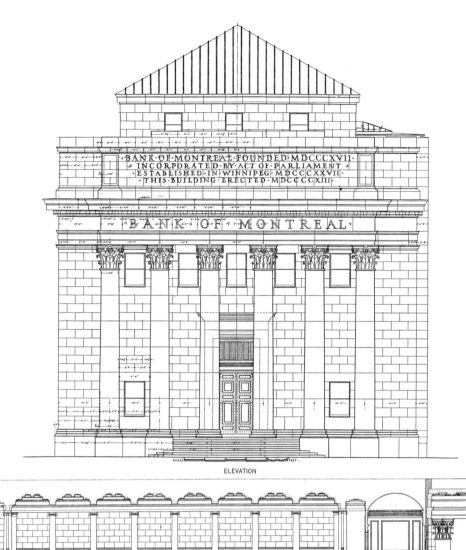

ELEVATION

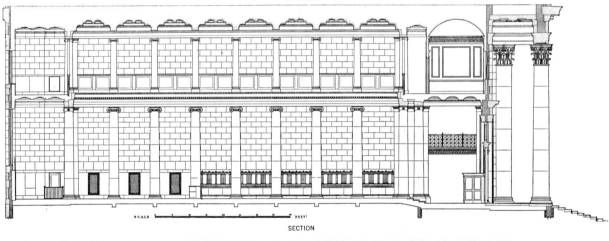

SECTION

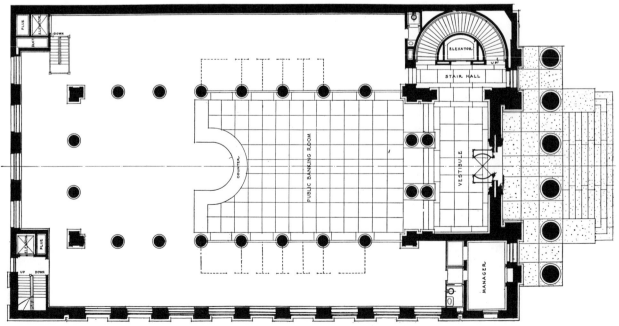

PLAN

Plate 356

THE BANK OF MONTREAL, WINNIPEG BRANCH

1911

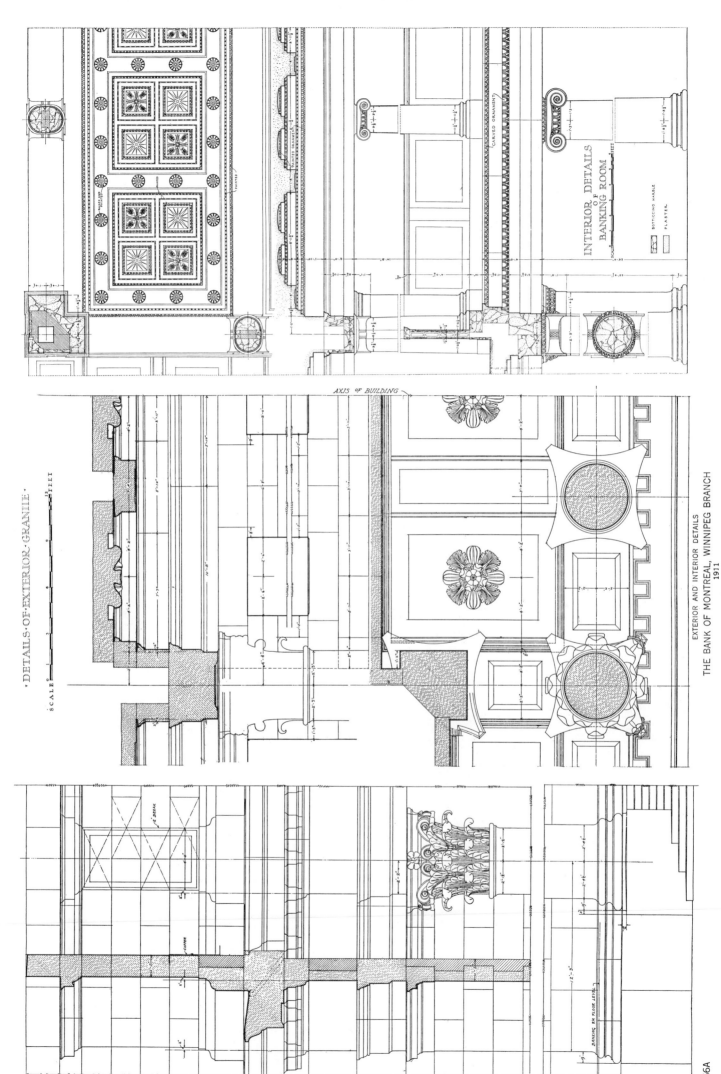

INTERIOR DETAILS OF BANKING ROOM

BOTTICCINO MARBLE
PLASTER

DETAILS·OF·EXTERIOR·GRANITE·

SCALE

AXIS OF BUILDING

EXTERIOR AND INTERIOR DETAILS
THE BANK OF MONTREAL, WINNIPEG BRANCH
1911

Plate 356A

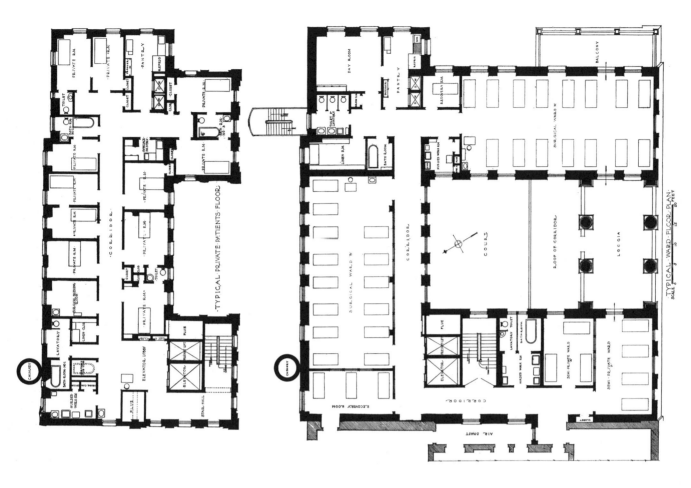

TYPICAL WARD FLOOR PLAN
SCALE

ADDITIONS TO THE NEW YORK POST GRADUATE HOSPITAL
NEW YORK CITY
1912

Plate 357

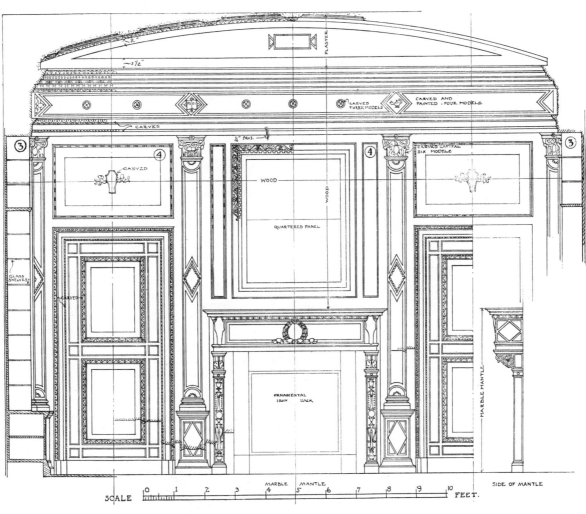

U. S. POST OFFICE, NEW YORK CITY
1913

Plate 360

DETAIL OF FACADE

PUBLIC CORRIDOR

UNITED STATES POST OFFICE, NEW YORK CITY.
1913

Plate 361

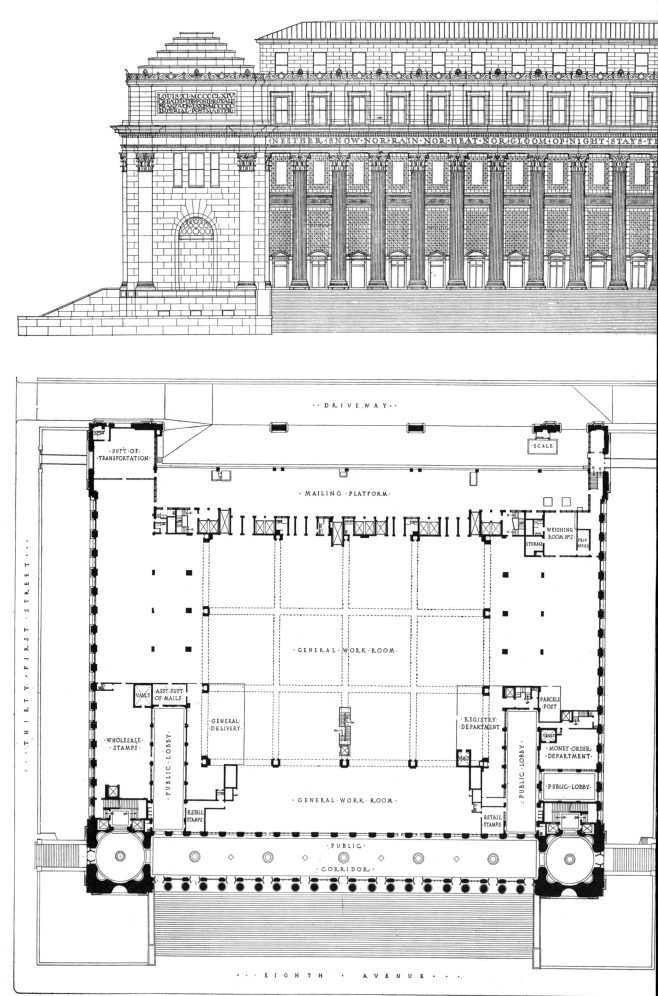

LOUIS·XI·MCCCCLXIV
CREATED·THE·POSTE·ROYALE
FRANZ·VON·TAXIS·MCCCC
IMPERIAL·POSTMASTER

·NEITHER·SNOW·NOR·RAIN·NOR·HEAT·NOR·GLOOM·OF·NIGHT·STAYS·TH

·DRIVE·WAY·

·SUP'T·OF·
TRANSPORTATION·

·SCALE·

·MAILING·PLATFORM·

WEIGHING
ROOM·N°2

PRIV
OFFICE

STORAGE

·GENERAL·WORK·ROOM·

·ASST·SUP'T·
OF·MAILS·

VAULT

PARCELS
POST·

VAULT

·WHOLESALE·
·STAMPS·

·GENERAL·
·DELIVERY·

·REGISTRY·
·DEPARTMENT·

·MONEY·ORDER·
·DEPARTMENT·

·PUBLIC·LOBBY·

·PUBLIC·LOBBY·

·PUBLIC·LOBBY·

VAULT

·RETAIL·
STAMPS

·GENERAL·WORK·ROOM·

·RETAIL·
STAMPS

·THIRTY·FIRST·STREET·

·PUBLIC·

·CORRIDOR·

·EIGHTH·AVENUE·

FIRST FLOOR PLAN

Plate 362 - 362A

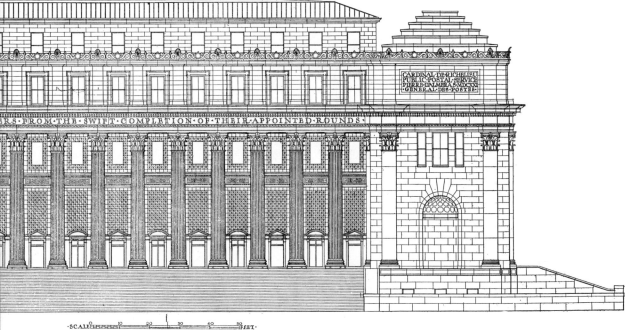

CARDINAL·DE·RICHELIEU
PUBLIC·POSTAL·SERVICE
PIERRE·D'ALMERA·MDCCC
·GENERAL·DES·POSTES·

····RS·FROM·THE·SWIFT·COMPLETION·OF·THEIR·APPOINTED·ROUNDS·

·SCALE· 10 20 30 40 50 ·FEET·

FRONT ELEVATION

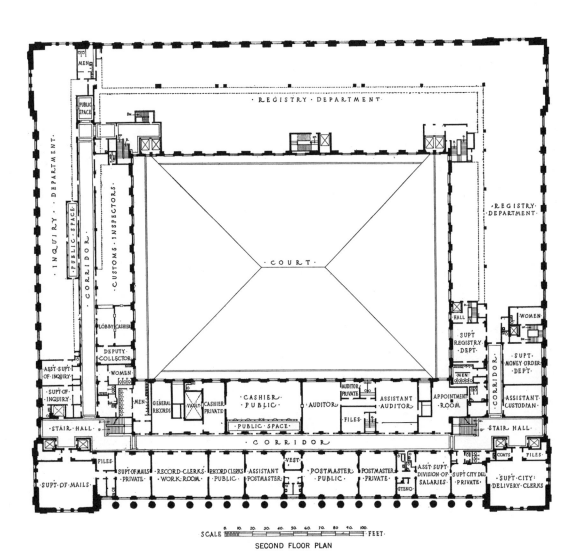

SCALE 0 10 20 30 40 50 60 70 80 90 100 FEET

SECOND FLOOR PLAN

UNITED STATES POST OFFICE, NEW YORK CITY

1913

DETAILS OF COLUMN AND PILASTER CAPS AND CORNICE - EXTERIOR

DETAIL OF CEILING IN PUBLIC CORRIDOR

Plate 363   UNITED STATES POST OFFICE, NEW YORK CITY.

· TERRA · COTTA · CHENEAU ·

· DETAIL · OF · ATTIC ·

GRANITE

· SCALE ·
0 1 2 3 4 5 6 7 8

· EXTERIOR ·
· DETAILS ·
· OF · THE ·
· U · S · POST ·
· OFFICE ·
· NEW · YORK · N · Y ·

GRANITE

· DETAIL · OF ·
· ENTRANCES ·
· THIRTY · FIRST · & ·
· THIRTY · THIRD · ST̄S ·

6'-1"

1'-0"

17'-11"

5'-4"

· DETAIL · OF · NICHE ·

· SECTION ·

CAST · IRON

CAST · IRON

· GRANITE ·

45'-0"

· PLAN · THRU · END ·
· OF · COLONNADE ·

4'-8"

1'-9"

4'-0½" 1'-3" 8'-2½" 4'-10" 4'-1¼"

· SECTION · THRU · COLONNADE ·

UNITED STATES POST OFFICE, NEW YORK CITY

Plate 364

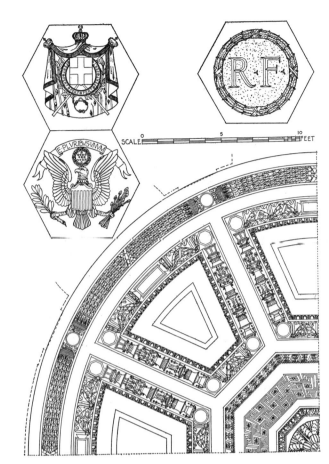

SCALE 0 — 5 — 10 FEET

DETAILS OF PLASTER CEILING

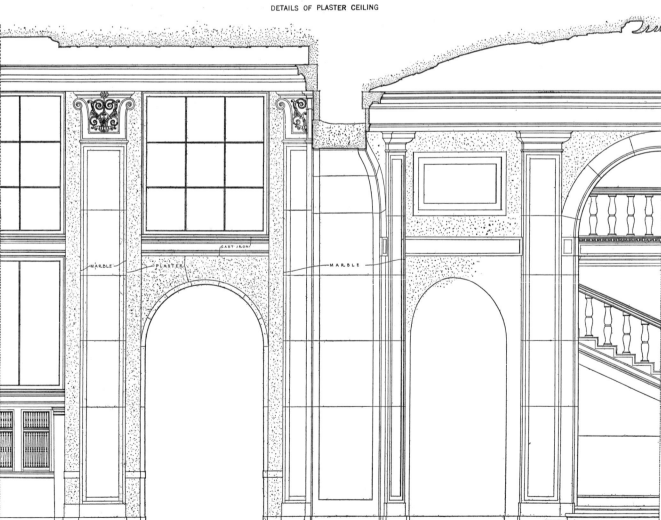

MARBLE — PLASTER — CAST IRON — MARBLE

UNITED STATES POST OFFICE, NEW YORK CITY
DETAILS OF PUBLIC CORRIDOR, FIRST FLOOR
1913

DETAIL OF ENTRANCE

BANK AND OFFICE BUILDING FOR THE ROYAL TRUST CO., MONTREAL, CANADA
1912

FACADE

Plate 365

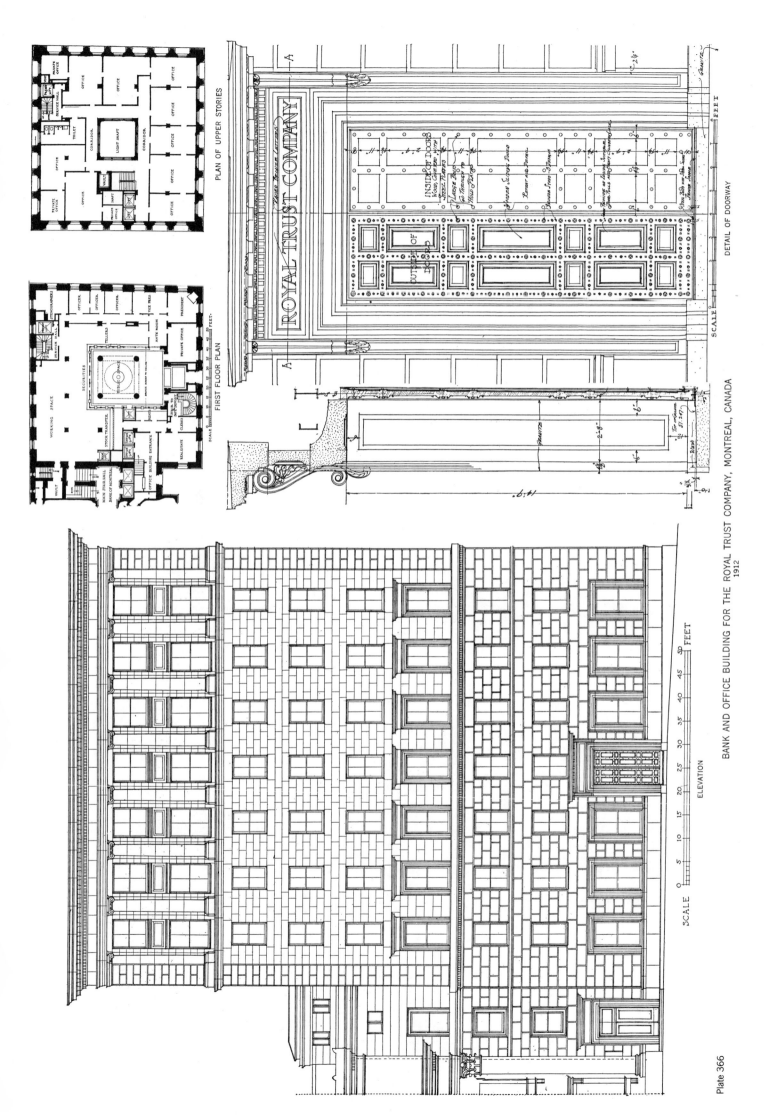

PLAN OF UPPER STORIES

FIRST FLOOR PLAN

ROYAL TRUST COMPANY

DETAIL OF DOORWAY

BANK AND OFFICE BUILDING FOR THE ROYAL TRUST COMPANY, MONTREAL, CANADA
1912

ELEVATION

Plate 366

AUDITORIUM BUILDING FOR VASSAR COLLEGE, POUGHKEEPSIE, N. Y.
1913

Plate 367

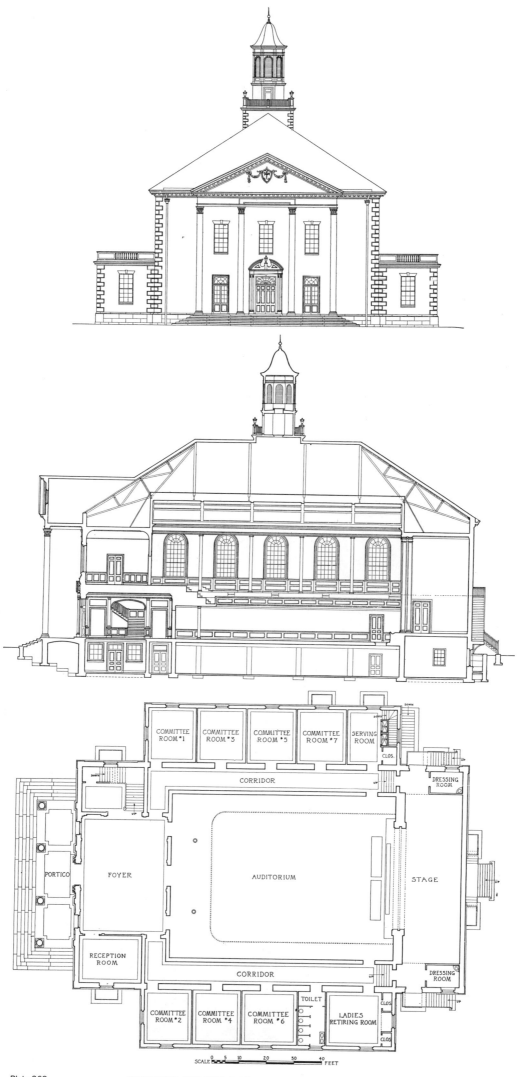

Plate 368   AUDITORIUM FOR VASSAR COLLEGE, POUGHKEEPSIE, N. Y.
                                          1913

VIEWS OF MAIN ENTRANCE, CORRIDOR AND STAIRWAY

NORTH ELEVATION OF FIRST SECTION

THE MINNEAPOLIS MUSEUM OF FINE ARTS
1914

Plate 369

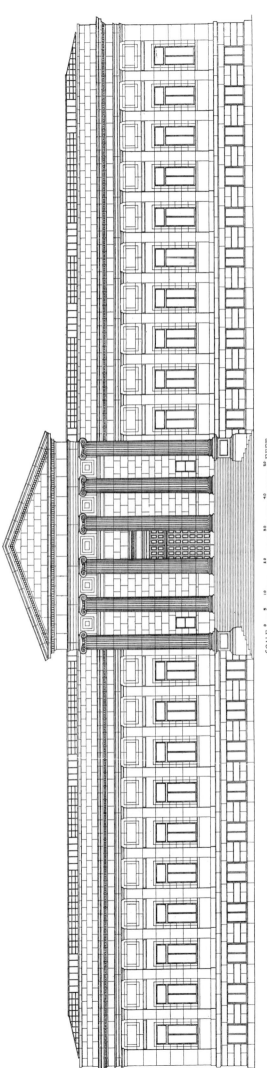

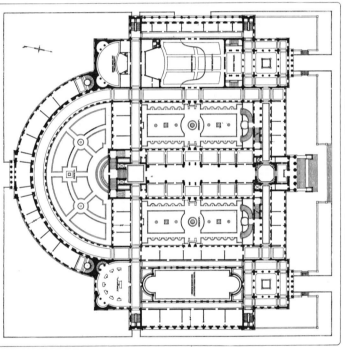

SECOND FLOOR PLAN

MAIN FLOOR PLAN

SCALE 0 10 20 40 60 80 100 150 200 250 FEET

THE MINNEAPOLIS MUSEUM OF FINE ARTS

MINNEAPOLIS, MINNESOTA.

1912

BASEMENT PLAN

Plate 370

BUILDING FOR THE AMERICAN ACADEMY IN ROME
1913

Plate 372

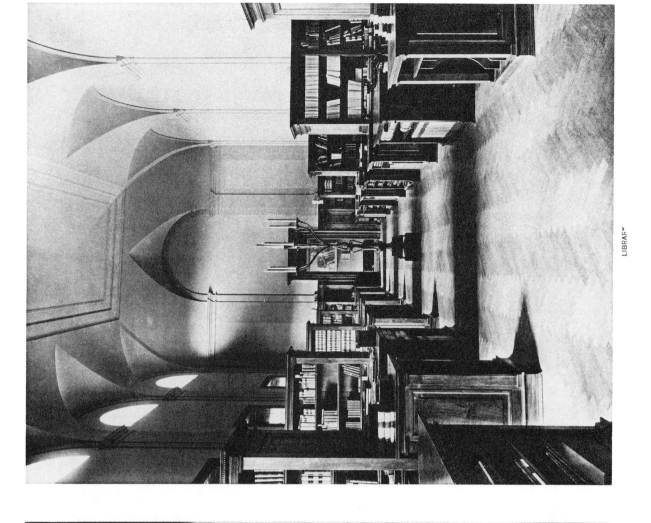

LIBRARY

ENTRANCE VESTIBULE

BUILDING FOR THE AMERICAN ACADEMY IN ROME.
1913

Plate 373

CORRIDOR AROUND COURT

THE COURT

THE AMERICAN ACADEMY IN ROME.
1913

Plate 374

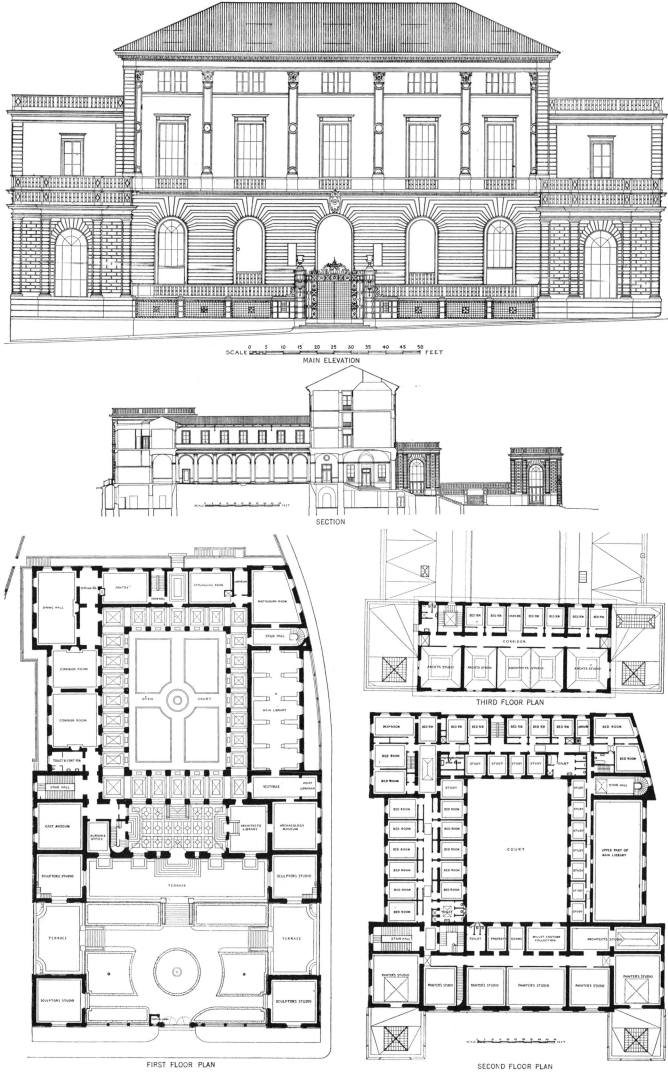

SCALE |10 5 10 15 20 25 30 35 40 45 50| FEET
MAIN ELEVATION

SECTION

FIRST FLOOR PLAN

THIRD FLOOR PLAN

SECOND FLOOR PLAN

Plate 375

THE AMERICAN ACADEMY IN ROME.
1913

FOUNTAIN OF THE GREAT GOD PAN - 1907
SCULPTURE BY GEORGE GRAY BARNARD

CLASS OF 1891, MEMORIAL GATEWAY. 1917.

COLUMBIA UNIVERSITY, NEW YORK CITY.

Plate 376

FACADE TOWARD GARDEN

FACADE TOWARD STREET

Plate 377   BOTANICAL MUSEUM OF THE BROOKLYN INSTITUTE OF ARTS & SCIENCES
1917

INTERIOR OF CENTRAL PAVILION

DETAIL OF CENTRAL PAVILION

BOTANICAL MUSEUM OF THE BROOKLYN INSTITUTE OF ARTS & SCIENCES
1917

Plate 378

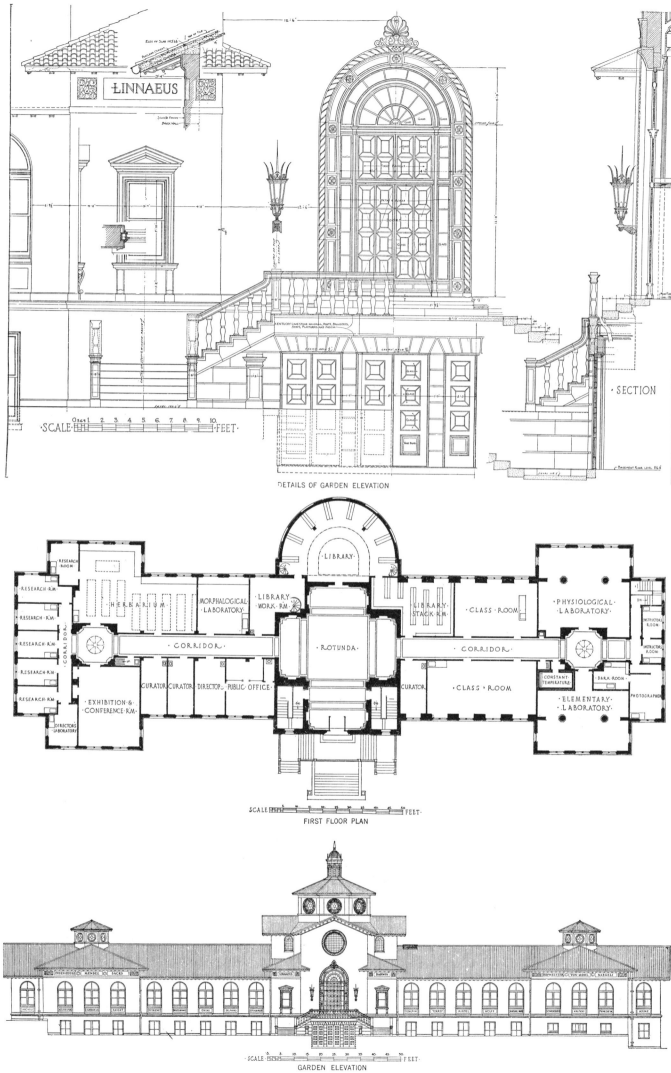

LINNAEUS

· SECTION ·

· SCALE · 0 ½ 1 2. 3. 4. 5. 6. 7. 8. 9. 10. · FEET ·

DETAILS OF GARDEN ELEVATION

RESEARCH ROOM · RESEARCH · R·M · RESEARCH · R·M · RESEARCH · R·M · RESEARCH · R·M · RESEARCH · R·M · DIRECTORS · LABORATORY

· CORRIDOR ·

· HERBARIUM ·

· MORPHALOGICAL · LABORATORY ·

· LIBRARY · WORK · RM ·

· LIBRARY ·

· LIBRARY · STACK · RM ·

· CLASS · ROOM ·

· PHYSIOLOGICAL · LABORATORY ·

DN

INSTRUCTORS ROOM

INSTRUCTORS ROOM

· CORRIDOR ·

· ROTUNDA ·

· CORRIDOR ·

CURATOR · CURATOR · DIRECTORS · PUBLIC · OFFICE ·

CURATOR

· CLASS · ROOM ·

CONSTANT · TEMPERATURE

· DARK · ROOM ·

PHOTOGRAPHER

· EXHIBITION & · CONFERENCE · RM ·

DN

DN

· ELEMENTARY · LABORATORY ·

SCALE 0 5 10 15 20 25 30 35 40 45 50 FEET ·

FIRST FLOOR PLAN

INGEN-HOUSE · MENDEL · SACKS

LINNAEUS

DARWIN

HOFMEISTER · VON MOHL · NAEGELI

· SCALE · 0. 5. 10. 15. 20 25. 30 35 40. 45. 50. FEET ·

GARDEN ELEVATION

Plate 379

BOTANICAL MUSEUM OF THE BROOKLYN INSTITUTE OF ARTS & SCIENCES

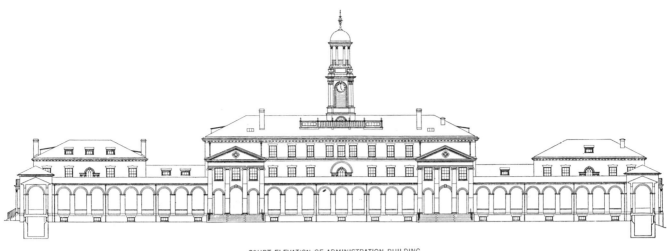

COURT ELEVATION OF ADMINISTRATION BUILDING.

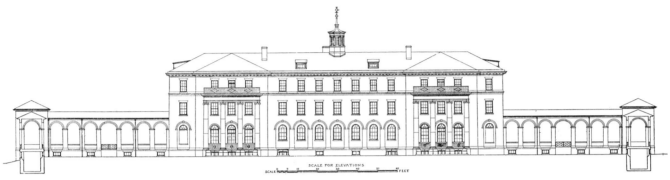

COURT ELEVATION OF DINING HALL BUILDING.

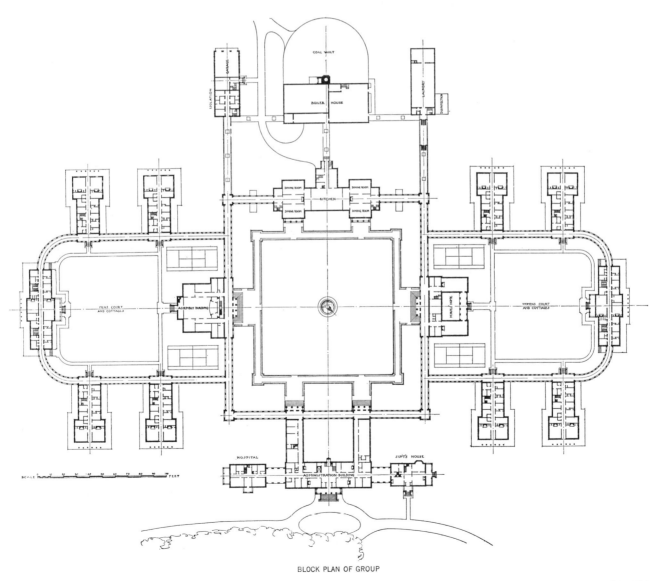

BLOCK PLAN OF GROUP

THE BURKE FOUNDATION HOSPITAL FOR CONVALESCENTS,
WHITE PLAINS, N. Y.
1914

Plate 380

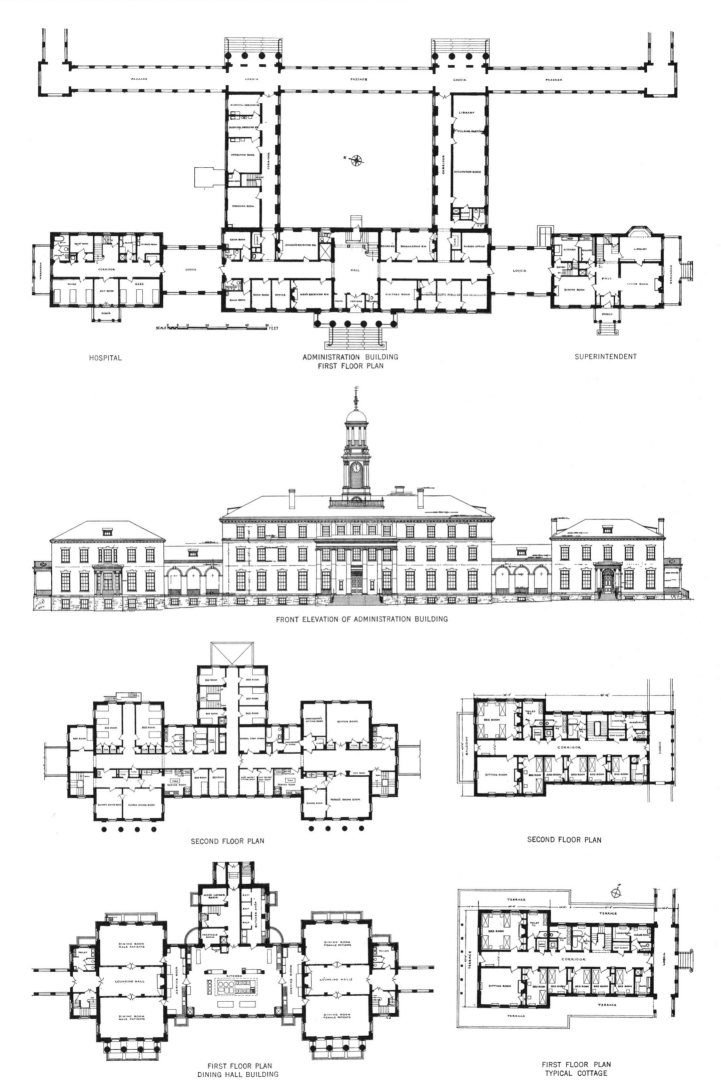

HOSPITAL

ADMINISTRATION BUILDING
FIRST FLOOR PLAN

SUPERINTENDENT

FRONT ELEVATION OF ADMINISTRATION BUILDING

SECOND FLOOR PLAN

SECOND FLOOR PLAN

FIRST FLOOR PLAN
DINING HALL BUILDING

FIRST FLOOR PLAN
TYPICAL COTTAGE

Plate 381

THE BURKE FOUNDATION HOSPITAL FOR CONVALESCENTS,
WHITE PLAINS, N. Y.
1914

MAIN ENTRANCE AND ADMINISTRATION BUILDING

DINING HALL BUILDING FROM QUADRANGLE

THE BURKE FOUNDATION HOSPITAL FOR CONVALESCENTS.
WHITE PLAINS, NEW YORK.
1914

Plate 382

ADMINISTRATION BUILDING, FACADE TOWARD QUADRANGLE

Plate 383

THE BURKE FOUNDATION HOSPITAL FOR CONVALESCENTS,
WHITE PLAINS, NEW YORK.
1914

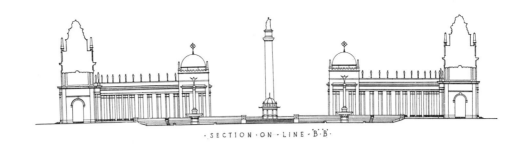

· SECTION · ON · LINE · B·B ·

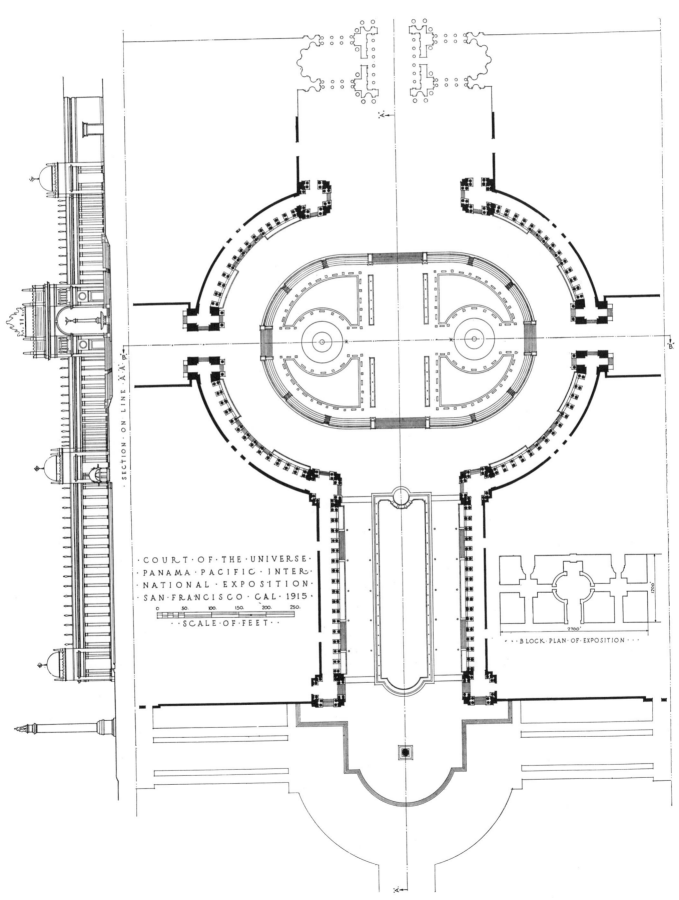

· SECTION · ON · LINE · A·A ·

COURT · OF · THE · UNIVERSE ·
PANAMA · PACIFIC · INTER·
NATIONAL · EXPOSITION ·
SAN · FRANCISCO · CAL · 1915 ·

0   50.   100.   150.   200.   250.
· SCALE · OF · FEET ·

· BLOCK · PLAN · OF · EXPOSITION ·

2700'

1700'

THE PANAMA PACIFIC INTERNATIONAL EXPOSITION, SAN FRANCISCO, CAL.

Plate 384

AGRICVLTVRE

DOOR IN COLONNADE

SCALE 0 1 2 3 4 5   10   15   20   25   30 FEET

THIS WORK WAS EXECUTED IN ARTIFICIAL TRAVERTINE, CAST AND PLASTIC, AND DECORATED WITH COLOR.

Plate 385

THE PANAMA PACIFIC INTERNATIONAL EXPOSITION, SAN FRANCISCO, CAL.
DETAIL OF PAVILION AND COLONNADE IN COURT OF THE UNIVERSE.
1915

Plate 386

THE PANAMA - PACIFIC INTERNATIONAL EXPOSITION
SAN FRANCISCO 1915.
VIEWS IN COURT OF THE UNIVERSE

PAVILIONS AND COLONNADE

FOUNTAIN OF THE RISING SUN

COLUMN OF PROGRESS

Plate 387   COURT OF THE UNIVERSE, PANAMA PACIFIC INTERNATIONAL EXPOSITION,
SAN FRANCISCO, 1915.

WILLIAM M°KINLEY

THE NATIONAL McKINLEY BIRTHPLACE MEMORIAL, NILES, OHIO.
1915

Plate 388

THE COURT AND MEMORIAL STATUE

DETAIL OF FAÇADE

THE NATIONAL McKINLEY BIRTHPLACE MEMORIAL, NILES, OHIO
1915

Plate 389

ELEVATION

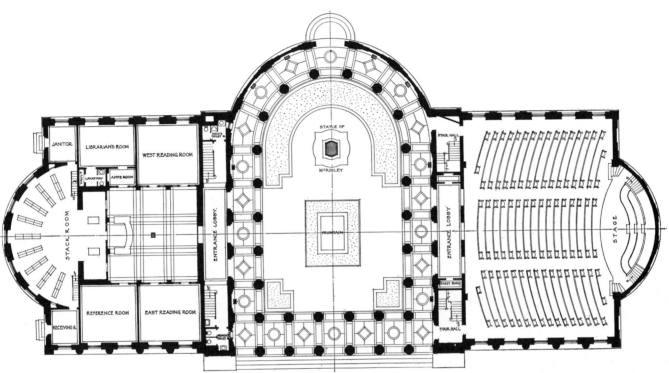

FIRST FLOOR PLAN

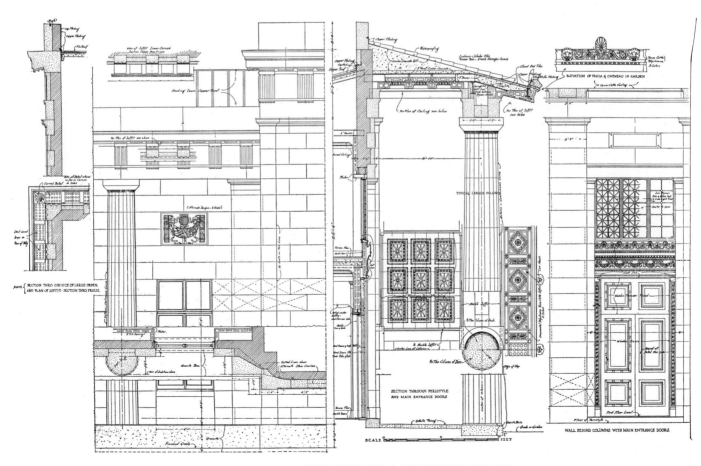

EXTERIOR DETAILS - GRANITE, WHITE GEORGIA MARBLE, POLYCHROME TERRA COTTA, ETC.

THE NATIONAL McKINLEY BIRTHPLACE MEMORIAL, NILES, OHIO.
1915

Plate 390

Plate 392 HOUSES FOR GERALDYN REDMOND ESQ. AND THE COUNTESS DE LAUGIER VILLARS
NEW YORK CITY
1914

SCALE ⊢ O. 5. IO. 15 20 ⊣ FEET

FIRST FLOOR PLAN   SECOND FLOOR PLAN

HOUSES FOR GERALDYN REDMOND ESQ. AND THE COUNTESS DE LAUGIER VILLARS   Plate 393
NEW YORK CITY
1914

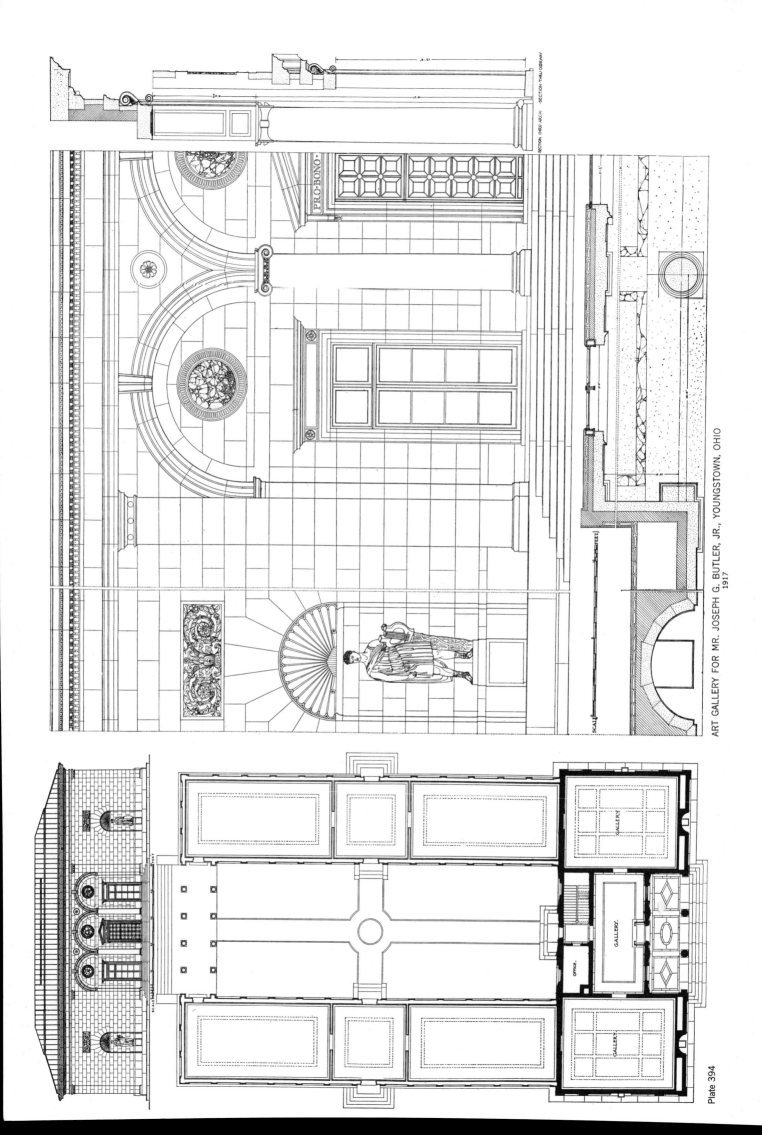

ART GALLERY FOR MR. JOSEPH G. BUTLER, JR., YOUNGSTOWN, OHIO
1917

Plate 394

ART GALLERY AT YOUNGSTOWN, OHIO, FOR MR. J. G. BUTLER, JR.
1917

Plate 394A

FACADE

INTERIOR OF BANKING ROOM

Plate 395

THE FRANKLIN NATIONAL BANK, PHILADELPHIA, PA.
1916

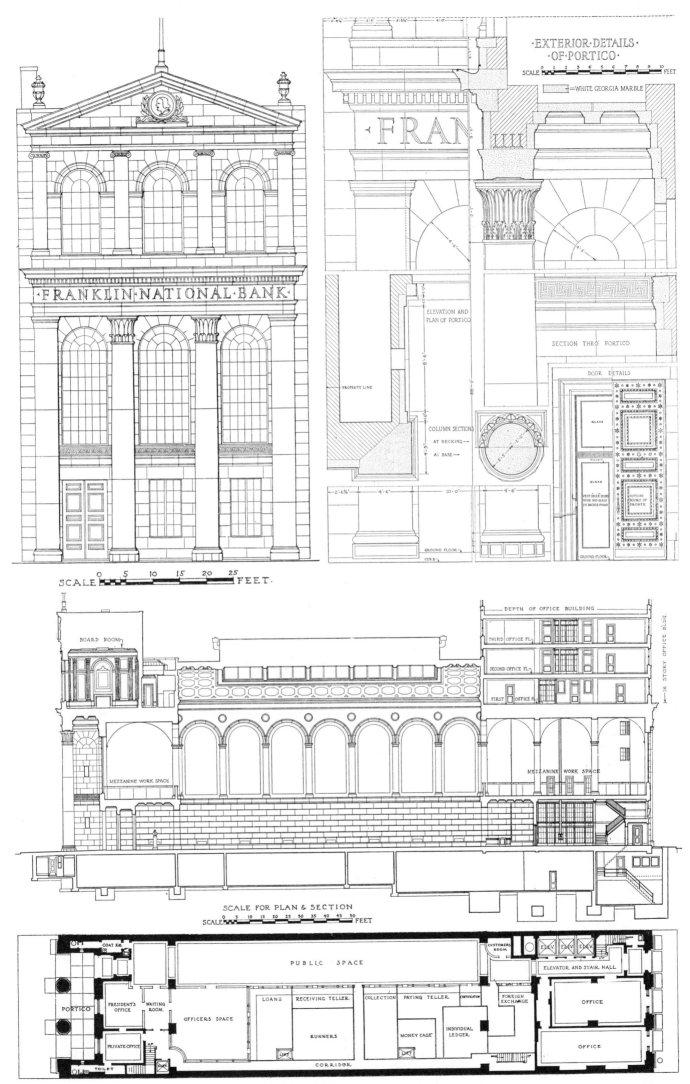

EXTERIOR·DETAILS·
OF·PORTICO·

SCALE 0 1 2 3 4 5 6 7 8 9 10 FEET

= WHITE GEORGIA MARBLE

FRAN

ELEVATION AND
PLAN OF PORTICO

SECTION THRO' PORTICO

PROPERTY LINE

COLUMN SECTIONS
AT NECKING →
AT BASE →

DOOR DETAILS

GLASS

WOOD

GLASS

VESTIBULE DOORS
WOOD AND GLASS
IN BRONZE FRAME

OUTSIDE
DOORS OF
BRONZE

GROUND FLOOR

GROUND FLOOR

CURB

·FRANKLIN·NATIONAL·BANK·

SCALE 0 5 10 15 20 25 FEET.

BOARD ROOM

DEPTH OF OFFICE BUILDING

THIRD OFFICE FL.

SECOND OFFICE FL.

FIRST OFFICE FL.

16 STORY OFFICE BLDG.

MEZZANINE WORK SPACE

MEZZANINE WORK SPACE

SCALE FOR PLAN & SECTION

SCALE 0 5 10 15 20 25 30 35 40 45 50 FEET

COAT RM.

PUBLIC SPACE

CUSTOMERS ROOM

ELEV ELEV ELEV

ELEVATOR AND STAIR HALL

PORTICO

PRESIDENT'S OFFICE

WAITING ROOM.

OFFICERS SPACE

LOANS

RECEIVING TELLER.

COLLECTION

PAYING TELLER.

CERTIFICATION

FOREIGN EXCHANGE

OFFICE

PRIVATE OFFICE

RUNNERS

MONEY CAGE

INDIVIDUAL LEDGER

OFFICE

TOILET

CORRIDOR.

THE FRANKLIN NATIONAL BANK, PHILADELPHIA, PA.
1916

Plate 396

LIVING ROOM

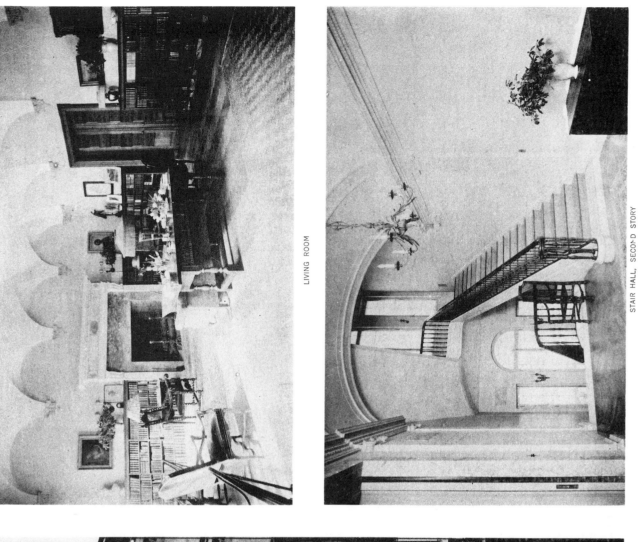

STAIR HALL, SECOND STORY

RESIDENCE OF THOMAS NEWBOLD, NEW YORK CITY
1917

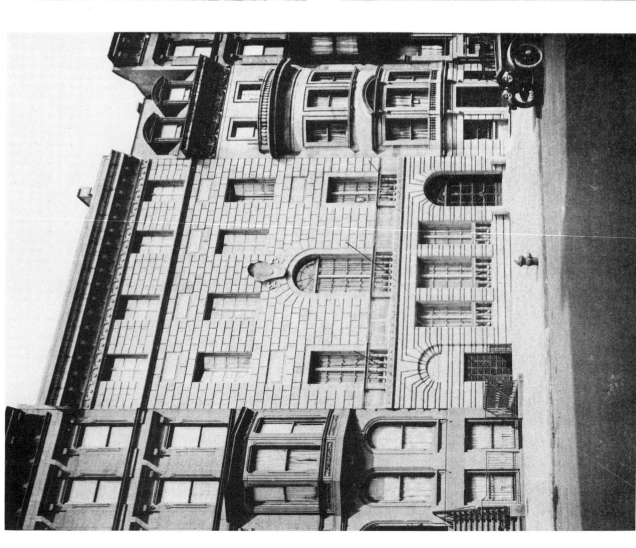

FACADE

Plate 397

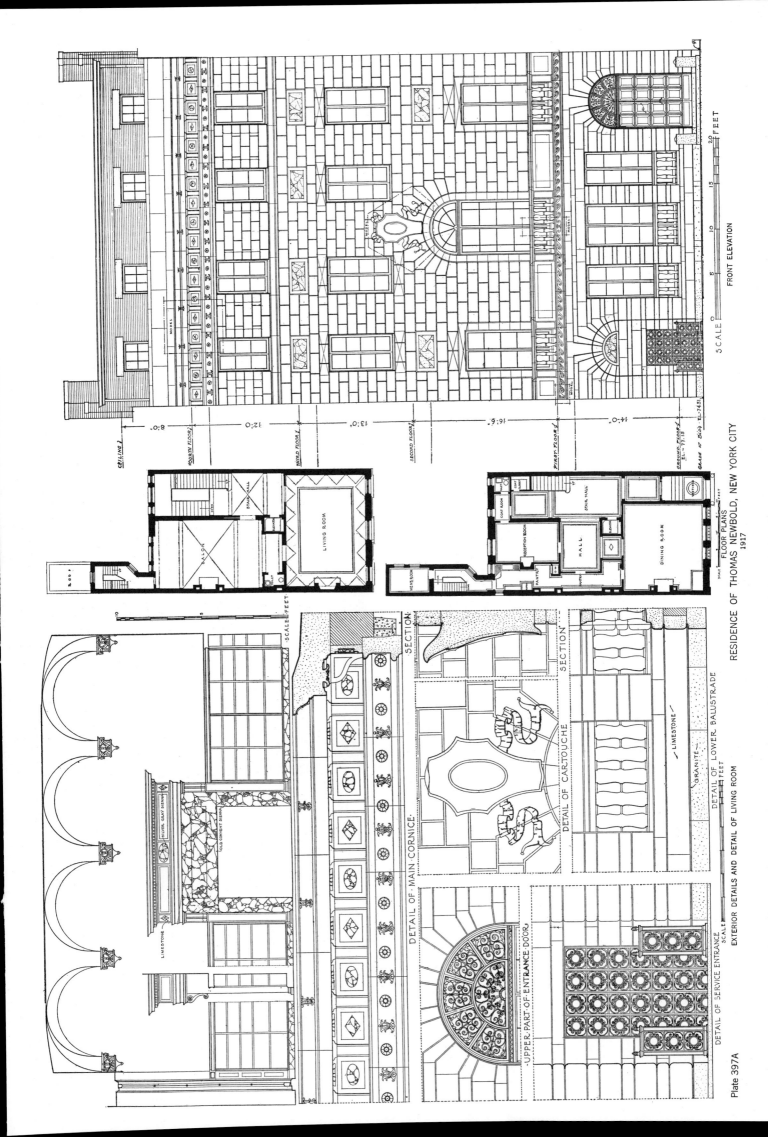

FRONT ELEVATION

SCALE

RESIDENCE OF THOMAS NEWBOLD, NEW YORK CITY

FLOOR PLANS
1917

DETAIL OF SERVICE ENTRANCE

DETAIL OF MAIN CORNICE

DETAIL OF CARTOUCHE

DETAIL OF LOWER BALUSTRADE

EXTERIOR DETAILS AND DETAIL OF LIVING ROOM

Plate 397A

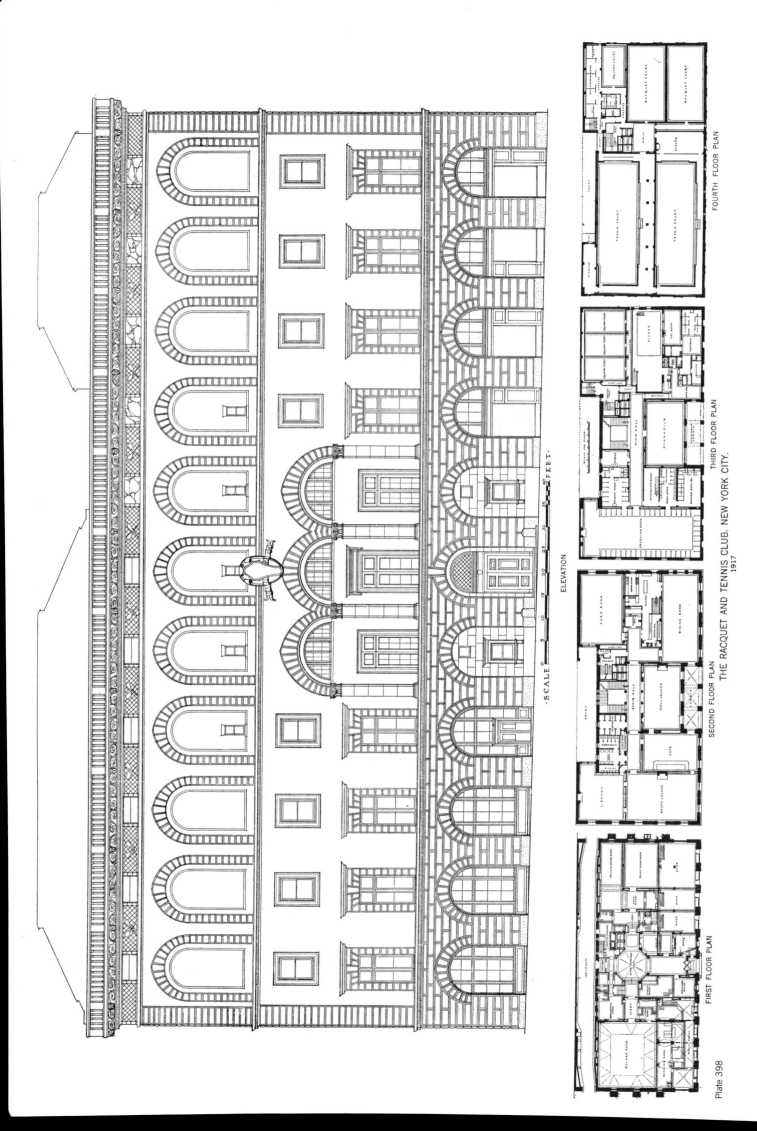

SCALE 0 5 10 15 20 25 30 35 40 FEET.

ELEVATION

FOURTH FLOOR PLAN

THIRD FLOOR PLAN

SECOND FLOOR PLAN

FIRST FLOOR PLAN

THE RACQUET AND TENNIS CLUB, NEW YORK CITY.
1917

Plate 398

FACADE

LOGGIA ON SECOND FLOOR

ENTRANCE HALL

THE RACQUET AND TENNIS CLUB, NEW YORK CITY
1917.

Plate 399

EAST LOUNGE, SECOND FLOOR

TENNIS COURT

HALL LOUNGE, SECOND FLOOR

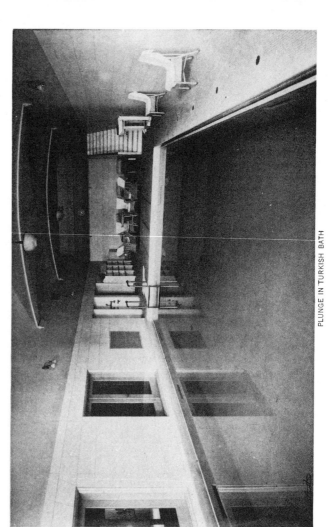

PLUNGE IN TURKISH BATH

THE RACQUET AND TENNIS CLUB, NEW YORK CITY
1917

Index to Plates